What Now?™
The Teen Handbook

An Uncensored Guide to School and Life.

By Chris DeCarlo

First Edition, 2019
Copyright © by Christopher DeCarlo

www.WhatNowTeens.com

Published by DeCarlo Enterprises Inc.
420 Mill St., N.E.
Vienna, Virginia   22180

Cover design by Tabitha Seipel-Meltzer.

Printed in the United States of America.

ISBN 978-1-7330054-0-1

Acknowledgments

I would like to acknowledge the many people that have helped me get to the point where I could write this book.

In particular, I would like to recognize and thank all of my wonderful elementary, middle, and high school staff, administrators, and teachers.

As is the case with all school personnel and teachers, students never really appreciate the concern for students' well being until they are far from your classrooms. Then, they often can't find these influential people anymore to say thank you and then it may be too late.

We still remember them and are forever grateful for everything they tried to do and for what they did do for us that we realize as life continues.

Thank you.

Table of Contents

Introduction

Written as a handbook, this is my attempt to help you mature so you can have a more meaningful life. To mature, you are going to need improved behaviors for getting along with people and improved problem solving skills for the events and circumstances you are going to encounter. My combination of being an entrepreneur and of living in the shadows of Washington, D.C., has served as a great environment for me to learn about and learn how to see the reality of how our society functions and why. Being a father of five teens provides me with an accurate perspective of today's influences, distortions, and pressures on you, our young adults, and your many challenges and options.

This handbook is only possible due to the combination of attending Fairfax County Public Schools while living in Northern Virginia with the tens of thousands of Federal employees and their families and of being fortunate in the starting and operating of an independent small family business that provides energy related products and services to the community. And, it is also only possible because of my marriage to my wife Kathleen with whom I have shared a large portion of my journey including the birth of our five children with current ages of 12 to 20 years. And it is only possible because I have participated in their growth, development and education during this epic shift to overwhelming digital communication. The combination of these unique events have provided me with insights that you, today's digital teenagers, need to know so you are better prepared to survive and prosper.

Washington, D.C., is a unique place for learning about many things such as how appearances differ from reality and what is important and what isn't because the industry here is information—and information is always subject to interpretation.

I was born in 1958 and became a teenager during the Vietnam War. I almost had to register for the draft. I attended public school with students whose parents worked at the White House, the Capitol,

Introduction

the FBI, CIA and Department of State, the Pentagon, and all the other government agencies of the Federal Government, as well as *The Washington Post* newspaper. Because of their connections, many elected representatives came and spoke at my school.

My mother was a teacher and returned to school in the early '70's and earned her Ph.D. in Education from American University, and my father was a scientist with a Ph.D. in Physical Chemistry from Catholic University. Both my parents worked in either higher education or for agencies of the Federal Government, but for many reasons I don't think they were ever happy. I received a Congressional nomination to the Air Force Academy but did not get ranked high enough for acceptance, so I studied Electrical Engineering at Georgia Institute of Technology for two years at the time Jimmy Carter was President. I returned home to Virginia in 1978 and began classes in Business at George Mason University. While still a student I started a family business by renting a former gasoline station in 1979 that led me to selling propane fuel which has carried me to where I am today.

This book is formatted to provide you with basic explanations, observations and real life stories regarding important topics that you should be aware of, while also providing you an opportunity to begin learning how to see things from a different perspective and to start questioning what you see and think. But first, you need to understand the importance of being able to disconnect from your digital world so you can look up and around to see and comprehend what is going on around you. And, secondly, you need to be able to protect your body from injury and disease, and, thirdly, to break the chains that social media and gaming are placing on your minds, perspectives and creativity.

I was very fortunate to have many mentors who helped me understand myself and society with some of the best advice coming from my German immigrant next door neighbor and auto mechanic Karl Eisenschmidt who taught me that, "You can't fix anything unless you first understand how it works." This is a reference to repairing cars, but his mantra can be applied to everything in life. It isn't

Introduction

that life needs or can be fixed but that each of us is always trying to understand why things happen to us and others so we can avoid the bad things. We must try to capitalize on the good things which is the driving theme and purpose of this book and how something that may seem like a good thing now may turn out to be a bad thing later and vice versa.

One of the keys to a successful life is to be able to look ahead. Another is to be able to see the possibilities when they come along. And another is to know when the right one is in your hand. I hope this book serves as another tool that you can use on your journey so that you will be able to see the multitudes of possibilities that pass through your hands and be able to catch and hold on to a really good one.

Notes to the Reader

This is a self-published publication so I can maintain legal control of the content and modify it as appropriate for future editions.

It is not complete and it never will be. It is my best attempt to put the best information together as quickly as possible for you to read, absorb, and consider so you can make use of it as soon as possible since, for you, time is of the essence. It is also formated and organized for easier referencing, and future modification and republication.

I have tried to present this material as my Freshman shop teacher Mr. Sam Derrick tried to prepare us as best he could for our life journeys by weaving his real world stories, insight and advice into his lesson plans. His method seems to have worked for me and I hope it will work for you.

"The Man," as described by Jack Black in the movie *School of Rock*, changed me into who I am today and how I think. I used to be just like you in that I always tried to do my duty and, for the most part, accepted what I was told. Not anymore.

Your positive and negative comments and feedback will be greatly appreciated as a means to improve future editions.

Warning

This handbook can be hazardous.

1) If you suspect yourself of laziness, it will likely be confirmed.

2) It may cause you to lose your immature friends.

3) You may accidentally become a role model.

4) The breadth of topics represents the bewildering level of complexity faced by modern teens.

5) This is an uncensored version which includes some unvetted descriptions, analysis, and remedies.

6) It was written for an audience of 16 to 22 year olds.

7) Parents are encouraged to read the book with your teen's mindset—no matter the age.

Continue with caution...

Disclaimer

This book is intended as educational information provided for entertainment purposes only. This book is not meant to be used to diagnose or treat any medical condition or ailment, and is in no way intended as expert advice of any sort. The author and publisher are not offering this as any form of advice, whether psychological, legal, medical, accounting, and/or any other professional and/or expert services of any kind.

The opinions stated herein are merely that of the author and not necessarily that of the publisher or others mentioned and/or quoted, and should not be interpreted as providing any representations, guarantees, and/or warranties of any kind, express or implied, and are provided assuming no liabilities of any kind with respect to their accuracy, completeness, and/or appropriateness for use in any particular situation. No warranty may be created or extended

Warning and Disclaimer

by sales representatives or written sales materials. No warranties or guarantees are expressed or implied by author's, or publisher's choice to include any of the contents of this book.

The author and publisher specifically disclaim any implied warranties of merchantability or fitness of use for a particular purpose. Neither the publisher nor the author shall be liable to any person or entity, for any physical, psychological, emotional, financial, health, and/or commercial, damages, including, but not limited to, any compensatory, direct, indirect, consequential, incidental, special, punitive, loss of business, loss of use or data, interruption of business, and/or other damages of any kind, or negative consequences from any information, treatment, action, application, or preparation, to any person reading, or following the information included in this book.

Any references to any intellectual property (IP) herein, are not intended to grant any license and/or right, express or implied, to use any such IP. References to any third party sources, websites, or opinions are included for informational and entertainment purposes only and do not constitute endorsement of any such source or website, and their contents may be subject to change over time.

Every person is different and any information, advice or strategies contained in these materials may not be suitable to a given particular situation. You are responsible for your own choices, actions, and results of your chosen actions.

You should seek professional services, and/or advice and counsel of a competent professional with appropriate expertise, such as, e.g., your physician, medical professional, lawyer, psychiatrist, and/or other counselor, before beginning any improvement program. It is important to note that past results are no guarantee of future performance, and your results may vary.

Welcome Message

Dear Teens (and Parents),

This is your handbook. Mess it up by making notes all over the pages and feel free to start anywhere and jump around. Read just one page a day or ten to give yourself a chance to think about what is here. Underline the parts you like and put question marks next to parts that don't make sense to you. Talk with your friends and parents about some of the ideas provided to see what they think.

Use this handbook to start conversations.

You can carry this handbook with you and read a few paragraphs when you have a moment instead of swiping screens on your phone.

You are to be commended for looking for answers and reading this far. It shows that you are interested in improving your life.

You are part of an amazing world at an amazing time and you have a whole life of fun and adventure waiting for you. To have the best adventure, you have to be careful that you don't make too many wrong turns.

I was your age once and now some decades later I see how really fast time goes by so I want to pass along to you a lot of the knowledge and insight that I have learned—some the hard way.

Life is a very complicated journey and each of you is a unique person with the capacity to procreate offspring who will be dependent on you for their care, support and development one day. When I was sixteen I told my mother, "I'm never getting married." For a long time I did not. Now I have been happily married to Kathleen for 24 years and we have five children ages from 12 to 20. I can say, "Expect the unexpected."

I can only wish that I could take what I know now and be in your shoes today so I could go through all the new experiences again. Since I can't, the next best thing is to pass some things to you so hopefully some of my ideas and concepts and ways of thinking can

Welcome Message

accompany you vicariously on your life adventure. As odd as this may sound, the best thing you can do at this stage in your life is to get rid of your phone—mostly in a figurative way. It is very hard for you to understand life without your phone. We all need our phone, that's understood. Nevertheless, it may be stifling your development and progress in many ways without you being aware of the massive amount of time spent on it.

Time seems free, but it is very valuable.

Your Real Challenge

You are a very important person with the power to control your life. What is hard is resisting the temptation to waste your time and mental energy on social media and digital entertainment which is, for the most part, short term "crap".

While some of it may entertain and inform, there is no making up the time lost on it. Communicate in person. Start to live like it counts. If you are in high school, start figuring out how you are going to move on to a vocational career or college so you can be more successful than your parents. If you are starting college, make the best of the great opportunity you have so you can be more successful than your parents, if you are lucky.

No matter where you are, don't let your dismal friends suck you into their rabbit hole of despair that's a dead end. You can still be their friend but set your own priorities and move on. Choose your friends wisely.

Adolescence is your chance to develop yourself as quickly and efficiently as possible. It is your chance to have the most opportunities. It is an exciting time that shouldn't be wasted on empty distractions and loser friends. Don't be afraid to grow up. There are a lot of people that will help you along the way and you will do just fine.

You know you need to make good choices. Now that you get to make choices on your own, you need to give all of them careful consideration because all choices come with consequences which can be good or bad.

It is important for you to understand that the choices you make now will affect your options for choices in the future.

This handbook is intended to help you make the right choices.

Be the best you can be, be resilient, work hard, and you will be just fine. You can do it once you put your mind to the task, set your goals, and stay focused.

Your Real Challenge

The world is yours for the taking and this handbook will explain how you can figure out what you have to offer, get ahead of your classmates, sweep up the money, and run.

Chapter one

Who are You?

**Take an inventory of who you are,
how you think, and what are your resources.**

What personality traits and characteristics do you have so that others will want to trust you?

Will clients or employers feel you are responsible?

Is your life in order so you can start reaping the benefits as soon as possible?

Your Characteristics

Topics listed alphabetically

Accomplishments

Thinking positively, make a list of everything that you have accomplished. It is kind of like your resume; what have you accomplished so far in your life? It is probably a good idea to ask one of your parents to help you with your list.

Write the list out so you can see everything together in one place. Writing it down makes you more tangible and real.

Describing yourself in writing is a start in showing who you are and what you are made of, and may reveal a direction—bad or good.

Anatomy

Your body is an amazing living thing engineered just right so you can live and function. What pieces do you have and how well developed are they? Take good care of all your pieces because you need everything to work together for the best results.

Imagine how your life could change without an eye, kidney, foot or finger or if you had a serious concussion. Of course, you probably know people who have learned to adapt.

Try not to put yourself in harm's way. Don't abuse your body with drugs and alcohol because you want to preserve it as long as possible and make it the best it can be.

Attributes

Think of your special qualities and the things that you want to promote.

What are they?

Brain - your processor

Don't fill your brain with trash.
Keep it clean. Keep it sharp.

Your brain is a very fast processor with lots of free memory when you are young. You cannot upgrade your processor or get a multi-core one installed so be careful with how you allocate your ram because you don't have any extra open slots.

Gaming and social media trivia are not the best use of your most prized computer. Critical thinking and interpersonal skills that you can use and apply for the rest of your life are a better application for your unique processor and memory.

Who are you?

Is there anything that you can do to make better use of your processor and random access memory storage?

_____

_____

_____

_____

_____

_____

_____

_____

Clearance Ready - aka - Background check

How clearance ready are you?

Clearance Ready is a term that relates to whether you have conducted and will continue to conduct yourself in a manner that you can be trusted with sensitive information.

Clearance relates to your being able to get a security clearance which means you are cleared to handle top secret information. Being able to get a clearance is very valuable because it is a ticket to almost guaranteed employment for life and up to a 20% boost in pay according to a panelist at a college career fair.

See the section titled Security Clearances for some really good and important information to consider and know.

Creativity

Since you have a processor in your head and you are human, you are born with creativity. Creativity is key to your success because it will give you the ability to imagine, innovate, create new things, solve problems, and earn money. Everyone has creativity. You might just not know how to uncover it.

Creativity is a very important characteristic but it is hard to quantify. It is important because if it can be harnessed and directed properly it can provide a special dimension for new ways of solving problems.

**Solving problems is the name of the game
in the competitive world of adulthood.**

Curiosity

This trait is very important because natural curiosity is an innate attribute that leads one to develop and utilize their critical thinking skills.

Curiosity is a great self-motivator. Your curiosity will help propel you forward in your quest to analyze and learn and employers value it because it is indicative of good skills in problem solving, especially in areas of personal interest.

Daily routine and routines

Get out of bed.

Get dressed.

Eat something so you have energy. Break the fast, that's why it's called breakfast.

**Plan your objectives for the day,
Don't idly waste your life away.**

Make a list and/or a schedule?

Write things down so you can be more efficient and you don't forget something.

Dances

High School dances were a lot of fun in the 1970's. We would have many formal and informal dances as well as reenacted 1950's sock hops each year and they were always a treat. It is unfortunate that today's dances at high schools have deteriorated into sweaty jumping contests where the music is so loud that even when you yell at the person next to you, you can't be heard and then are hoarse the next day.

These aren't real "school dances," they are often just dress up, during which you take lots of pictures, eat out, and appear briefly at

Who are you?

the "dance". We used to show up much earlier and enjoy the whole evening.

It is unfortunate that you have been denied the experience of real adolescent dances like in the movies.

I took some tap dancing lessons when I was in my early 20's and Kathleen and I took dancing lessons before we got married for fun and so we would be in sync on the dance floor at our wedding reception. I have always liked all kinds of dance.

Dancing is great exercise and a great way for socialization.

Even today I would love to be able to shuffle but my knees may not be able to handle it.

You already know the shuffle, but here's a neat example.

YouTube: Genesis - I Can't Dance (Remix)

Deficiencies

"In most workplaces, you need more than raw intelligence to get ahead. And only focusing on your greatest strength, rather than also addressing your weaknesses, tends to be self-sabotaging." *Harvard Business Review.*

Deficiencies are your weaknesses, which we all have and which can be improved.

It is a good idea to recognize and try to correct some of yours— sooner than later.

List some of them here that you can work on.

_____
_____
_____
_____
_____
_____
_____
_____

My verbal SAT score was lower than my math and I was never very interested in English so during my senior year of high school and during the summer before I went to college, I attended my local community college for three quarters of evening classes in English composition to try and improve my writing skills.

The classes were very helpful and helped me to mature a little faster because I was in an environment with adults and I had to be extra careful not to act juvenile.

Discipline

Be careful with how you allocate your free time.

How much do you push yourself to accomplish specific goals versus procrastinate and seek entertainment? How is your free time divided between productive activities and entertainment activities?

Disposition

What kind of person are you? How would you describe yourself? Are you more an introvert or an extrovert, a doer or a procrastinator, a dreamer or a realist?

It is helpful to be in touch with your disposition so you can have a better understanding of your strengths and weaknesses which will help you to have a more balanced personality.

Dress

You don't have to dress for success but wear clean clothes and don't look like you just got out of bed. It doesn't look good to wear your pajamas to class or in public. Slides, which are kind of like slippers or other casual wear, send the message that you are too lazy to put on shoes and tie them.

An unkempt appearance reflects an unkempt mind.

Who are you?

Guys, you look much more presentable if you shave your face every day and keep your hair and nails trimmed. If you do have a beard, keep it neat and trimmed.

Consider keeping your tattoos covered because they might send the wrong impression. It's better if you don't have them in the first place as health issues can result from viruses and messages can cause embarrassment. See section on tattoos.

Dress Suit

Every male should have a standard black suit and black shoes and black socks and a white button down shirt and a nice tie for those special occasions such as funerals, religious celebrations, school dances and interviews.

It is always better to be overdressed than under dressed.

Education

What is your level of education?

How well trained is your brain and what problem solving skills do you have?

How fast can you solve problems and get the correct answers?

What do you know? Are you a specialist in anything?

Chapter 2 has a lot of information about education.

Etiquette

Avoid appearing lazy and uncouth.

Manners matter because they are a reflection of your personality and your personality is everything.

You know good manners from bad so show your respect for others and conduct yourself accordingly.

My fifth grade teacher, Mrs. Soderquist, at Cedar Lane Elementary, in Vienna, Virginia, had a poster over the door titled, *The Golden Rule* The 3 foot wide round poster kind of looked like a baseball and it read very simply, *Do unto others as you would have others do unto you.*

I have always tried to follow *The Golden Rule* and I think it has served me well.

Executive Function

Executive functions are a set of cognitive processes. The processes function like a controller for your brain. Your controller helps you to manage yourself and your resources in a way that you can achieve your goals as they are related to mental control and self regulation.

Executive function is synonymous with the term "critical thinking" and to some degree maturity.

Exercise

Good mobility is essential for sustained healthy living but don't exercise so much or so hard that you injure yourself. Injury kind of defeats the purpose of exercising in the first place. Build up weights slowly if you lift and don't try to prove anything to yourself or those around you.

I recently attended many hot yoga sessions and they are a fun way to condition yourself. Try a hot yoga session. With a room temperature of 105 degrees, they are an ultimate challenge and very rewarding when over.

Food

Do you eat regular meals that are nutritious so that you take care of yourself?

What are your favorite foods?

Are they good for you?

Do you stay away from soda and sugar?

Garages

Do you have access to a garage or a space that you can use to create or take apart things? This space can be a great asset for learning.

Many successful people got their start in garages.

Who are you?

If you live in a house with a garage, consider asking your parents if you can use part of the garage for developing your creativity and expanding your learning.

Goals

What are your goals?

How well do you set and try to achieve them, big and small? The goals can be academic, sports, music or other simpler objectives such as how fast you can type on a keyboard without looking at the keys or whether you can build a drone from scratch, not a kit.

Developing your creativity is a beneficial activity and goal. What other goals do you have?

Take a moment to list some of your short and long term goals. They can include goals related to school, your career, family, sports, personal or other areas of your life.

_____

_____

_____

_____

_____

_____

Habits - Good and Bad

Ask your parents if they have any ideas if you're not sure what to write here. They probably know you better than anybody.

_____

_____

_____

_____

Hustle

This is an innate characteristic for people who are achievers and it has to do with one's level of enthusiasm for projects and objectives. Do you have hustle? Are you always trying to keep yourself and others moving along?

Employers like this trait—it is a step above initiative because initiative is more about you and your individual motivation whereas hustle means that you are pushing yourself as well as others to perform. If you have hustle be careful to manage it because in the extreme it can alienate coworkers and friends.

Individuality

This is who you are, what makes you unique. Will people see your qualities and want you to be on their team?

Individuality is composed of all your pieces assembled. The tangible and intangible parts. The intangible parts include your behavior, reputation, etiquette, and trustworthiness. The tangible parts include your skills and problem solving abilities.

Realize that with the traits of consideration and thoughtfulness that you will be well liked by your peers and if you are well liked by your peers you will be able to go farther in life.

It is a holistic view. Who are you?

Initiative

The concept of one's ability to motivate him/herself. It can be contagious. How much initiative do you have? Do you like working with people that have initiative?

Intelligence

How do you define intelligence?

_____
_____
_____
_____

How do you plan to use your intelligence? Write two possibilities.

_____
_____
_____

Who are you?

Investing

What does investing mean to you? Also see Resources.

_____

_____

_____

Knowledge

In what areas do you have knowledge?

How are book skills different from practical skills?

What skills have you acquired through experience or education?

How is your education more or less rigorous than that of your parents? What has changed and are the changes for the better or worse?

We thought that we needed to know a lot before, and now we need to know even more.

The expectations for you are higher. Often, students hear "you are not your test score." That's just obvious. Move on to showing your intelligence in other ways.

Maturity - Age Maturity vs. Emotional Maturity

Age maturity just means you have had more birthdays and are older; it does not mean you are emotionally mature.

Emotional maturity requires accepting responsibility for yourself.

The benefit of accepting emotional maturity is that it leads to more freedom.

Who do you know that is older than you but acts immature for her/his age?

How does your level of emotional maturity compare with your age?

Keep developing your natural maturity. Today you need to mature faster than before because society is more complex and moving at a very fast pace. Be careful that the distractions are not stifling your maturity at the time it will be most beneficial to propelling you ahead.

Some ways to help achieve maturity include reading a classic, going to the theater after preparing yourself with the drama's plot, and going to local lectures on topics that inform you on various topics. Colleges have lectures about many different topics which will expand your thinking. Check them out, they are always free.

When I was at Georgia Tech, which was a Navy ROTC school, I noticed flyers promoting a presentation by a four-star General. I thought it would be neat to see a four-star general because I had never seen one before.

I attended the presentation and learned about what the General thought about America's troop presence in Korea. I was surprised at how critical he was about the current policy especially because, I thought, Generals were not supposed to speak critically of their Commander-in-Chief. Then, during the question and answer period I was even more surprised at how informed the ROTC students were about Korea, based on the depth of their questions. As a side note, President Jimmy Carter had attended Georgia Tech.

It wasn't until the following day that I realized I had witnessed history when the newspaper headlines read that the general had been recalled to Washington and then a month later he resigned.

Still somewhat confused about what I saw many years later, eventually someone explained that the student questions were planted.

Mental Health/Stress

Examine how you try to think and behave in a rational and normal manner. Do you have difficulty when you are under pressure and what can you do about it? Do you know how to break problems down logically so you can try to develop rational solutions?

Mentors

Mentors are people who take an interest in you and who try to guide you on your way based on their experience and insight.

List some of your mentors.

Who are you?

_____

_____

_____

_____

What special qualities do they offer you?
Why do you have fun talking with them? _____

_____

_____

Money

Money becomes the currency of life.

It drives behaviors and rules supreme.

How much money do you have available to you and what is your plan to protect what you have and to earn or acquire more?

_____

_____

_____

_____

_____

If all you are after is money you will never have enough.

Music

My grandmother Vincenza was a piano teacher and she would give me lessons when I visited over the holidays. I was willing to play at home as a child but I only had a small electronic organ that wasn't any fun to play and my mother never asked if I wanted to take piano lessons or ever talked about getting a piano. My parents told me that I needed to demonstrate an interest in playing before they would purchase a standard piano for me. I taught myself simple songs on the electric keyboard but the problem was that it didn't sound good and wasn't any fun to play. Eventually I just gave up because nobody was interested in what I was trying to do and it seemed hopeless. I don't know if I would have had the discipline to take lessons and play, but I was willing which is a big part of the equation.

All our children started taking piano lessons when they were in kindergarten continuing through about twelfth grade.

I never did see the sense in music education until I started working with Eric Weinberg, our family music teacher, as he taught Mary Jane how to play the electric guitar, John drums and Mike bass guitar. Vince was already on piano or keyboard. We had our own rock'n roll band just like the Partridge Family.

I learned a lot from Eric about the importance of music and how learning to play helps your brain develop more synapse when a person is young and the brain is still growing.

Eric was able to get all our children to play as a rock'n roll band and they even competed in a high school competition (at a local high school where nobody knew who they were) when the oldest, Mary Jane, was in eighth grade. Mike was in fifth grade and his bass guitar was almost as big as he was. We didn't know what was going on when the crowd started chanting Mike's name at the beginning of their third song. They played three songs and did a great job.

Eric explained later that Mike has the "it" factor. We didn't even know what the "it" factor was. Eric explained that "it" is something that either you have or you don't.

Later, Eric helped me with my rap songs which were a lot of work and fun to create and from that experience I learned how to create music videos which are really neat.

From the business side I was most impressed with how much money the right songs can produce and I found it interesting as to how much money some performers have been able to earn. I wish I was eighteen again so I could try to be a rock star. Oh well, in another life.

Granted that it is rare that someone can make a lot of money as a music performer, but it really isn't that hard to create songs and you never know unless you try. Just don't put your whole life into it because it probably won't pay off; there are so many uncontrollables and it is a dirty business.

Who are you?

Music is a skill that you should keep up with and be sure to include on your resume because it demonstrates that you have the discipline to stick with something and that you will push yourself to improve. That says a lot to employers. And if you were in a band that shows that you can work with other people as a team, another critical component in business. And I learned from working with my kids that it takes a lot more discipline to work as part of a band than it does to be a player on a sports team. In a band everyone has to pull their weight and do it on the same beat.

Now, I think that schools should promote music more than they promote sports. And, nobody gets a concussion or a broken bone from playing an instrument. Studies reveal that music even helps students get smarter. What better activity could you ask for?

It is interesting to note that David Grohl, who was the drummer for Foo Fighters and then Nirvanna grew up in Springfield, Virginia, and went to high school not far from where I live. I would never recommend it but he dropped out of high school so he could go on a European tour with the band Scream when he was 17. He lied about his age.

David is a rare musical success story especially for someone from Northern Virginia, and he is a good example of what can happen when a young person has a tremendous amount of initiative, discipline and talent and a special mother, who was a single mom, school teacher and a musician herself that could help him along to make it all happen with just the right timing.

I would also like to point out that David's success happened at the phase in his life when he had the innocence of youth which is a critical component to get one's start in music. He discovered the guitar when he was nine and he founded his first band when he was in the fifth grade.

David was able to apply and focus his creative talents and invest his time when he was young to create some music products that keep on paying royalties such that he now has an estimated net worth of over $250 million.

Networking

The sum of your relationships make up your unique network.

To be successful in your future endeavors, including employment and other pursuits, you are going to need to develop your research skills so you can have and be able to maintain a more continuous and complete picture of as many of your options as possible as things change. Phones and the Internet are only going to provide a very limited view. To get a more complete and in-depth perspective you are going to need to be able to establish relationships with people.

Reliance on smart phones, texting and the Internet will diminish your ability to meet, converse, learn and ask questions from people that have the answers to what you need to know.

Objectives/Resiliency

Start small to learn to accomplish small goals that lead to more challenging goals.

Persistence

This term was used and applied very well in the 2016 movie "The Founder" about how the McDonald's franchise chain began. It is a great story. Be sure to watch it.

It doesn't matter how much money you have, you are nobody important if you can't be nice to other people especially the ones that are close to you. Remember, money does not make you a good person, but it can give you the means to help others.

Personal Assessment

By going through this list of characteristics and skills you are making an assessment of who you are just as prospective employers are going to be doing when they consider you for employment.

Would you want to hire yourself?

Who are you?

Personal Hygiene

Wash and take care of yourself every day including all the details. Make a good impression.

You don't want to have body odor. Deodorant won't work on its own.

You need to brush your teeth every morning and night. Don't use mints or gum to hide bad breath.

Brush your teeth. Especially the ones you want to keep.

Perspective and Relativity

Focus on the positive instead of the negative.

The past versus today—today versus tomorrow. The choice is yours. Everything is relative and perspective is everything.

Don't get hung up in thinking how you have less than others in that your car is too old or your house is too small. Everything you have is better than the people that lived before you and everything you have now will be less than others have in the future, so don't waste your energy complaining.

Be happy with whatever you have because there are probably millions of people worse off that would gladly change places with you not to mention all the people that have passed on and are not here any longer to enjoy any of it.

Is the glass half empty or half full?

Professional

How professional or amateurish do you act?

Do you prefer to associate with people that are professional or amateurs for life because they lack follow through?

Reading and used books

I used to collect used books on different subjects because they were an excellent source of knowledge and then the Internet came along greatly diminishing my need to buy so many used books. However, be that as it may, used books and books in general are a great resource to further one's understanding.

I rarely read entire books but they still serve as a resource for me when I have an idea that I want to explore further. Tangible books are much better than what you get from the Internet because they are interactive and you can annotate paper. Books provide a lot more depth of information and are easier to read, and used books can be really cheap for the amount of information they provide.

Don't discount reading books. They are a great source of unlimited knowledge and a great resource for personal development and maturity. Reading about the trials and tribulations of real and fiction characters will help you to better understand yourself and those around you, something that challenges all of us for all of our lives.

**Books should be your best friends
and you can never have enough friends.**

Resources

What resources do you have and how will you invest them?

Time is one of your resources. Money is another resource as is your future earning capability. Your relationships are another resource as in your knowledge in a particular subject or special problem solving skills. Your school and its teachers are resources. A library is a resource of information for you.

You have lots of resources   List some of your special resources and why they are important to you.

_____

_____

_____

_____

_____

Who are you?

Scholarships

You won't know unless you try.

Don't be afraid to ask about scholarships. Just ask.
Mary Jane asked about them and applied for several and received two her freshman year. One scholarship was for four years.

Asking shows initiative. It might also help to make new friends. You might learn something and every little bit helps. What better way to practice your research skills. What do you have to lose in asking? Make the effort. It is another opportunity to start conversations and establish relationships.

There are lots of people interested in helping those that are willing to help themselves. Go for it.

Self-sufficiency

You need to learn and practice self-sufficiency so you are as prepared as possible to take care of yourself if something happens to your parents.

Think of your parents, foster parents, and grandparents as your Guardian Angels when you are little and how they try to train you and your own Guardian Angel as you get older.

How are you going to avoid making mistakes as you age if you lose your parent(s)?

Listen, learn, and practice as much as you can while you have the opportunity, just like Luke listened to Yoda and Obi Wan Kenobi. Concentrate and you can be a Jedi Master, too.

Sitting

It is going to make you older and fatter sooner rather than later.

A doctor told me about a study where professional athletes were placed in bed for two weeks and they lost fifty percent of their strength.

How much strength are you losing because of your sitting?

You have to keep you body moving or your muscles are going to turn to mush. Even after a matter of weeks in a cast or brace, muscles atrophy. Imagine your brain without exercise, too.

Sleep

Sleep is very, very important.

Don't let phone or computer use get in the way of your sleep. It is very important to have a good normal sleep routine of 8 hours which does not include going to sleep at 2 a.m. and waking up at 10 a.m.

You may want to try paying particular attention to your dreams by writing them down as soon as you wake up and then thinking about what they mean. It is a helpful way to try and get in touch with your subconscious.

At Georgia Tech I had an English professor that was also an expert in dream analysis. He taught us about the importance of sleep and dreaming and he instructed us in how to capture our dreams and then how to try and analyze all the symbolism all in the context of improving our writing.

We were told to keep a notebook and pencil next to our bed and to begin writing our dream down as soon as we woke up. It was fascinating as to how once I would start writing the story and how my mind would keep recovering bits of the story. The faster I wrote the story down, the more complete story became. Then, he had us use the material as the subject for our compositions.

I learned a lot about the importance of sleep and the need for deep sleep. The knowledge and experience I gained has improved my understanding of who I am and what may be bothering me and why.

There are many books about dreaming that can help you to understand this phenomena that is critical to your brain. It is a fascinating subject.

Who are you?

Social Media - Part I

How do your social media accounts portray you?

The psychological impact of your words on another child's feelings cannot be under emphasized. As you are aware, many suicides have been credited to hurtful comments and postings.

Is it possible that your posts or use of social media could cause you embarrassment sometime in the future?

Sheila Gunter, from Virginia Beach, Virginia, and a mother of four adult children, is one of my friends from Camp Friendship.

Sheila emphasizes, as VERY IMPORTANT, the dangers of social media. She said, "One of the most dangerous aspects of social media is that when you post something, you can never get rid of it. Once it's out there, it's out there. And it follows you.

"Colleges and universities, as well as HR departments, scrutinize your social media before admitting, hiring, etc. If you wouldn't say it or show it to your grandmother, don't post it."

What may seem funny now may not seem so funny later and it might be a poor portrayal of your character or show your immaturity.

BE MATURE.

Sports in school

The proliferation and intensity of in-school sports activities often seems extreme, and perhaps it has gotten out of hand. It has become more of a means for students to work off their youthful energy than a beneficial personal development activity. Have sports programs developed to a point where they are consuming too much time? Are they creating unnecessary distractions as well as physical risks for the students relative to the benefits of participation?

The push for sports seems to have shifted the boundaries and priorities of what is supposed to be an educational system. It has intensified the physical competition among students to unhealthy levels. Moreover, it appears that the pressure for increased intensity is coming more from the parents than the students themselves—sometimes for the mere entertainment value. Perhaps some parents rely on it for a way to spend time with a child—observing him or her on the field or gym floor—and also observe their friends, but may not make one-on-one time, otherwise.

Teeth

What is the condition of your teeth? Do you keep them sparkly and clean? Be careful when playing sports to wear proper mouth protection to avoid chipping or losing a tooth.

It is a good practice to brush your teeth at least twice a day and to floss at least once to help keep your gums healthy. I didn't realize it until I was participating in a presentation about getting a knee replacement with my mother (she was the one getting one of her knees replaced), but diseases can get into your blood via poor gums. The issue with knee or other joint replacements is that if the bacteria sneaks in and you have an artificial joint, the bacteria can collect at the joint which could require another operation to replace it.

Not that you are going to be getting any artificial joints any time soon, but the risk illustrates the importance of good dental hygiene and care.

Make sure you replace your tooth brush when the bristles start to spread and go for a cleaning every six months.

You can buy a lot of floss and tooth brushes for the cost of just one cavity.

Be careful that you don't get hooked on soda with all its addictive sugar or caffeine drinks that act as a stimulant.

When my mother taught first grade, I would visit her classroom and sometimes she would have a paper cup on her desk filled with soda and a tooth that one of her students had lost. She put the tooth in the soda so the students could see how quickly the sugar would dissolve the enamel and create a cavity. It was a very good demonstration.

We never drank soda at home and we still don't to this day except during parties.

Test scores decreasing

SAT and ACT tests scores are dropping at the same time that

Who are you?

there are so many more opportunities for students to learn and improve their skills.

Do you think the tests are getting harder or is student motivation and performance decreasing?

It is hard for you to compare the past with today but what do you think some of the reasons scores are decreasing considering schools are trying to improve your ability to learn? Why aren't the schools succeeding more than they are so test scores increase? As someone with first hand knowledge of the current state of education, to what extent do I think the decrease is due to the students, teachers, teaching methods, or testing organizations? Answer: Quite a lot. What do you think and why?

I think test scores are decreasing because _____

_____

_____

_____

_____

Values and ideology

How would you describe your values and ideology?

Ideology is a word that isn't used much today. It is the essence your system of ideas, ideals, beliefs, principles and morals.

Your ideology is apparent in how you find it more comfortable to have friends that possess a value system that is similar to yours.

Ideology isn't as important to you now because you have so many friends to choose from but it is helpful to consider yours.

Similarities and differences in ideology with others will become more important when your circle of friends and associates begins to shrink as you enter college and/or the professional work place because you will encounter other people with ideologies that don't align with yours.

The difficult part will be that you will have to work with them which will create friction and uncomfortable or stressful environments. Being open minded allows space for others.

A big part of leadership and being a good leader is being able

36

to build a team of people that has similar ideologies so they will get along and work together to accomplish their objectives. This is easier said than done.

What do you value and how would you describe your ideology?

Write some of your ideas here.

_____

_____

_____

_____

_____

Weight

What you eat is more important than how much you eat. Watch your weight and adjust your diet and exercise plan accordingly. Be careful if you start to slouch, shuffle when you walk, and lose muscle tone from excessive sitting and staring at a screen. Your body is very resilient when you are young but it won't stay that way forever.

Monitor and keep a daily record of your weight so it doesn't start to creep up on you, especially if you go to college. Once you put it on, it is really hard to get off. Don't eat high calorie breakfast cereals and pasta for lunch and dinner.

Eat healthy and in moderation and avoid the Freshman 15. Exercise your will power. Keep it strong.

When I went to college the food was hardly edible so the term Freshman 15 had not be coined yet. Today, colleges have five-star dining halls with unlimited food. I think today's campus dining halls are doing the students a disservice by tempting them with so much tasty and high calorie food that is accessible 24/7.

What is your current weight? Establish a baseline.

No fudging.   _____lbs on ___/___/___.

Your Time

Time is fleeting and there's never enough of it.

Time gives good advice.

In other words, the right answers to past decisions are a lot clearer as time passes. As time passes you can see what else happened and what you did and didn't know at the time of your decision.

Time is unique for each of us.

Time isn't the same for everyone even though that is what we are taught to think since we all live by the same minute, hour, day and year. In reality, we each have our own unique clock that started when we were born and stops when we expire.

Slow down, and don't get caught up in the fast pace. The earth is going to keep spinning and the sun will come up each morning and your clock will keep running.

Computers and the Internet have changed people's behaviors, perspectives, and attitudes so much that you can only understand what it was like if you lived without them at an earlier time.

Relax and slow down. You are not going to miss anything that important that you have to drive yourself crazy trying to keep up with everything. It's impossible.

Think, talk with your friends, and calm down.

Pace yourself

You don't want your life to be a sprint to the end.

I ran cross-country in high school for three years. It was a great experience and I made a lot of great friends and learned a lot from my coaches.

Part of our conditioning for the 3-mile races was to practice running a lap around the track at a consistent and specific pace. It was called interval training.

We might be told to run three laps at 74 seconds, then a couple at 72 seconds and then maybe two at 70 seconds and than back to 74 seconds. Anything under 70 seconds was a killer.

Coach John Schlögl would be calling out the seconds as we approached and crossed the line so we could gauge how we did in hitting his mark. The goal wasn't to run the fastest possible. The goal was to try and get comfortable with a specific speed so that we would have an idea of how fast we were running in a race and be able to pace ourselves. In races you don't want to start too fast and burn out or too slow and not be able to catch up. The interval training helped with body awareness also.

Life is kind of the same as cross country running. It will go better if you can establish a steady pace for what you can handle instead of trying to run as fast as possible and then you burn out. Find the pace that works for you and you will be able to enjoy and stay in the race to the finish.

The fastest I ever ran a flat out mile was 5:05 which was pretty good. A football player had challenged me to a race of four laps around the track. I couldn't resist the challenge and some of my teammates joined in the competition. There was no way he was going to beat us.

The fastest I ran the first mile in a 3-mile meet was 5:20 which really surprised me since I still had two miles to go. It was at a big regional race and my speed at the mile showed me how much the adrenaline and excitement for the big race had kicked in. I was relieved when I crossed the finish line and it was over.

Time investment

How and where are you investing your time?

_____

_____

_____

_____

Who are you?

Time management and daily schedule

How do you manage your time? Keep track of how you use your time in 15-minute increments and see where it goes. One thing about time is that you can never get it back.

Twenty years ago, Ron, one of my older truck drivers who was always very impatient went to get some tires replaced on his truck. Ron was always impatient and he had to wait a while for the tires to be installed. He got so mad that they forgot about him for some reason that he said, "I wasted two hours of my life here and I can't get it back."

"Yes," the service manager said, "and at your age I guess you don't have much left do you?" That only made Ron madder.

Life is too short to be in a hurry or get mad. Relax and spend a few minutes just looking out the window. What do you see?

What is your daily schedule?

How do you allocate your time?

How much do you have left?

Time value

Time is money.

What is your strategy for converting one to the other?

What is your time worth if you think you have a long time to live versus what it is worth to you if you think you have less time to live?

Do people use their time differently depending on their age and their perceived value of time? I don't know the answer, I'm just posing the question.

Is time less valuable to a younger person than an older person?

Younger people think they have more available, right?

If a person only has three weeks to live, how valuable is each day compared with if he has 30 years to live?

Your Skills

More skills, more money.

What skills do you have to use, and what tools do you have at your disposal to improve yourself and be productive and efficient?

You have an unprecedented amount of resources available to improve yourself. Use the technology to improve your brain, not to retard its natural development, but don't forget about old school exercises for your brain like reading books.

Analytical approach to solving problems

How are your analytical problem-solving skills? How well do you know how to use of an appropriate process to break a problem down into the smaller pieces necessary to solve it?

Boredom

A necessary and healthy component of life, boredom, can be beneficial.

How do you handle boredom?

What do you typically do when you are bored?

Boredom gives your brain a chance to decompress and absorb what is around you.

Communication and words

Words are your means of communication and the words you use and how you communicate says a lot about you and your critical thinking and interpersonal skills. Learning and knowing how to use words properly is beneficial because they help you to understand and to explain yourself.

Vocabulary building does not end in English class.

Use words to unleash the true power of your brain.

Who are you?

Computer programming and coding

Programming is the best foreign language you can learn.

A basic class in programming should be a requirement for high school graduation and definitely for college. How can anybody go through school today without a class in programming?

Programming is so simple. All you are doing is telling the computer what to do with a series of instructions.

Programming is the best foreign language to learn because it is easy and you can do so much with it.

I learned my first programming language when I was a senior. It is called Basic and it still works today and is very simple and easy to learn. Learning it teaches the main concepts of how to write code to program the computer to do what you want it to do.

All students should learn a computer language so they have an understanding of how to give a computer instructions.

There is nothing hard about programming. It is all logical. You just have to learn the different computer commands for the different computer languages which are specially designed for different applications like scientific or graphics applications.

Don't be afraid to learn programming.
Try it, you might like it. Its really not that hard.
It may even become one of your best friends.

Computers - then versus now

When I was growing up in the 1970's, a mechanics toolbox with screwdrivers, open end wrenches, a socket set and ratchets were what I carried along with an electrical meter.

The laptop is the toolbox of today and the computing power of today's cell phone is the 1985 equivalent of what was an industrial computer called a Cray-2 super computer. In 1985, the Cray-2 cost $12 million. Accounting for inflation it would be worth $28 million today. And if you had one you couldn't carry it in your hip pocket.

In 2014, I signed two of my children up for a one-week summer camp on cybersecurity at George C. Marshall High School in Falls Church, Virginia, which is my old high school. As I was driving them to the class I had an out of body experience as I realized that I was driving my offspring to my high school for an Internet class and that instead of carrying hand tools they were carrying laptops.

It was a very bizarre feeling and then the feeling compounded itself when their class was held in my former wood shop classroom where Mr. Sam Derrick was my teacher. All the woodworking benches and equipment were gone and they were replaced by tables where 75 teenagers sat with their open laptops.

I went across the hall to my old electronics classroom and all the shop benches, voltage meters, and oscilloscopes had also been replaced by tables with teenagers and laptops. I had not been to either of the classrooms since I had left school so I felt caught in a time warp.

It was a scene I couldn't have possibly ever imagined 35 years earlier and I felt like a ghost who was moving between then and now as I stood in the doorway and listened to the discussion regarding computers and the cyber world. I could feel the presence of the ghosts of the past moving among the real students of the present.

I stayed for about thirty minutes to see how the information was being presented and to see what I could learn. The session was started off by displaying a public website known as map.norse.com which represented the world and all the known cyberattacks live. It was fascinating to see the representation which was compiled visa-via sensors in the fiber system that are detecting known attack packets. Norse company was sold and the same map isn't available now.

I left bewildered that I had aged so much, that I could move back and forth through time so quickly, and that my vocational classes had been replaced by cybersecurity classes. All of it, including the technology and the presence of my children were completely unimaginable to me when I was there in my teens.

Who are you?

Conversations

You won't have real friends or mentors if you can't have conversations. Make a point to enjoy three or four actual long conversations a day. It's fun and an irreplaceable social skill exercise.

Financial responsibility

This is a very important topic that you need to learn about and pay attention to.

You need to practice being economical and not wasting your money so you can make good investments which will earn more value for you.

Learn how to be fiscally responsible which means you can save your money, live within your means, and be secure enough with yourself that you do not need to lead an extravagant lifestyle to get acceptance by your peers.

Money doesn't guarantee happiness but it does provide you with more freedom as long as you don't use it to buy drugs. Be careful, money easily distorts relationships.

You will begin earning money with entry-level positions. They may be called entry-level, but they will provide you with a lot more than just money. These beginning jobs will reinforce your values of responsibility and teamwork and you will make new friends and find new mentors to name some of the benefits.

Most people keep their money in a checking account and have a debit card. Keep track of the withdrawals and deposits and have the discipline to balance your check book so you don't get charged overdraft fees if you accidentally run out of money in your account.

Think of banks as legalized and protected loan sharks that try to entice you to use their money now so you can pay them a lot for the money you use. Interest of up to 24% is robbery but they charge that percentage and more. Avoid credit card debt at all costs.

Don't let yourself get played by the banks and their credit card companies. Think of them as legalized loan sharks.

Hand-eye coordination

Hand-eye coordination and hand dexterity are practical skills that are very important in some professions like surgery, assembly and fabrication, machine repair and flying airplanes.

Be sure to stay active in creative and construction projects so you have experience with tools and using your hands to make and repair things. Maintain a rounded education including artistic subjects and activities that require hand and finger coordination and manipulation.

Surgeons, as an example, need dexterity and skill in sewing or stitching, skills that used to be learned at school or at home in play. Technicians need to be natural in the use of their hands as they manipulate tools and install parts. Unfortunately, many schools are cutting back on creative and manual activities in favor of academic ones where performance can be measured with standardized testing.

Watching two-dimensional flat screens and operating a mouse and game controllers do not provide the hands-on skills needed to carry out tasks that can only be learned with practice in manipulating your hands and fingers in the handling and use of tools and parts.

Improvise, Adapt and Overcome

"You improvise, you adapt, you overcome." You have the smarts and the power to apply the Marine Corps' motto and succeed just like Gunnery Sergeant Highway, played by Clint Eastwood, told his recruits in the movie *Heartbreak Ridge*. Yes, you want your independence but you also have to be creative in solving problems as you comply with your parents' wishes and work within your educational system and more.

Practice with obstacles you face today to learn how you are going to solve tomorrow's problems. Don't try and take the problems on whole. You have to analyze and break them down into smaller pieces and overcome them bit by bit. That is the big thing that school is trying to teach you.

An example that you are very familiar with is your school grades. You want to get in "A" in all your classes but to do so you

Who are you?

need to go to class, do the homework on time, read and study the assignments, ask questions and prepare for the quizzes and tests. When you breakdown what it takes to get an "A" you can see the obstacles that you need to overcome so that you learn and can be tested on the information.

The information is always presented to you ahead of time and there are no secrets as to what is going to be on the tests. It is up to you to make the effort to learn the material so you can get an "A"

Life can seem difficult but at least you have life so make the best of it. Adjust your frame of reference from "I can't" to "I can" and you will succeed.

We all have a tendency to blame others for things that seem challenging or to feel sorry for ourselves when the going gets tough. As an alternative, use today's difficult situations to practice your problem solving and critical thinking skills. First, identify the problem; second, consider alternatives; third, formulate a plan with contingencies, and fourth, implement the plan. And, if that doesn't work, learn from your mistakes and try again.

It is easy to procrastinate, to blame the teacher or the school or the school board or to implicate social media or any other number of reasons as to why we feel down or why we didn't perform as we know we could have but the real reason rests with each of us. We didn't keep our wits about us and put out our best effort. I always say, "As long as I did my best, nobody can ask any more of me."

If you are having a problem with school—get on the ball and focus on the problem. If a friend in class is distracting you or if you are not doing your homework, then recognize what is holding you back and address it. Don't let the problem take you down. If you can't see the smart board or are easily distracted, move to the front of the class. If you are tired in school then go to bed earlier. I am sure that you are resourceful and smart enough, but you may just need to start to think of school as your job—train yourself and overcome the distractions and difficulties.

Seriously, have you made a sincere effort to analyze the possible causes for the problem? Is it you or something or someone else?

Is it a controllable or an uncontrollable? Write it out, break it down, examine the pieces. Look at your online assignments and digital resources for help. It's like a mindset—go with the mindset that you are going to accomplish something even if you are not interested.

Arrive at your classes prepared because you have work to do just like a carpenter has work to do when he frames a house. He needs to be prepared by having his plans, materials and a hammer each day otherwise the house won't get built. As a student you are like the carpenter because you can't construct your house if you don't bring your plans, materials, and hammer each day.

Keep your immediate objectives in focus. All you have to do now is go to school and learn so you can have the necessary skills to apply tomorrow when you want to make a lot of money.

You don't have to work as child labor in factories making textiles like in the 1800's because your family doesn't have any money. You may want to speak to issues where adults can help. You don't have to worry about being sent to fight in a war and getting injured or killed. All you have to do is go to school and learn so you can have a fun life.

Keep it all relative and you'll see that you might not have serious problems and if you still think that you do, then think about how you can overcome them just like your ancestors strove to overcome theirs.

Turn problems into a game or a list. Don't make perceived problems bigger than they are and remember it is all relative.

Stand up for yourself and take charge of your life and do what you need to do to help yourself and move on. Advocate for yourself—try not to leave it to others to take care of you. This is called maturity.

My grandfather on my mother's side was named Adolfo Carbone. His clock started in 1898 and it stopped in 1993 when he was 94 years old. I lived with him for ten years in the same house I live in now. I know that his ghost is still here and that he is always looking out for us just as your ancestors are looking out for you.

He was a neat grandfather with a tough childhood. He was born

Who are you?

in Genoa, Italy and he started working as a cabin boy on a steam powered merchant ship when he was 16 years old. He came from a family of mariners.

He was still working on merchant ships when WWI started and Italy was allied with America against Germany. At that time, one of his jobs, when he wasn't shoveling coal into the boilers, was to oil the bearings that ran along the 16-inch solid steel propeller shaft from where the shaft started at the steam engine all the way to the very back end of the ship where the shaft went through the hull and attached to the propeller. To access all the bearings, he had to walk in a small low tunnel which ran next to the shaft, checking the oil reservoir for each bearing about every 10 feet or so for about 150 feet.

"One day," he told me, "shortly after the ship had left port in Genoa I finished checking the bearings and came out of the tunnel. I sat down on the concrete platform that supported the electrical generator. At that moment the ship was hit by a torpedo from a German submarine. The ship shook violently and quickly started to sink. We all ran up the stairs from the engine room to get out of the ship as quickly as possible.

"If I had still been in that tunnel when the torpedo hit I never could have gotten out fast enough. I would have been trapped. I escaped the ship as it sunk and was able to swim to shore and run back home in my underwear. My family was surprised to see me return, but I soon signed up onto another ship. It was also sunk by a torpedo one night when we came out of the Suez Canal.

"We were asleep when it hit and Marcello, one of my good friends, calmed us down and told us what to do. When he didn't follow us out I asked him where he was going and he said he had to help someone else. That was the last time I saw him."

None of this really applies to your education except to show that his school was a hot steam engine room on a ship on the sea where he shoveled coal into the boilers with the shadow of death always present; it almost killed him twice but he was a survivor that could improvise, adapt, and overcome whatever problems he encountered. He was also lucky; otherwise, I wouldn't be writing these words today. He had to survive or he was dead. My grandpa wasn't going to be defeated, except when it came to cigarettes.

Grandpa was addicted to smoking cigarettes. He probably started when he was 15-years-old. After the war in 1923, when he was 25-five-years old, he was employed on the Dante Aligeri, another merchant ship. When it docked in New York City, he decided to "jump ship," which means he didn't return to the ship, and he became an illegal immigrant. He was so addicted to smoking that he smoked the strongest cigarettes available which were Camel brand, non-filtered. By the time he was in his 60's, the cigarettes were quickly killing him and he struggled to quit but couldn't. He was smoking two packs per day and there are 20 cigarettes per pack. That would be a cigarette every 30 minutes.

He would tell me the story of how the cigarettes were affecting him so badly that he couldn't catch his breath and that he was having difficulty recovering when he got sick. He would cough and feel horrible and he knew that the cigarettes were going to slowly kill him, but he felt helpless in the face of the problem. Two torpedoes full of gunpowder didn't sink him, but those little white cigarettes were slowly taking him down.

He told me in his broken English, "One day I was laying in bed sick and I felt so bad. I kept coughing and coughing and couldn't stop. I could see the pack of cigarettes on the table next to me and I asked himself, "Am I going to the cigarettes or are the cigarettes coming to me."

He told me, "I kept watching them and they never moved. They stayed right there on the table.

"I stopped smoking that day."

I still have his very last pack of Camels, the ones that didn't move. He saved them as a reminder.

The same applies to you.

Look at your problems, break them down to see what is causing them, and address the problems in small steps.

My grandfather realized that the problem wasn't the cigarettes; the problem was that he kept reaching for them. He just had to stop

Who are you?

reaching for them so he could solve his problem and feel better.

He improvised, adapted, and overcame, and you can also.

Interpersonal Relations

Getting along with people is a critical soft skill. It doesn't matter how book smart somebody is; if people don't want to work you, you aren't going anywhere—unless you own the company and then you started at the top.

Surprisingly, people skills are just-if not more-important at the top. People like to be treated with respect, bottom to top.

Journal Writing

**A journal is a great way to document
what you did and your concerns.**

Keep a journal that you write in every evening. It has a lot of benefits even if you miss a few evenings. Something is better than nothing.

Then, take some time to review it periodically so you can see how your life is progressing and what you are doing with your time. Notice any patterns and gain any insight about your life and how you are using your time?

Journal writing will help you to unload your concerns and fall asleep.

Write a letter to yourself about where you think you are headed that you can read to yourself in the future.

When my daughter graduated from high school, she received an envelope in the mail with a letter that her sixth-grade elementary school teacher had posted to her with a letter that Mary Jane had written to herself. She enjoyed the time capsule from herself and felt part of an experience just like in the movie *Back to the Future*. She didn't even remember writing the letter.

The letter created a priceless moment from when she wrote it and now when she received it from her former self.

Remember that the more you write, the better you get, and the better you get, the more you will enjoy writing.

I never consider myself to be a writer, but since I wrote this book I guess I am.

Here is a journal entry I wrote about my future wife, Kathleen, before I went to sleep the evening I met her.

As background information regarding the entry, the "Fallon's" were friends of my parents with children the same ages as me and my sister. Bob Fallon, the dad, was my godfather and of Irish decent. We called him Uncle Bob. He was always the life of the party and would keep everyone laughing with his wit. Unfortunately he died in 2016.

December 28, 1985

Tonight dad, mom and I went to the Fallon's for a small holiday party. I had hoped to talk with Kathleen (Bob's daughter) since it had been a couple of years since I had seen her but she stayed with her group of friends.

Instead I talked with Patrick (Bob's son) about school and work. After a while I went to see what mom and dad were doing and I started talking with Matt Travers again and found his sister Kathleen to be very friendly, interesting, and energetic.

We talked about work and she just graduated as an occupational therapist and now works for Fairfax County Schools. The conversation turned towards Europe when she mentioned that she had 3-month summer vacations. Kathleen had spent two months in Europe last year backpacking through five countries and she did very well with her Euro-pass.

She has pretty green eyes, short blond hair, and a cute figure. But best of all Kathleen had large dimples and loved to smile.

Meeting her made the evening worthwhile and I hope I can see her next month sometime. I could invite her to the play at the Kreeger Theatre.

As it turned out, Kathleen's parents know mine and she is from a family of four children. They live in Mantua and knew of Fairfax

Who are you?

Propane.

She invited me to Europe with her this summer to which I quickly accepted.

Now I just have to wait and see what happens.

Journal entry one year later.

January 13, 1987

Kathleen and I continue to have a good time together. She is a real star, shinning ever so bright. I have never felt so comfortable as I do with her.

It is hard for me to believe that it has been a year since we met. I am so glad we did. She has made life much more enjoyable by being my close friend and companion.

Kathleen has everything I could possible look for in a woman. She is intelligent, playful, patient, adventurous, flexible, and happy. Kathleen is very loving and understanding and independent. I cannot think of anything I would change about her. She is very special.

I'm glad I was keeping a journal during the time I met and started dating Kathleen so I had the opportunity to look back and relive my feelings and insights and see how things worked out.

The events became priceless moments in my life and you can capture your own daily life events if you take the time to write them down as they occur so you can see what insights you may gain way off at some unknown time in your future.

Language - spoken, and learning another

The reason it is so much easier to learn your first or second language when you are young is because your brain is receptive to all sounds and has not been conditioned to only hear specific sounds such as of your first language. It can hear all the unique different sounds used in different languages because it doesn't discriminate from the repetition. As you get older. your brain gets trained to only hear the sounds associated with your primary language and it starts to exclude the others.

Learn another language while you are young because it is relatively easy compared with when you get older. Watching movies and listening to music in another language is very helpful also and the way that most children outside the U.S. perfect their English.

Foreign exchange students hosted for the summer.

We have had many foreign exchange students live with us for a month during the summer. It has been a great experience.

It is easier to bring Europe to your family than to bring your family to Europe. And sometimes the student returns the following summer and then one of my children returns to the native country with them for a reciprocal adventure.

Leadership

Leadership is a very important and valuable skill, and if you have it you don't get credit for it in school because it can't be measured in a standard classroom environment.

The difficulty with leadership is that it is comprised of many intangible skills including being able to earn respect and flexibility in relationships. You can be given authority, but that does not mean you have leadership.

Leadership is an attribute colleges routinely look for in applications. Businesses will make note of your responsible decisions.

Learning

So many ways to learn, lots of money you can earn.

Technology has provided you with unlimited ways to learn about every subject conceivable from Java and C+ programming to caring for hamsters, video editing to macro economics, linear calculus to cybersecurity, and building drones to recording songs. Your classroom and personal options are incredible.

There are so many online classrooms, free or with a cheap

Who are you?

monthly subscription, that there is no reason why you shouldn't be able to get an A in every class you take but for a lack of persistence.

Granted, computer learning takes discipline, but the trade off in knowledge gained is so valuable. The best part is that since you have so few responsibilities now, you have lots of time for learning and then lots of time in front of you to apply what you learn today.

When my son Mike was in seventh grade, he became interested in building drones and every afternoon when he got home from school he would sit and watch videos by a guy in Australia about how to build them. Learning from YouTube videos was such a new concept that I didn't catch on as to what he was up to right away and then I realized that if I just bought him the parts that he could apply what he was learning.

It blew my mind to see how cheap the specialized electronic parts were and that with just a few clicks and my credit card number he could order direct from China. The packages showed up in about 10 days—something that was absolutely inconceivable when I was his age. Back then, I thought it was neat just to have a transistor radio from Japan.

He did a great job on his drones, which he built with the help of his cousin who was also interested in drones. He was able to fly the one he build outside our home until we got placed in a drone no-fly zone which kind of killed his drive.

My advice for hands-on learning is to find something that you can build or take apart so you can learn about the parts, what they do, how it goes together, and how it works. Look around and see what you have or just buy the materials that you need which are usually pretty cheap if you are resourceful.

There are unlimited opportunities for you to learn and explore. Whether it is how to run a software program to make an online game or how to create an animation to amuse your friends, an old lawnmower engine or an old dishwasher to take apart or some left over lumber that you can saw and nail together to build something or use bricks so you can try bricklaying, the possibilities for you are endless.

Learning is a life long skill and when tied with curiosity and persistence, it will be very financially rewarding for you.

Listening

It is important to have good listening skills. If someone is talking with you, stop what you are doing and look at them. Put your phone down and engage with them in a conversation. Don't act impatient.

Give them your full attention no matter how hard it might be. They are talking to you for any number of reasons and not paying attention to them is very disrespectful.

Machines

What machines can you operate, maintain, and repair, and why are they important to you?

You know how to operate your phone, run your computer, and drive a car. What else can you do with machines? Running machines increases your productivity, and adds to your quality of life and your value to others.

Machines are defined as an assembly of parts that together perform work.

Do you know how the car you drive works? Have you tried to fix your computer or understand what ip addresses are and how they are used by the Internet to route traffic through routers? Have you taken a teen living class and used a sewing machine or taken a shop class and used wood working tools and other types of machines?

Machines are very important in helping you maintain the quality of your life. The more you know about them and how they function, the better you will be able to use and maintain them so they can keep working for you.

Organization

How are your organization skills rated and do you keep yourself organized?

Who are you?

Problem solving

It is also known as critical thinking. This is what you will be doing for the rest of your life.

I always thought that everyone else approached problems the way I do but then, when I was in my twenties, I realized that they didn't and I needed to take that into consideration when I was working with other people so we could achieve better results.

I might need to explain my thoughts to them and they might need to explain their thoughts to me or I needed to ask some questions so that we had better communication and together we had a better understanding of what each of us was thinking. It's a better way to solve a problem.

Reading

Reading is the best way to improve your critical thinking skills without any risk of physical injury compared with sports which is counter productive.

Reading is like watching TV in your head.

Reading is a very efficient way for you to learn because you can gain a lot of in-depth knowledge with the only cost being the time you spend reading. So why don't you read more?

It is the best exercise for your brain to keep it trim and fit. To keep it exercised.

Electronics and gaming are like sugar for your brain.

Do you want a slow, fat brain or a quick one?

Do you want to score points and win?

How are you training your brain for the big game?

Skin

How well do you take care of your skin? It is the biggest organ that you have.

Are you exhibiting responsible behaviors by taking measures to protect it from the sun so you don't get skin cancer when you get older?

56

How you take care of your body says a lot about you and your priorities.

Strategic thinking

Write a strategic plan on where you are trying to go. Try to stay on track and periodically review and update it.

Saving your money by living at home after you graduate instead of rushing out to get an apartment is just one example of strategic thinking. By staying at home you can use your saved money for a down payment on a house and once you have a house you can rent out rooms to help make the mortgage payment.

Surroundings and personal security

How aware are you about your surroundings?

I noticed when I ate at a restaurant with another friend, Don Goins, who worked for Arlington County Fire Department, that before he would sit down he would stand next to the table and look around the restaurant.

Finally one day I asked him, "What are you doing?"

Don responded, "I always check to see where the fire exits are located before I sit down at a restaurant."

That was a new one on me and so I think of him every time I go out to eat. I always take a second to get a reference as to where the exits are located, too.

Personal security is a growing need and skill in today's world.

Telephone use

You need to practice your skills in initiating and responding to telephone calls. As kids, we would race to see who could answer the phone first. Now, my kids won't answer the phone. What changed?

Thank you cards

Do you make a practice of sending hand written thank you cards as an expression of gratitude when appropriate?

These very simple forms of expression are still important and

Who are you?

get noticed now more than ever. They can carry a lot of weight about who you are, how you express yourself, and your maturity.

Buy some and use them if you are not already and emails and texts work too but are not as tangible.

Typing

Get rid of your bad typing habits as soon as possible and focus on proper touch typing where you won't have to look at the keys, including number keys. You might not think that this is very important but it is.

Touch typing and keyboarding is easy to learn and you are going to be typing or entering data of some kind all your life. It is important that you fix your bad habits. It isn't hard, you just have to practice the muscle memory and then you will be very efficient. So make correcting your typing a priority and then move on to something else.

Keep in mind that gaming keyboards are easier and neater to use because they have mechanical switches instead of plastic ones and they even make more noise kind of like a real typewriter.

I learned how to type in high school. My teacher was named Mrs. Rowe and we had manual typewriters. Manual means they didn't use electricity to type, just finger power. And yes, they made a steady click, click, click snapping sound.

It was fun when we would take a test because there was a lot of noise with all of us banging away as fast as we could at the same time trying to get the best score.

Typing served my grandmother, mother, and mother-in-law very well and was critical to their successful careers. And typing skills could have saved my friend Joe's life because he didn't have to carry a gun in Vietnam. Instead he carried a typewriter because his assigned duty was to be a clerk. His was a case where something as simple as typing not only got him more comfortable accommodations in a war zone but it probably also saved him from serious injury or death.

Touch typing is probably the easiest thing that you can learn relative to how much it will benefit you the most throughout your life. For the little amount of effort it takes to learn, you can't go wrong.

I even bought some old typewriters for my children to practice on because it is more fun to practice typing when it makes noise and we have typing books that stand up next to the typewriter for practice.

My oldest son John took typing class and received a certificate that he could type 61 words per minute. I took the test at the same time and we tied. The certification test is a timed five minute test. You are only allowed five errors but you can correct as you type. Now he can include his typing certification on his resume.

Schools would serve their students well to promote typing and even have sports competitions as to who can type the fastest with the least errors. The students would be better served with typing sports than running around with a stick chasing the person that has the ball.

There is resurgence in interest of using typewriters and I have a small collection of them that I collected when we used to go to yard sales. They are neat machines.

Touch typing is especially important for computer programmers because as a programmer writing code you want to focus on the process you are developing more than where the keys are; you want to be able to type as fast as possible so you can be efficient, and you don't want to make typing mistakes or your program will have errors that you have to go back and fix.

Quoting Holden Caulfield in *Catcher In the Rye, It kills me* when I see that everybody is struggling to use their keyboard without simple, easy, and proper typing skills. It doesn't make any sense to me as to why so many young people are torturing themselves to do something that, with a little effort, can easily become natural.

There is no way I could have written this book if I didn't know how to type and to be able to type quickly.

Who are you?

Writing 101

Writing is a way to collect your thoughts and to make a permanent record of them. How are your writing skills?

Writing is kind of like speaking but when you write for yourself such as in your journal, you don't have to worry about whom you are writing for or what they might think or whether you will be embarrassed by what you would say. When you write it is for you and you can play with the words and ideas as you wish to see what suits you.

If you want to remember something, you have to write it down.
Clear and concise writing is essential for communication.

You can't take the time to make funny videos or take a photo with a sentence in it every time you want to communicate with someone.

If you give someone instructions to follow, take the time to write down the steps. Otherwise, the tasks won't be completed quite the way you intended, and you can't blame them for not following your verbal directions.

Writing creatively

I wish I had discovered creative writing sooner as a possible productive endeavor. We have all been told that writers don't make any money, so I dismissed it. I recently learned that creative writing is a sub-discipline of English in school and that it is about story telling. I had thought that it all fell into the same "English" subject that always seemed to torture me. I didn't know there was a science to creative writing with aspects for character development, plot, conflict and resolution.

Writing this handbook has been creative writing for me and I have enjoyed the process immensely even thought it would fall under self-help which is considered non-fiction. Sharing my story and ideas with you has been very therapeutic and a lot of fun. I have enjoyed putting all of this together for you.

I have a novel that I started writing in 2016 about a sheriff that wants to save America and democracy by fighting corrupted governance.

Stay tuned. Every week now, I seem to create new story scenarios!

There are a lot of positive aspects to creative writing of which I was not aware. One of the neatest ones is being able to express your story or ideas in a creative way. Another is being able to document your own personal story of growth and experience. The best reason for creative writing is the sense of accomplishment you feel as you take all the ideas that are running around in your head, get them out and on paper, and organize them so they can be seen and understood.

Practicing creative writing is a very fulfilling experience because you quickly get to see what you created. Then, you have room for more ideas. Writing also, as said earlier, keeps the mind engaged and exercised. Creativity builds abstract thinking skills.

Driving skills

The goal of driving is to deliver the load safely.

Actual driving isn't hard, it's the discipline to pay attention that's the problem. You need to focus, pay attention, and anticipate.

How do you drive? Driving is also a reflection of who you are. Do you think like a truck driver would when you drive?

The mentality of a truck driver is different because when you drive a big heavy truck you have to use an opposite skill set than that of say a race car driver whose goal is to get there as fast as possible. The goal of a truck driver is to get the load delivered safely no matter how long it takes.

When you drive a heavy truck you have to have to take your time or you are going to have a crash and equipment is going to gt damaged and people are going to get hurt.

I remember that there was a tractor-trailer driver who rolled his

Who are you?

tractor-trailer truck with 10,000 gallons of gasoline on an entrance ramp to Interstate 95 in Newington, Virginia one night. The gasoline caught fire and he was killed. A few years later I was taking an overnight MegaBus from Knoxville, Tennessee to Washington, D.C., and we stopped in Christiansburg, Virginia for a break at 3 a.m., and I started a conversation with one of the team night drivers and learned that he used to haul gasoline and I mentioned the recent accident. He said that he knew the accident well and that he was the last person to talk to the driver because he had been loading his truck at the rack at the same time as the driver that was killed and the last thing the driver said was that he was in a big hurry so he wasn't surprised when he saw the explosion and fire.

When you drive a truck you have to pay extra attention to what is going on around you because you need more time to slow down and stop or to maneuver if there is a hazard in your path.

So whether you are driving alone or your little brother or sister to practice or yourself to a party, always take your responsibility to deliver your load as seriously and with as much care as if you were driving a truck loaded with nitroglycerin or explosives. Drive defensively and gently.

Another tip you can use when you are driving on a highway is to get in behind a tractor-trailer so you can have a more relaxing trip. The truck driver will keep a moderate pace and nobody will cut in front of you, and if anything happens in front of you, the truck will take the impact and push it out of your way.

Don't crowd trucks.

When you encounter them on the street give them room and be patient. Stop if it looks like they are trying to maneuver and give them a chance to position their truck. Let the cars wait behind you. Don't try to quickly sneak around the truck. Your courtesy will be much appreciated by the truck driver.

Don't challenge trucks on the road. Be aware that they might not see you when you are beside them. Cars always lose.

As you have been told, texting is a dangerous aspect to driving. Falling asleep while driving is another with disastrous consequences.

Do not push yourself when you are tired because it only takes a second to nod off and lose control of your vehicle, crash, and die.

When you feel your eyes closing, opening the window and turning the music louder won't help. You are, as we truckers say, "zoning out." You need to get off the road and take a nap. Don't push yourself even if it is in the middle of the day. Stop and take a rest somewhere safe.

Always approach traffic lights as if they are going to turn yellow just before you get to them. Do not approach them as if you are trying to beat the yellow.

Driving with the windows down gives you more information as to what is going around you because it allows you to use your sense of hearing as you drive. You can hear other vehicles as they approach or drive by you without having noticed them in your mirrors. Listening to music, while entertaining, is a distraction from what could be important.

Coast up to red lights and don't wait until the last minute to hit your brakes when stopping. Start braking sooner so anybody behind you will hopefully have a longer chance to see that you are stopping and they will be less likely to run into the back of you because they were not paying attention.

When driving keep in mind that you have anti-lock brakes so if you brake hard you will not lock up the tires and skid. The anti-lock mechanism will keep your wheels turning to try and help you maintain control of the car even as it seems like it should stop faster. All the recent cars are engineered so they won't skid because the coefficient of sliding friction is less than the coefficient of braking friction so supposedly you will stop faster if the wheels don't lock up. You will not be able to steer with your front wheels when they are skidding.

Do you have good driving habits?

Most importantly, stay focused on what is in front of you at all times. Be careful as you crest a hill because you don't know what is on the other side. If traffic is stopped when you top the hill you might crash into whatever is in the road. It could be a truck that is stopped

Who are you?

while it is backing into a driveway. It could be a line of traffic from an accident. Be especially careful when cresting a hill if there isn't a car in front of you that will provide an indication with their brake lights when they crest the hill that there is a hazard on the other side.

Staying focused and seeing the hazards before it is too late is key to accident free driving.

Even if you happen to notice something that is very unusual or unexpected while driving, such as some furries that just happen to be walking on the sidewalk, stay focused to what is happening in front of you. Don't take your mind off of your driving. They're just furries.

Be especially careful if you drive a car to school because a lot of accidents occur in school parking lots because of so many inexperienced drivers and distractions as to who might be watching you drive and how cool you are. Chill and pay attention because you are going to be embarrassed and look a lot worse if you have an accident because you are in a hurry and/or not paying attention.

You also need to be careful when approaching and driving by accidents on the road because if you are paying more attention to what happened at the scene of the accident than your driving it is very easy to drive right into the car in front of you when they slow down because they are more curious than you. Stay focused on what is going on in front of you and don't slow down to rubber neck which slows up the traffic behind you even more. Don't contribute to the traffic by causing even another accident and looking really stupid. Pay attention to what really matters and realize that the accident was probably caused because someone wasn't paying attention in the first place.

The worst accident I witnessed was about 2004 when I was driving a tractor-trailer loaded with 9,000 gallons of propane south just past the Key Bridge in Baltimore at about 45 mph. It was about 1 a.m. as I was traveling up and down over some small little hills in the road, when a guy that was racing somebody else passed me on the left driving about 90 mph. The little hills blocked the view of the lead driver so he never saw the car in his lane. He crested a hill and creamed right into the back of the car that was traveling at about 50 mph. As he hit it from the rear it spun out of control into to my lane and headed for the concrete wall on my right. There wasn't anything I could do but drive straight and pray I was going to get through it as I waited for the car to bounce off the concrete wall on my right and into my truck. Thankfully it didn't come back toward me or my trailer. It all happened very fast.

When the guy that was leading the race smashed into the back of the car that was in his lane, he hit it so hard that the complete front of his car was smashed in and it had lost all its power and all its lights. He was just coasting at about 20 mph as I passed him. I pulled on my air horn to let him know where I was so he didn't decide to pull into my lane to get off the road. I'm sure he was stunned.

The buddy he was racing was driving so fast that he had passed his friend's crashed car and was parked on the left shoulder waiting for him to catch up as I drove ahead further.

I really felt sorry for the driver of the car that got creamed from behind because the driver was just minding his own business probably heading home and never had a clue about the danger that was coming up quickly behind him.

Another sad story is that I knew a very nice firefighter who helped me in the winter part-time driving propane trucks. His name was Harold Sisson. One Saturday Harold helped some friends move their belongings and he was so tired that on his way home he fell asleep and crashed into a tree and died.

Another incident occurred in 2002 when, driving at 55 mph north of Dulles Airport, I had a driver in a small SUV with a short wheelbase and a high center of gravity pass me on the left because she was in a hurry. The car in her lane was driving too slow for her so she pulled into my lane and then when she saw another car farther up in my lane that she wouldn't be able to get around she quickly pulled back into the left lane. She was in such a hurry and made such quick lane changes that she over compensated on the pull back into the left lane losing control of her car. It started flipping at over at 60 mph, bouncing right in front of me as it careened off the right side of

Who are you?

the road with car parts flying off into the air. It flipped over one time completely in the air, just like in the movies, and then at least three more times as it hit the pavement before it came to rest in a ditch. It was flipping so close to me that I had to brake hard as it spun and bounced into my lane and onto the shoulder to avoid hitting it.

The female driver was dazed she was able to get herself out of the car by the time I had stopped and ran back to her and her male passenger. I got the passenger out after I ran back to my car for a tool to try and pry his door open. Fortunately, the car landed right side up. They survived, but I am sure that the passenger got more than he bargained for in that ride.

So, please be careful when you drive or even when you are a pedestrian or when you are standing on the curb waiting for a bus to arrive. Pay attention and think about what is going on around you and take care of yourself.

Another aspect to driving is to drive with consideration and recognition for the people traveling behind you. You want to be driving your car and paying attention to what is occurring in front of you so you can avoid having to brake quickly which may catch someone driving behind you by surprise. You could be hit from behind if that driver is following you too closely, driving to fast or distracted.

As a rule it is best to drive slower and begin braking earlier so the person traveling behind you will have been put on notice sooner that you are slowing down. This will help in preventing your car from being hit from the rear which is going to damage the back of your car and the front of theirs. Sometimes just being involved in an accident can cause your insurance premium to go up even if it wasn't your fault.

You also need to drive with consideration for the people to your side so that you have sufficient time to adjust your driving if you or they need to change lanes unexpectedly or quickly. Don't drive just thinking about yourself. You need to take the perspective of the other drivers around you into consideration so that you can try to read their mind as to what indicators their driving is showing. Are they driving slow because they are confused and, therefore, getting ready to turn or are they tailgating someone which means they are in a hurry and could get in trouble and suddenly jump into your lane if the person they are following decides or has to stop suddenly?

Anticipate. Anticipate. Anticipate.

Do you think about what you can see and what others can't see? Do you think that they see the traffic slowing down in front of them or that there is a hazard in the road that might surprise them and cause them to swerve and set up a chain reaction of events?

Driving is a continuous exercise in monitoring all the events in a dynamic environment and considering all the what-ifs. It isn't about thinking how important you are and how you have the right-of-way. Definitely, it isn't about trying to find the right song on the radio or making sure your phone is accessible. It is about driving in a way that you can deliver your load safely taking into consideration all the other possible hazards along the way and people that are driving at the same time with you and the problems they may cause.

The best way to avoid problems is to **anticipate and drive slowly** which increases your time to react. Then your reaction to un-expected circumstances doesn't have to be as radical and severe.

Physics and momentum

Driving is all about physics and Newton's first law of motion which is referred to as the law of inertia. It is often stated as, "An object at rest stays at rest and an object in motion stays in motion with the same speed and in the same direction unless acted upon by an unbalanced force."

Just think of the car you drive as the object in motion and that it will continue in the same speed and in the same direction unless you apply the brakes or turn the steering wheel to change its direction.

So, pay attention while driving. There are no "undo" or "back-space" buttons for car crashes.

Another thing to consider is that your car only does what you tell it to do. Cars are engineered and designed so you are in control. You control where your car goes so it doesn't run into the tree. Trees don't just grow up in the road and the cars smash into them. The driver was supposed to have been in control of the car before it hit the tree. The driver can't blame the accident on the car or the tree.

Riding—with a friend driving

It is also important to be very careful about who you get rides with and the roads you are traveling. A lot of times it is the passenger that pays the price for the drivers deficiencies.

As a youth I had several very scary instances and close calls when I was a passenger in a car because I didn't know better or because I was put in bad situations. You need to try to recognize and avoid potentially hazardous situations ahead of time so that you can avoid putting yourself at risk in the first place. If you end up in a situation where someone else's driving is making you uncomfortable, you should assume some leadership and politely ask them to slow down and to pay more attention or to stop so you can get out.

My friend from school, Simon Thompson, whom I reference in the section titled death, was the passenger in a car that crashed eight days after we graduated from high school at 4:39 in the afternoon. He died at the hospital seventeen days later on July 6, 1976. He was only 19 years old.

I have included a copy of his typewriter prepared death certificate at the end of the book in the addendum.

My best advice is to take your time and not rush and be careful with whom you trust your life and future. You have a whole lifetime in front of you.

Be very careful not make a rash decision that could cause your life to be shortened unexpectedly.

Stay in control.

Chill.

Chapter two

Phases of Life; Education, Career, Timing, Alternatives, and Beyond.

It is important to understand that there are many phases of life and what is important in each of them, how they build on each other, and how they are linked.

It is also important to understand how happiness is defined and changes as priorities and life changes. You need to be thinking about tomorrow's happiness, not today's, and you need to have a plan for how you are going to get to your happiness zone.

Think about tomorrow's happiness today.

The Road Not Taken
By Robert Frost

Two roads diverged in a yellow wood,
And sorry I could not travel both
And be one traveler, long I stood
And looked down one as far as I could
To where it bent in the undergrowth;

Phases of Life

Then took the other, as just as fair,
And having perhaps the better claim,
Because it was grassy and wanted wear;
Though as for that the passing there
Had worn them really about the same,

And both that morning equally lay
In leaves no step had trodden black.
Oh, I kept the first for another day!
Yet knowing how way leads on to way,
I doubted if I should ever come back.

I shall be telling this with a sigh
Somewhere ages and ages hence:
Two roads diverged in a wood, and I—
I took the one less traveled by,
And that has made all the difference.   (1916)

Phases of life - in general

Your life can be divided up into different distinct phases. It is important for you to understand each phase and to understand what you should be accomplishing as you progress through each and why each is important to your future.

Life is a competitive endeavor. You are always competing for something and you can stay in the game if you stay competitive. Just like a baseball game, the game of life has many innings or phases that you progress through. You want to stay in your game and play it with your teammates as long as possible.

Your continued progress through each inning or phase will help prepare and position you as best as possible for the opportunities of your next phase. You need to keep advancing through the phases so that you don't get hit with a setback in your progress. It is impossible to make up for lost time because many phase related opportunities are associated with a narrow age window so it is important to keep them in relative sync or you will miss out on a lot of opportunities.

There are many phases that you may or may not move through or ones that you may skip and or repeat. Career and relationship phases can be dependent on each other and can run concurrently.

The major phases, simplified, are listed as;
>Learning—High School/College
>First Part-time Job
>Internship option
>Job searching
>First Full-time Job
>Career Development
>Dating
>Marriage
>Children
>Empty nest
>Retirement
>Senior

Right now you are in the Learning—High School/College Phase.

Understand the phases: what is unique and important about each one, how you are progressing and what is coming next. Staying in the game will help you to live your life to the fullest for the longest possible time.

Watch out for delays that can cause you to have a setback or get stuck in a phase. Getting stuck for too long may cause you to not be as successful in securing the best employment opportunities or the right mate that was available to you had you continued on schedule. And, missing your best mate might cause you to miss out on the best possible family and missing out on the best family may cause you to miss out on the best children and on your best possible life. Keep moving along and stay on schedule. Keep up with the game and ev-

Phases of Life

erything should fall in place for you.

Setbacks can be caused by stress and stress can be caused because you didn't perform as you expected. Be careful in how you manage stress and don't let it make you feel discouraged. Stay focused on what is important and make the effort. You have to find the right balance between entertainment and working to stay in the game. Do what is right for you because you are what matters. Not everyone else. Don't make excuses for not putting out the effort. Don't get distracted.

Your family and society in general put a lot of pressure on you so you can successfully move through the phases of life and become an adult, a family person, and then a senior. As you know, it is a complicated process with many factors. It takes time to build one's self- esteem and confidence, and it takes time to learn and gain experience, all of which is part of maturing.

Your maturity isn't black and white, all or nothing. It is a gradual transition and you need guidance and reassurance so you feel confident in your progress. Watching YouTube clips and keeping Snapchat streaks going will not help you grow up because growing up is about figuring out your identity, gaining experience and establishing and developing relationships with other people. Snapchat streaks don't count because they are a distraction from what is important and all of it becomes one big blur.

As you mature you will develop your research skills. You are going to need these skills so you can improve your choices, decision making, and your life. One example of developing your research skills is how you start considering your future career and employment options even though that phase may be many years away.

What do you think you want to be when you grow up? Try making a broad list of your top 10 top ideas and see what it looks like. Rank your ideas by different factors such as what are the most appealing and then rank them by which probably pay the most money or offer a more interesting lifestyle. See how you would you prioritize these career options today and then, as new information becomes available, you can see how your perspective changes in the future.

Relying on your phone and the Internet for information is only going to provide you with a small piece of what you need to know. Don't limit yourself. To see a more complete picture of what is available to you, you are going to need inside information from experienced people with specialized knowledge in the areas you are considering. To learn what they can tell you, you are going to need to establish relationships with these insiders. Establishing these relationships is called networking. As you meet new people, you are creating a network of relationships unique to you.

I was studying electrical engineering but I didn't know any engineers or have much of an idea of my options or where I was going. They didn't have any career fairs that I knew of at school so I didn't have anyone in the industry that I could talk to. My interest in electrical engineering came from my curiosity of how radios worked in that I thought it was neat how electricity could be used to transmit and receive electromagnetic waves carrying information that could then be convert to sound.

Ruth, the mother of my high school girlfriend, worked with some electrical engineers and one day, after my freshmen year in college, she invited me to her office to talk with them about what they did.

I went to her office in Crystal City, Virginia, near Regan National Airport, and talked with the two engineers. From what I remember, they were designing antenna systems for the Navy in small and dreary offices. They explained what they were doing and it didn't seem very interesting to me at all and it seemed that they were not that excited with what they were doing either. The experience made me apprehensive about where the road I was on might be taking me and that meeting was probably the beginning of my eventual realization that I did not want to continue in electrical engineering or remain at Georgia Tech. Conversations with her husband Clair helped also.

I didn't have anyone to coach or mentor me with my college track or career other than my parents. I was pretty much on my own and knowing what I know today, I would have been approaching my career track a lot differently. But that was the way it was then.

Phases of Life

Today, I am trying to pass my knowledge and experience to my children, and with this handbook, I am trying to help you get and stay pointed in the right direction for you.

Most importantly, try to keep your personal growth on time and on track so you don't get hung up in a phase and miss future opportunities because of a delay. I bailed out of electrical engineering in time and was able to find something else that worked out. My two years at Georgia Tech did teach me a lot and I gained a lot of confidence in myself so it was not time wasted. No education is really wasted, but some times your time is a consideration. People who change majors more than twice probably needed more coaching before deciding their initial starting point.

Keep thinking and keep talking. Do research and have conversations. It is a huge world out there with lots of opportunities. Make the effort to think ahead about your next phase so you can be better prepared for it as you complete your current one. Visit your career center often while in college. See section titled Your Career, p. 119.

An example of getting really off track in your progression might be going off on an adventure that could take a year or longer that isn't going to improve your skills or marketability when you return other than to have given you another new life experience. I am not saying not to go on the adventure but before you do you should consider what future employment or higher education opportunities might pass you by because of your hiatus and how future employers might consider your adventure an indicator of your overall behavior to avoid responsibility.

Your very early twenties are the best time to get established in a profession that can provide you enjoyment for the rest of your life so make the most of this time period to get established. Put yourself and your future first before you rush off to try and save or explore the world. You can always go on an extended vacation after you are more established in a career and your future employer might even fund it and your interest in traveling or working in another country might be a plus in their recruitment process.

Think ahead and try to be clairvoyant so you are as educated as possible as you make your choices. Try to think through all the what ifs of your different options. Think strategically.

An example of how you can start thinking strategically is to attend college, career and higher education seminars. I have seen students in the college phase not giving much thought to their options in their next phase of career, professional or graduate school work. And, of course, high school students are just trying to navigate high school without much thought to the multitude of career options available.

Don't become a student that isn't thinking about their next phase. Be sure to attend as many of your school's sponsored career and advanced education events as possible. Ask questions, learn, and be an informed student.

These events are organized by the Career Services Department to make the resources and their information available to you, but you have to attend, be interested and motivated, ask questions and have conversations. When you engage you will find very qualified staff from all the various departments and companies that are happy to provide their specialized guidance and to answer your questions and more.

In October 2018, I attended a Graduate and Professional Fair at George Mason University that was held from 4 to 7 p.m. where every department was represented at a table on the floor of the sports arena. I don't think there were more than 40 students in attendance for the whole event. What a wasted opportunity for the students that didn't participate. Make sure you are one of the 40 at your fairs and then you can be privileged with the inside information and be that much further ahead faster.

I have also seen dismal attendance by students at numerous panels of industry professionals that were organized by George Mason Career Services. The panels are composed of well-connected professionals who are invited to offer students their inside experience, knowledge and the real scoop on what lays ahead. Unfortunately, very few students attend. Sometimes less than 10. The school has 25,000 undergraduate students. Why aren't they paying attention?

Phases of Life

What are they thinking?

I don't understand why today's students are so resistive to participating in these events. One reason may be because they think that they don't need the information because it is available to them in via the Internet when they go looking for it. Another reason may be because they already know what they need to know and they think they are as smart as the presenters. What ever the reason, don't be one of them and miss out on these opportunities to learn outside of the classroom.

What you learn from the panelists may be a lot more important to your future than what you learned in class all week or all month or all year. A lot of what they say may not be specifically relevant for you but they have lots of tidbits of good information. You just have to wait for it and then write it down so you don't forget what they said. And take notes so you can keep up with the flow of information. You need them to help you draw your map.

When these outside classroom learning opportunities are available to you don't stay trapped in a personal bubble only thinking in a linear fashion where you don't know how or you can't think about moving on to your next step until you finish the current one. Don't become a student who is on a journey of taking classes without a good road map of where your road is leading. Don't rely on Google maps to get you where you are going. Start drawing your road map of where you can go.

Life might appear linear where you have to finish step C before you can move to step D, but that doesn't apply in high school and especially after you graduate from high school. You have to be multitasking about your future.

You have so many opportunities in front of you that with each step there will be more options that you didn't see before. You need to be thinking and looking a few years ahead so you will be better positioned and prepared for that special intersection in the road when you arrive there.

Recognize that you are at a critical period the multitude of options you have now are going to start diminishing as you age and become more specialized.

And be sure to double check how your guidance counselors are guiding you. Don't take their advice verbatim. I heard a story recently of a student that was on track to get automatic acceptance from a four year college after completing their two-year Associates Degree at the community college. Unbeknown to them, even though they had laid out their plan with their guidance counselor two years earlier, they were not taking all the right courses for acceptance to the four year school so they had to attend the community college for an additional year. It was a big disappointment. Check and double check.

As a high school or college student you are in the learning phase now. When you graduate, you will probably be transitioning to the Job Searching Phase which will lead up to your First Full-time Job Phase.

Assuming you want to have a successful career and get paid lots of money so you can buy a car and a house, get married, have a family, go on vacations, save some money and live comfortably for the rest of your life, you want to be as highly qualified as possible for that first future prospective employer. Have a strategy so you will enter your next phase of First Full-time Job as far up the career ladder as possible and be able to earn a higher salary commensurate with your qualifications. When you are developing your plan remember that you will only have educational qualifications, not experience qualifications so don't think you are super smart and should get paid top dollar to start. It is only as you prove yourself and gain experience that you will slowly graduate to the Career Development Phase. Then with accumulation of even more specialized skills you will become more valuable to employers and be able to earn a higher salary.

One of your challenges is to avoid losing time taking classes or going down a career path that you are not interested or one which could become a dead end. Doing so for an extended period of time will cause you to miss opportunities that you could have had and then you will have to back track on your learning which will delay your entry into your next career path. Of course, you need time to explore

Phases of Life

your options and that is why the more you explore those options while in the learning phase the more informed and better career path decision you will be able to make.

If possible don't delay in choosing or finding your career track if you are comfortable that it is the right one for you because careers take specialized skills that can only be learned on the job and which take time. The sooner that you can understand what is right for you, the faster you can start applying yourself and accumulating those skills for your career and then the faster your earnings can progress and hopefully you will have higher job satisfaction.

You can't think in a linear step-by-step fashion anymore. You continually need to be multitasking and collecting information about the possibilities for your future while in the Learning Phase so you have a better sense of where you are going and what options are available to you as you enter the First full-time job phase.

To find those future options you have to talk with professional people about the employment opportunities they have available now or the ones they see coming in the near future. You always need to be gathering research for your next phase because your options are going to be difficult to assess and very important to your career and there is no benefit in waiting. The sooner you begin establishing relationships with the people that have the information the better prepared you will be.

The best way to learn about these career options is to make relationships with the people in specific fields of interest or learn about the paths students with similar interests have followed. You should be going to all the career fairs and talking with everybody about what they might have to offer, what they are hearing from others, and what is available for you to consider or what they are seeing in their area of expertise.

Think of yourself as a secret agent on a mission to gather intelligence about the mission that lies ahead. The mission is your life.

The intelligence you collect from your sources will provide you with a better and bigger road map of where you can go. And don't be so focused on one specific subject that you miss other things that might be worth considering. Keep an open mind and ask people what opportunities they have and what opportunities they see coming.

Your side job as a secret agent is really easy because the people you approach are ready, willing, and able to give you their information, whatever it is, because you are not a threat and they want to help you. You don't even have to bribe them for it, all you have to do is ask.

Keep in mind that you are going to need employers to help you on your path to a career. Nobody is just going to discover you, hold your hand, and dump money in your lap. You are going to have to promote yourself. You can't have a career on your own and no one is obligated to provide a successful one for you.

I have helped many people in their career paths by providing them employment opportunities and with it the opportunity to gain specialized skills and knowledge that they wouldn't have been able to get on their own. Some people have continued to work with me and others have moved on to work at other companies applying and building on the skills they learned with me. You will follow a similar path and some day you will be helping others on their career paths also.

My disappointment at the career fairs I attended was that so many students don't seem to have the wherewithal to even attend and ask questions. I could be wrong but it seems that today's students don't have much of an ability to look ahead or the initiative to try and find opportunities both of which are essential characteristics for all successful careers.

Don't make the same mistakes. Put your phone down, look up, and engage. Only then will you find a great big world of friendly people looking to talk with you and to help you draw your road map so you can stay in the game and win.

I recently met a truck driver who lives in North Carolina when we were both loading our tractor-trailers with propane. He told me about his second daughter who is 20-years-old and who just moved back home. He said that she recently told him, "I should have started listening to you a lot sooner, dad."

Phases of Life

I added, "Yes, but she missed the critical developmental phase of her life and now she can't make it up."

He shrugged his shoulders and said, "Well, better late than never. She wouldn't listen. At least now she gets it and realizes that I do have experience."

"And that counts for a lot," I added.

Train of life - your ride through the phases

You're the engineer for your train and you will have an easier ride if you can keep your train running on the right tracks and on time.

You don't want your train to be arriving late. As with all trains, it is important to stay on schedule.

Timing

Timing is everything.

Timing can work in your favor and against you also.

During one of the periods when my father was unemployed, my mother sent him to the store for a gallon of milk and while there he happened to meet an acquaintance who knew of a job opening at a government agency for someone with my father's credentials. Acting on this intelligence, my father was able to get a job with the agency because his work experience and educational background truly matched the agency's need.

Unfortunately, my father couldn't get along with others so when there was an opportunity for a promotion and my father applied, he didn't get the promotion. His co-workers didn't think he was a good fit for the supervisory position. My father got mad at his boss and the agency for not promoting him so he quit to prove his point and he was unemployed again.

This was at the time that the agency was new so it was destined to grow a lot and my father was in the right place at the right time. He was already making a lot of money as a GS-15 and he could have grown with the agency, but his ego got the best of him.

He needed better interpersonal skills to work with others and so the opportunity passed him by.

Your Life

Ancestors

Your ancestors came before you. They blazed a trail that you get to pick up as you turn 18 from where they left off.

Birth - Your first phase

Your birth certificate marks the beginning of your ride.
Your birth certificate is your ticket to an education, drivers license, passport, marriage, and all the other neat things that come with your life opportunity to explore and experience the world.

YouTube: Patrick Hernandez - *Born to Be Alive* - HD

Cars

Having your own car is a new phase of life. You have mobility that you have never had before, except when you started riding your own bicycle in the neighborhood.

Cars should not be thought of as a status symbol, they are a tool to help you go somewhere. Any new car today will be old tomorrow and new cars cost a lot of money. If your self worth or your image is dependent on having a car or a new car you have problems.

If you don't have a car, instead of fretting over the fact that you don't have one to drive, you, especially you guys reading this, study the mechanics of how cars work because they are relatively simple machines and you are going to be dependent on them for the rest of your life so make good use of your time now and begin learning about all the terms and systems so when they break, you can talk intelligently with the person that is going to fix it for you and so they won't take advantage of you and suggest a diagnosis that is flawed or repairs that can be put off or isn't really needed.

Phases of Life

Cash flow

It is as important to understand your cash flow as it is to understand how much money you have. If you are earning a lot and spending a lot, then you don't have much of a positive cash flow. If you are spending more than you are receiving, it is a negative cash flow. You don't want a negative cash flow.

Cash flow is very important because one of the criteria for loans is how much positive cash flow you have so you will be able make the loan payments as they come due. Loan amounts are based on your excess cash flow.

To buy a house you will need enough excess cash flow to make the payments and if you have a lot of other loans such as for student debt or a new car payment then that will reduce how much you can borrow for your house. You always want to conserve your cash and minimize your debts. And when you want to make a major purchase like a house you will also need a down payment of five to ten percent.

How much extra cash do you project that you will you have coming in that you can put towards savings so you can build a down payment for real estate?

It is not prudent to rush off and use all your money for an apartment just because you have the money to spend when you can still live at home with your parents. Renting an apartment when you don't have to is a poor use of your earnings.

You need to have a good understanding of your finances so you have something to show, like lots of money in the bank for all your work. You can't blame your employer if you are not earning what you think you are worth. You either need to increase your skills or take on more responsibilities so you are a more valuable employee or you need to look for another employer.

And if you think you are really smart and you want to try and earn even more money then you should take it upon yourself to take the risk and start your own company and then you can see what it is like on the other side as an employer.

Choices - by your parents

Look at your parents lives to see if they are happy with their choices in life. What worked well for them and what were their mistakes? What would they do different if they had a second chance? Who helped them in their life journey and how? How would you advise them?

Critical thinking and creativity

Creativity and your ability for critical thinking are two of the best things that you have going for you. Your challenge is to try and develop and learn how to use these innate attributes to solve problems—not so much with standardized problems like in math, or chemistry, or physics, or biology, but the more abstract and ever evolving everyday problems you are going to encounter in life. Not that life is a problem, but in your daily life you are always being presented with situations and information that you have to be able to analyze and act on. These situations are where your creativity and critical thinking skills can really come into play. The standardized problems you practice in school provide a means for you to practice without real life consequences.

More specifically, you can apply your creativity and critical thinking skills so you can recognize and understand the traditional and logical progression that society has established, promotes, and teaches whereby you follow the requisite steps for knowledge, conformance, and acceptance. Yes, you need basic skills and to be familiar with the standardized procedures and processes of living, but better yet, you need to be able to think outside the box in trying to find alternatives that may work for you so you can move ahead of the traditional and institutionalized thinkers.

Educational institutions, a fancy term for schools, teach standardized problem solving processes and techniques, condition, and train you in this logical thinking progression. Their mantra is to train you to complete A, then B, then C, then D, then E and then, if you have successfully and properly completed each step and mastered the subject, the magical doors will open because the teachers and their

Phases of Life

school will have prepared you with the requisite skill set to achieve your career and life goals. Unfortunately, you will probably discover later that it is not that easy and diplomas don't come with a guarantee.

Yes, you need to know and to follow the standardized steps laid out for you in the field(s) that you are interested in, but at the same time you always need to be thinking of how you might be able to get out of line and jump ahead and in doing so seize opportunities that are available to you now that might not be available to you later. This line of thinking is counter to how you have been conditioned because ever since you were little you have been told to follow each step and to wait your turn in line.

It is important that you begin practicing this new method of trying to put yourself first because as you mature, trying to be first is going to be the new game you are going to be playing. People are going to be trying to cut in front of you, so you need to be ready and you need to be able to cut in front of others. It's going to be ok to cut in front of the line now because you are entering the world of "survival of the fittest."

Listen and watch:
The Message **by Grandmaster Flash and the Furious Five**

Just as described by the chorus of *The Message*: "It's like a jungle sometimes; it makes me wonder how I keep from goin' under," the sooner you can begin developing and practicing your critical thinking and problem solving skills, the sooner you will be able to refine them and put them to good use.

Questioning the status-quo and promoting contrarian methods of thinking and problem solving are very dangerous and difficult for teachers and their schools to teach because it goes against their creed. This method of thinking "outside the box" runs counter to what "The Man" can tolerate because it is a threat to his protected status-quo. This aspect is depicted best in the movie "School of Rock" where creating a rock'n roll band that secretly competes in a competition quickly propels the students ahead.

Teaching you to challenge the "The Man" is not promoted in schools because to teach such skills could create a threat to the people who are in positions of power and their support base. Furthermore, it is not necessarily something that could be taught by all the teachers that have adopted and are conditioned to adhering to and promoting the standardized way to comply and succeed in life.

Schools will not teach you how to challenge authority and test the limits of established life processes and institutions because to do so would be counter-productive to their personal balance of power and the perpetuity that is expected from and which these institutions depend on. It would be a conflict-of-interest.

One simple example of the influence and power of the status quo over what, and how you are taught, is to consider the paradox that for all of the hours you will spend in civics and/or government class learning about your government, how concerned it is about you, and how inclusive it says that it tries to be. You will likely not be taught how or encouraged to participate in the political discussion by getting your name on a ballot and running for office as an independent candidate, even though it is a very, simple and free process. Any discussion about this or the actual procedure to get on a ballot is excluded from every government class textbook and it is rarely discussed anywhere else.

Why would something so critical to the foundation of our government be excluded? Is "The Man" trying to hide something from you? Wouldn't more participation and another voice be construed as beneficial for good government? Instead, you will be relentlessly indoctrinated with information about the status-quo and its great very limited two-party system.

In reality, it is the power of the "Iron Triangle" that rules. As a ballot candidate for Congress, I just happened to learn about the term from a government teacher in Prince William County who was teaching her class about it using a handout because "Iron Triangle" is excluded from textbooks, check for it in yours, even though it represents the very real and powerful subculture foundation of how our

Phases of Life

governments function. Gee, I wonder why the term is missing and we are not taught about it?

Iron Triangle refers to the triangle of relationships between, lobbyists, administrators and elected officials. I refer to it in my *Calling All Jedi... Rap Song #2* at 2:12 on YouTube.

Don't be confused and misled by this foe,
They're only lookin' to snatch all your dough,
A cold dark secret, don't want you to look.
Runs the nation, never mentioned in books.

A fiend with the power to twist and mangle,
Goes by the name of the Iron Triangle.

What about all the unsolicited calls to cell and home phone numbers for health care that you are powerless to stop? The "Iron Triangle" rules and so even though the calls are have become an epidemic, our government won't save us. Help! The robots are relentless.

Another simple example of traditional thinking and how a status quo protects itself is how student writers are told that they have to perfect and practice their style before they should expect to get noticed and how writing book reviews and submitting short stories are two of the steps they can follow in order to establish their name and build their brand so they can become accepted by and into the world of book writers and publishers.

Promoting such a one track standard process for professional development is how the network, in this case of seasoned authors and their book publishers, seeks to protect themselves and promote conformance when, at this time in a young student writer's life, the author actually posses privileged information about the new and unique world where he or she lives. Only they have the knowledge which can be leveraged for their success because older writers can't enter or even conceive today's adolescent world.

Today's young writers have the best opportunity ever to write stories that can be successful for their age because they can incorporate their unique insider perspective of the effect technology has had on their generation. These student writers posses privileged knowledge which can be used to craft stories about how technology, and everything that has come with it, has changed the adolescent world from what it was like before.

Young writers are the only ones with the familiarity of this new world with its unique new lingo. If young writers are told that their works would not be adequate or qualified until the established process for professional development is followed, he or she will miss their once-in-a-lifetime opportunity to try and capitalize on the opportunity they currently have.

Unfortunately, that is how young writers are being directed.

Listen to the establishment but you need to be able to think on your own.

Keep in mind how a continual abuse of power will lead to a loss of trust and confidence in our governments and our social institutions. A blatant example of a status quo gone wild is the missed pass interference call in a recent and very important sporting event. I saw a video clip where a disgusted famous actor very profoundly explained, "It's the bookies, it's the bookies". The blown call is a prime example of how, indirectly, we as citizens are being manipulated with the complexity of the various rackets for their profit.

Yes, you should listen to what your parents, teachers and advisors suggest and recommend but don't just accept what they say carte blanc as the best or one and only way for you to grow, think, mature and progress. Just because they are older does not mean they are correct. It is just their perspective and they may have subtle biases.

What trails are you blazing for yourself?

To teach yourself how to make good decisions on your own you need to learn how to look for the inconsistencies, and in a very

Phases of Life

nice way, raise questions as appropriate. Think. Use your brain. Engage in discussions.

Most of all, do not be afraid to ask questions when it appears that something does not make sense so you can try to extrapolate and recognize the inconsistencies or disconnects. Then you will be able to recognize those special opportunities where you can jump to the front of the line.

The best way to learn is by applying your creativity and practicing your critical thinking skills. You can't get anywhere unless you take some risk, it's part of the game. You are going to make mistakes but you will learn from them as you go.

Begin training and developing your creative problem solving skills now so you are can begin capitalizing on what might be obscured from your view. Use your critical thinking skills and creativity in observation and problem solving and the opportunities will start to become visible for you. Note, playing Clash of Clans is not an exercise in real creativity nor do you receive real gold.

**There is only one person that can make
you successful and that is you.**

Financial plan and Investments - your

Where is your money to live going to come from and how successful do you intend to be and how do you think you will be able to get there?

Research how much things cost and how much money you will need to support yourself and what will be left over after you deduct your taxes and expenses from your earnings.

Children are a huge negative cash flow and divorce is very destructive financially to all families.

It used to be that a larger more expensive house was a good financial investment because it would increase in value at a faster proportionate rate relative to the interest rate of the mortgage. But those days of rapid appreciation ended in 2008 and do not seem likely to return any time soon. Incorporating the risk that bigger houses create poor family synergy and general elitist attitudes in children, they have become more of a detriment than a benefit.

Rights and Freedom - Constitutional

These are given to you at birth but that doesn't mean that you don't have to fight to keep them from being denied or taken away.

Your rights, and the expectations that go with them are going to change as you turn 18 so you need be extra careful in how you conduct yourself after you turn 18. Once you turn 18 you have increased freedom and with it comes increased responsibilities for how you conduct yourself. You're not considered a kid anymore and you should know better. Be careful.

Youth

The special time of life that you are experiencing now because of your age, relative maturity, innocence, lack of income requirements and most of all your undiscovered potential.

When you are a teen you have a lot of benefits over everyone else. You still get support from your parents so you don't need to work or earn enough money to live on. You still have the option to live with your parents which is usually free as long as you help with the family and are working to improve yourself.

You have the flexibility to explore different subjects and possible career paths to see what opportunities are available and where your interest lie. You can try to develop your own product or service and you can fail without disastrous results knowing that failure is part of learning.

You can get a summer job to get an inside view of part of how the world works or, if you are in college, an internship that can lead to employment once you graduate. You can hone your skills in working with others by coaching teams or instructing other children or teens younger than you. Best of all, you have the perfect excuse if you make a mistake because nobody is going to get really mad at you if mess up, as long as the mess ups are small and it was probable that

Phases of Life

you didn't know better.

When you are young, people will be happy to help you because you still have some innocence and they won't think that you are trying to take advantage of them or a waste of their time and money. And they will embrace your youth as if it was theirs and try to guide you on your way because they can see all the opportunities waiting for you over the horizon and they know what you are going through because they were in your shoes once.

High School

You have a lot of freedom and minimal responsibility. Don't miss out on the many opportunities to improve yourself before you graduate.

It is a time of your life when you get to hang out with the most friends you will ever have and you can easily explore lots of types of school activities. Your circle of friends will never be as big as it now.

Shakespeare and his tales of humanity.

Recently my son Mike was studying Shakespeare in his high school English class at the same time my other son John was studying it in college so it became more prominent in our family discussions. The discussion shifted to how difficult it was and I began to reflect on the time I spent with Mr. Shakespeare in high school.

I remembered that with some direction, help, and interpretations from a very animated and wonderful English teacher named Mr. Edwin Vergason, that all of a sudden it started to click for me. But it wasn't without reluctance and pain. And I remember thinking that it was unfortunate that once Shakespeare clicked we were just about done with the unit.

Shakespeare builds comprehension skills that YA novels don't.

What I realized by the end of the class was that his writings have so much power because the characters are fully developed and the stories play out over and over, again and again, every day and you can learn a lot of important lessons about yourself, human nature, people and life in general by reading and having the stories interpreted for you. "The Taming of the Shrew," was my favorite and the one I liked the best.

An example of how a very high profile modern day Shakespearian story has been unfolding now is the one about the owner of a very large company whose mistress threw him under the bus.

Nothing changes with humanity and it's much easier to learn from someone else's mistakes in a story instead of your own.

High School Reunions

Attend all your high school reunions. They are a lot of fun and even better when you help organize them because then you have a reason to talk with your old classmates ahead of the event.

You never know what you will learn from hanging out with your friends and you can reestablish old friendships and make new ones because you will see your old classmates with different eyes and they will see you as well and you never know what you will learn.

My biggest surprise occurred at about my 15 year reunion when I was talking to an old female friend that used to sit in front of me in Physics class.

"Who was that girlfriend you had in high school? Whatever happened to her?" she asked me.

"Oh, in the end it didn't work out," was my response.

"Well, you know there were other girls that were interested in you but they thought you were taken."

I was speechless. Who? What girls? Who did I miss out on? I'll never know.

Networking and power, the real world and what you need to know.

It is very difficult to explain all the intricacies and nuances about networking and power but your network of relationships is and will become your foundation for your livelihood, success, and

Phases of Life

happiness. Networks have many aspects and you need to understand how you work within them and how they work around you.

There are different types of networks: public networks that serve public institutions such as government or the schools and private networks such as in business or among individuals. Unfortunately, schools do not usually teach this concept or its importance placing more emphasis on measurable academic success instead. Just because schools don't teach something doesn't mean that it isn't important for you to know and understand.

There are many reasons why this concept of developing one's network is not promoted or taught in schools. One reason is because the status quo is not going to empower others in how to build a power base which could conceivably challenge its position in society. Another reason is because many public organizations are in actuality closed networks with ulterior motives that are obscured in how affairs are conducted.

Personal and political power are predicated on networks of mutual support relationships and those relationships are not going to expose themselves or their structure because to do so would make them vulnerable. Accessibility to the top is controlled and restricted. Obscurity protects power. Trust is essential.

The real agendas and workings of power networks are very well organized and hidden. There are no membership lists or publicized chains of command. It is natural that these organizations would not promote the development of other organizations that could threaten their business model. Throughout the world each group is trying to protect and develop its unique business model in their pursuit of perpetual security, employment, financial gain and sustained power. Whether it is a group of students, faculty, an administration, elected officials, business associates, or criminal gang, they are all composed of networks of people. I am sure that you belong to many already and not the last one.

No base of power is going to expose itself because to do so would expose its vulnerabilities which could then be exploited and threaten its objectives and existence. Recruits move through these networks of relationships to positions of higher responsibility and trust with the understanding that as one is accepted into higher levels of the organization that one will increase their commitment to protect the status quo with the risk of being outcast and possibly blacklisted if they don't. As one moves up, one will be given access to more privileged information about the real workings and motives of the inner circle and see and understand its strength and its vulnerabilities. The closer one gets to the inner circle, the more the employee will be rewarded for contributions and loyalty.

You should be aware of how these unique private and public components of society function so that you can avoid being exploited by them and so, if and when the situations present themselves, you may find your own opportunities as part of their inner working labyrinth. More importantly, you need to be building your network of associates with and without similar interests to yours so collectively you can all help each other.

Fight fire with fire. Inside information is always helpful in positioning yourself and in being able to make the best decisions. How else are you going to get that inside perspective and information without inside sources.

At this stage of your life you will receive a lot of help and guidance from your parents and family as to what is and is not important in interpersonal relations and their perspective on how people and society really function based on their experiences. Your family is your tribe. Pay attention and listen. With their insight and guidance you will start to see and understand things that you couldn't see before. You always need to be listening, considering, thinking, and questioning the who, what, when, why, where and how of your surroundings.

The subjects of biology, chemistry, physics and calculus might seem complicated to you now, but it is the subject of human behavior and its relationships that is the most complex of all. Being able to understand and work with and within its myriad of parameters and variables separates the winners from the losers. Always keep in mind that anything is possible because human behavior is predicated on

Phases of Life

relationships and people and their relationships are always changing.

Schools offer the best place for you to begin establishing your network of relationships as you engage with fellow students that you do and don't share a common interest or goal. You should make the effort to meet and get to know as many people as possible even if you are not sure why the relationships are or could be enjoyable, rewarding or important in your and possibly their future. Don't pre-judge others, make friends with everyone. That is what life is about. Making friends.

It is always easier and more enjoyable to engage with people who are interested in subjects that you are familiar with, but it is the subjects that you are not aware which will provide you with a more broad perspective and base. As an example, even if you are interested in engineering, you should make friends with people interested in medicine and law and education and theater because you can learn from everyone and they can learn from you. That is the neat part about relationships, you engage and learn together which is a big part of what makes life fun.

Schools are the key place for you to be exploring and making this variety of relationships because schools support and facilitate the best environment for non-competitive relationship development. Contrast it to a work environment where you will have very limited and restricted exposure to other people or subjects and everyone is more competitive. With graduation you will transition from one extreme to the other.

Work environments are more competitive because employees compete with each other to either get a promotion, which usually results in more authority and money, or in doing less work or both together. Getting a promotion can mean someone does less drudge work and gets paid more money. And a lot of times they do not have the requisite interpersonal skills for advancement or supervision, but that is what happens. It doesn't always make sense.

And as with all relationships, keep in mind that we are all human and nobody is or can be perfect. Being flexible and able to work with others is key. We are all unique. Share the best and dismiss the worst.

Schools are the best place to begin developing your network of relationships and ideas because they are a great big playground of people and activity and you need to experience other people and their ideas to grow and achieve. Schools could promote more learning about human relationships and networks but to do so could expose the foibles of the faculty, its administration and its school board which would be very risky, especially to an energetic young group that is well-connected digitally. Schools will not discuss or encourage you to practice how to organize and challenge the power of a status-quo.

Learning how to build relationships and the benefits of building them may not seem very important to you now because your academic grades are being emphasized since you are in an academic environment. But once you leave high school or college academia and move into more financially orientated endeavors, you will find that your success or failure is going to be based more on whom you know and what they think of you and whether they can trust you, more than on what specialty knowledge or experience you have. You can always find specialty; it is trust that really counts and whether you will be a committed member to their team.

Practicing these interpersonal relations is why it is important to make use of the opportunity while you are in school. Establish relationships, gain diversified skills, and explore different subjects while you have the opportunity because it is the most conducive place to grow and mature and you have the time.

Wealthier families have these relationships in place and more experience with them, which helps them to protect and grow their resources, while others of less means are left to do the best they can with their limited experience and resources. It isn't that the wealthy are smarter it is more that they have the connections to make things happen to benefit them and they have the resources that they can put to use to help themselves and others in their tribe or circle of relationships. And, having more resources leads to more connections and so it builds on itself while the less fortunate are left struggling while

Phases of Life

they are being told, "You just need to work harder to realize your dreams." The deck is already stacked against them.

The situation can come to a head when, Dean Haldeman, my propane mentor, explained some of the injustices of society to me, "We lose trust in our governments when power becomes consolidated to such a degree that it can legislate, interpret and enforce."

My interpretation of what Mr. Haldeman means is that once the establishment, another word for the status quo, "The Man," achieves complete control of the governing process, such that the essential independent checks and balances are broken due to political obligations, the citizens are exploited and at its mercy.

An example of this is when laws and regulations are able to be written and enacted with such complexity that they appear one way but in actuality they can be interpreted in a way that benefits the true sponsors of the legislation. A way that only the insiders who drew the maze are aware.

Keep Mr. Haldeman's explanation in mind as the text books provide you with a very simplified description of the structure for how society and government are supposed to function in our democracy/republic. Compare what you are being taught with everyday events and you will start to see where the pieces don't fit. This disconnect may cause you to question why the checks and balances you are being taught don't seem to match the reality you are experiencing.

It is very confusing to try and understand why things are the way they are and you never will unless you have a crystal ball and are privy to the real inside objectives. Don't get caught up in the way you are being pulled one way and then the other by society and pressured to take a position. Just keep an open mind while remaining skeptical of everything you are being told.

Just because our schools and teachers teach us subject matter does not mean that what they are teaching has not been skewed or that we have to accept it verbatim and as true and complete. Learn how to take into consideration other aspects regarding how the information can be influenced by the school boards who purchase the text books that students use and how that content, especially in the books about history and government, can be controlled and manipulated via the purchasing process.

The school boards control the purchase money and they are calling the shots about what is in the text books and how it is written. Recognize that it is incumbent on text book manufacturers to present material and concepts in a manner that is acceptable to the school boards or the school boards won't buy the text books.

School Boards are supposed to have the interests of the students at heart but that does not mean that the students well being is at the top of the list or a high priority. Maintaining political power and control is always first for any political body. Nobody can ever know the whole picture unless they are a member of the majority on the school board with inside access to the decision making process.

The political power structure in a county or locality is a microcosm of how it works at the national level. Behind the scenes, the local party machine and its minions are directed by the local Congressional representative that is seated and that person calls the shots across the board just as Boss Tweed called the shots throughout his solid network of Irish immigrants, in New York City in the 1860's.

Your Congressional person, or the highest locally elected person in the other party, decides whom they want to win the local elections, will put that word out on the street, and this is how the political machine is built and maintained. Then once elected, those elected individuals will be indebted to the person that supported and called for their election. And that is how part of how "The Man" works. Then if someone who was elected crosses the political boss, they are out.

Even though the political parties appear divided, they are actually working with the same strategy for the same objective. Divide and conquer to stay in power. So who are they dividing?

The power structure of governments is the ultimate power base because, as a united organization, it has the power to control and divide up and authorize the spending of all the money collected from taxes as well as the power to legislate, enact, interpret, and see to

Phases of Life

the enforcement of laws. These political organizations may appear ideologically based, but in actuality they are monetarily incentivized. These organizations are composed of networks of individuals who are enamored with self preservation as well as the accumulation and maintenance of power over all others at all costs.

How else do elected officials become so wealthy so fast? They support changing laws that will help investments of other elected officials and then they will support laws that will help your investments. It is a racket of inside information and favors. See the Iron Triangle for more about these relationships.

Get laws changed to benefit an industry and all of a sudden you can make a lot of money if you own stock in that industry.

Campaign finance and speaking fees of hundreds of thousands of dollars are two of the biggest con jobs being run on the American public.

They are bribery, plain and simple, developed, legalized and supported by the political network.

The intricate combination of relationships of elected officials and their staff provides strength to their power which is manifested in the form of political parties and its respective candidates, elected legislators and appointees all of whom work together to increase their personal wealth, control agendas and influence decisions and spending throughout all branches of the government. As an organized network they can bend or make their own interpretations and rules as they please. They say one thing but are really doing something else. That is why politics is called a dirty business.

The real inner workings are completely whitewashed for the public including how school curriculum and textbooks are developed. You will be part of similar networks as you and your associates strive to meet personal objectives. This is how the world works.

A friend who used to work for Forestry, which is part of the Department of Interior, explained to me, "We have a lot of expertise on staff and we could accomplish so much more if it wasn't for the political appointees that put pressure on us to accommodate the agendas of their special interest groups."

Political power is all about money, not about doing what is right and avoiding what is wrong because everything is subject to interpretation.

Always remember: The political network uses legislative complexity to achieve its ulterior goals.

That is why schools will never teach the reality of how influence money effects how things really work in all levels of government because to do so would expose their real agendas and undermine their power network.

Having an ability to recognize and understand networks and how they function at the micro and macro levels of society will serve you well.

Don't delay in having conversations, making friends, and learning how to build your own network.

Ownership

As you get older you are going to be able to buy and own more things. Some of these things you will consume like food or gasoline, other things, like a new car, will decrease in value as you use them and some things may increase in value like a home.

Many years ago I was talking about the concept of land and what we each own with Mr. Richard Chiles, a much older neighbor-farmer. He set me straight when he explained that, "We don't own anything, we just get to use it while we are alive."

I had never thought of it like that, but what he said made sense.

Value

Value is defined as what someone would buy and someone would sell so keep adding value to yourself so you can earn more money and buy more assets that will be increasing in value while you continue earning more money.

Phases of Life

Value is created when demand for something increases relative to the available supply. And the opposite is true where value decreased when there is too much supply or a diminished demand.

Divorce

The vows of marriage are a legal and binding agreement, or contract, that society recognizes. Divorce is a breaking or dissolution of that agreement and breaking the contract comes with penalties, sometimes severe. The contract of marriage is very easy to enter but it is extremely difficult, complicated, and expensive to dissolve especially if there are children involved.

Society encourages people to enter into marriage and stay married because it is a healthy institution for family and child development.

What happens when one of the spouses doesn't want to be married to the other spouse? After much turmoil and anguish usually the property is divided in half and whoever is earning income has to provide spousal and child support. It's always ugly and you want to avoid getting into this situation at all costs.

Divorces are always unfortunate and messy and statistics show that 50% of the married people get divorced?

Why is the percentage of divorces so high?

What didn't they know before they got married that they found out later?

Everyone is different and no two marriages are alike, so do not stress.

How careful are you going to be in choosing your spouse?

My father left my mother when she was 57 years old and almost destroyed everything they had spent a lifetime building.

You have to be very careful of who you date and especially who you marry, and once you get married, you need to work hard to help and be nice to each other. When you are dating you need to think about the long term, not short term, and you need to be careful so you can get married for the right reasons instead of because you have to such as in the event of an unexpected pregnancy.

Finding a mate is very difficult to do, especially when you need to be able to allow plenty of time together to make sure that the two of you are compatible.

Senior Orphan

Relationships are everything throughout your life.

It is way past your wildest imagination but as you get into old age you don't want to become a senior citizen and not have any family or friends. It will be very lonely.

Death

Your death certificate will mark the end of your ride. It is your last official document and is prepared by the local medical officer after a death. You will never see your death certificate unless you come back as a ghost.

The addendum has a copy of the death certificate for Simon Thompson who was a friend of mine in high school.

Simon was an especially cool friend because he had a British accent and he spoke with proper English. He was very friendly and he was in my graduating class from Marshall High School. We graduated on June 15, 1976, and as you can see from his death certificate, he was injured in a car accident on June 19, 1976 at 4:39 in the afternoon.

The death certificate lists that he was the passenger in a car that struck a tree. He died on July 6, 1976.

I don't know who the driver was but as Clint Eastwood says in the movie *Unforgiven*, "It's a hell of a thing killing a man, you take away all he's got and all he's ever gonna have."

That's what the driver did to Simon.

His parents, family, and classmates were devastated by the loss.

Another very nice and helpful man that I knew a long time ago was named Harold who was in his 20's, a fireman and worked for

Phases of Life

me driving trucks part-time. Harold died after helping some friends move on a Saturday. He was tired and fell asleep driving home and was killed when his car hit a tree.

Another part-time employee asked a friend to come to a party with him even though the friend didn't want to go to the party. The friend eventually relented and on his way home from the party the friend crashed his motorcycle and was killed.

You always need to be thinking about the what-ifs and be as responsible as possible so that you don't cause or contribute to someone's injury or death or so that someone doesn't contribute to yours.

My thought is that when you die everyone moves over to occupy what was your place and all your stuff is distributed. Please make careful choices so you can stay on your train of life as long as possible and not go off the track and crash into a tree.

Dean Haldeman, one of my best friends and mentors, told me, "We all go out of this world with the same amount of money in our pocket."

With that in mind, I asked Kathleen to make sure that she puts $20 in my casket as my easy way to guaranty that I will leave with more than anyone else.

Slowdown and chill.

Focus your attention and energy where it will pay off for you.

You will make it just fine if you pay attention to what is important, take your time, think through what you are going to do before you do it, and ask yourself why?

Chris DeCarlo

Your Education

Nobody can ever take it away from you.

Your education is a key component to your happiness and success in life and it is something that nobody can take away from you. There is a legal requirement for you to attend school and get a primary education because your education will help you develop the problem solving skills that you will apply for the rest of your life. It is important to be developing those skills while your brain is still growing because it will be much harder if not impossible later.

The more skills you have the more valuable you are and the more valuable you are the more a company is willing to pay for your services. What's so wrong with that?

Education is the key to scoring in the big game.

To have a special perspective, you need to know how to think outside the box.

Your education should continue throughout your life.

You and your educational system

As a student in today's school system you are caught in the fastest and most unprecedented change ever to an institutional educational system and you are the guinea pig for how the changes will be assessed some time way off in the future. However, you can't wait for tomorrow's results to see how you are going to turn out. Your time is now and you need to make the most of it while you can.

The pressure that you are feeling at the end of each day is probably similar to battle fatigue because just like in a real war, the educational and social war that you are part of in school is being fought around you all day. You have to sit still in uncomfortable chairs, pay attention, and stay awake. It isn't easy.

Phases of Life

To cope in your battle zone which has lots of land mines that you have to avoid it is helpful to separate the real threats from the imaginary. Turn your battlefield into a game, don't take it so seriously, strategize a plan, and take the pressure off yourself.

There are lots of negatives to your real world and there are a lot of positives, too. The challenge in your daily battle is to figure out how to avoid the land mines and go for the cup of gold. Win enough battles so you win the war and the game.

Another way to look at it is like Rhett Butler says to Scarlet O'Hara in the movie, *Gone with the Wind* as they ride off in a wagon with Atlanta burning behind them. "I told you once before that there were two times for making big money, one in the up-building of a country and the other in its destruction. Slow money on the up-building, fast money in the crack-up. Remember my words. Perhaps they may be of use to you some day."

What he is saying is that you need to keep thinking and looking for the opportunities ahead of everyone else even when it seems like everything is lost. To succeed you need to outsmart the competition and make your life work for you. You have the smarts — it isn't that hard. You just don't have the training or experience. So apply your smarts and begin gaining experience avoiding the imaginary land mines and focus on the real cup of gold.

Your real world game is being fought in the battle field of an educational system gone wild and an Internet that is sucking up everyone's time. What opportunities does this create for the young, creative, and strategic thinker?

New methods of teaching are being thrown at you at the same time your head is kept spinning as you try to watch what everyone else is doing so you can keep up with them. It is hard to stay focused on a battlefield when so much is coming at you.

Forget about everyone else and think about yourself. The real battlefield is only what you make it. Formulate your strategic plan for success by recognizing the mistakes everyone else is making as they step on land mines that destroy them. Seek opportunities just like Rhett Butler was doing as Atlanta burned and all appeared lost.

He had seen the destruction coming and figured out how to position himself before Sherman burned it so he could profit from its reconstruction when lumber and building materials would be in short supply. He had already lined up lumber suppliers ahead of time. It wasn't that hard to figure out.

So as the educational system is burning around you and consuming itself and all its students and teachers in a whirlwind of technological distractions you need to find the path for how you can win the war and out smart them all and prove that you can do it.

You might feel like the educational system is your oppressor, but to survive, make it your best friend. You can make it work for you by gaining the skills and experience it can provide you as quickly as possible while your friends get sucked into the information quicksand of the Internet. They are stuck and sinking deeper and deeper while you can use your special insight to climb out and gain new skills as fast as you can and then you win the game. You get the cup of gold. It's not that hard. You just have to keep your wits about you and not get sucked in with them.

Your classmates know that they shouldn't be engaging in inappropriate and detrimental behaviors like drinking alcohol, vaping, excessive gaming, sex, and smoking weed, but the temptations are too strong and they can't resist. It's fun. They are caught in the quicksand of over-information and don't know how to turn it off to pull themselves out. You don't need to go down with them.

Recognize that the educational system isn't perfect either and that it is consuming itself with confusion as it tries to turn teachers and students into robots. You know you are not a robot but you have to play the game on their field so you can outsmart Big Brother just like Winston did in George Orwell's book *1984*. He figured it out and survived with his sanity as best he could; look at school like your military boot camp for life. Go for the good parts and you will come out a better, smarter, more disciplined, and experienced person.

About seven years after I had graduated from high school, I complained about one of my English teachers to my former high school principal, Mr. John T. Broaddus Jr. after he had retired. He

Phases of Life

stopped me in my tracks when he told me, "If there were no bad teachers then you wouldn't appreciate the good one's."

We all have to accept the good with the bad and move on just as it is easiest to survive boot camp if you know what it is really about. You've seen the movies. You get some training and learn how to march but it's real objective is weeding out recruits that can't take the pressure so only the best survive. Life then gets much better for those that graduate. If you take bad experiences personally they will destroy you. You just have to take the bad and make the most of the good. The same goes for school.

In school you are told that grades are what separate the winners from the losers. But, that is not always true. Grades are indicative of test scores, but if you have skills like creativity that are increasingly valuable and which tests don't easily measure then you might be led to think that you are sub-par. Remember, that is in the world of school and academics.

The world of business and life is different and you are graded differently. Some graded skills do translate into better life skills such as improved problem solving and critical thinking skills, but in real life survival is key and being able to fight the competition determines who wins and loses. That is where the problem solving skills you learn and practice now will help you.

You are going to be using these skills for the rest of your life and they don't cost you anything to learn in school like they will later.

In the educational environment that you are in now there are written and unwritten rules as well as many interpersonal forces at play. It is very confusing.

As a student you only understand the written policies and rules that are being applied to you, and you have to accept and follow them to finish school and be awarded a degree just like a military recruit has to do what the drill sergeant tells him to do or his life in camp will be even worse and he might not graduate.

At school you nor your parents are privy to all the behind the scenes maneuvering that happens because of personalities, individu-

106

al behaviors, personal preferences or deficiencies by the adults at the school and in the administration as they maneuver in their world of work preparing you for your life adventure. They can tell you some things about what it is like on the other side, but they can't tell you everything and this is the part that schools don't prepare you for. Adults can act just as petty as children; they're just more experienced in disguising and controlling it.

You would be well served to have a better understanding of the behind the scenes events at school and in the work place so you can have a better understanding of how the real world works and why things are being imposed on you. Educational systems won't teach those things but books will.

The goals for all of us is to work the least amount, efficiently when we do, and earn the most. It is a fact of life and it holds true in educational systems and everywhere else — money rules. School boards are trying to cut how much they have to spend to educate you by holding teacher's salaries stable and trying to measure their performance, eliminating take home textbooks, adjusting and blending curricula, changing the lunch menu, providing less money for music, and shifting human resources around. Change is part of life.

At the same time the teachers don't want to be taken advantage of for the work they are providing and their union is fighting for more money and fewer students per classroom so there can be improvements in instruction and less load on the teachers.

Take all that society is making available to you and embrace it for the opportunity while it is yours for the taking. Play the game and do the work that they ask, get the good grades and play along just like Winston did to survive, and you will come out way ahead. You can't go wrong. What do you have to lose?

No system is or will ever be perfect, but having an improved understanding of how and why it works like it does will give you a better frame of reference to have more realistic expectations and see the real value. Success isn't that hard in school, college included. They tell you what you need to know, give you a test on the material, and then they grade the test so you can see how you did.

Phases of Life

By comparison, in business we have to figure out what we need to know every day, test ourselves and grade our own tests. We have to do it every day all the time or we lose our customers, our business, our resources, our investments, and our livelihood. So get used to it, you might graduate out of the classroom but the tests are going to keep coming.

Relax, enjoy school, and do the work that is expected. School isn't that hard compared to what is on the other side. I would love to be able to go back to school full-time but I can't because I have too many responsibilities and it isn't as important for me now because my clock started a lot sooner than yours. It might stop sooner than later so I don't have as much to gain from the additional education as you do now. However, I do keep current with my business practices in my field. The homework of life and business never stops if you plan to thrive.

You are the one with the opportunities, not me anymore. Don't get hung up in the politics of school and your friends. They are not important. You and your future are what is important.

Focus on what is important to you and get over any hangups that you might have about the educational system, like having to get up in the morning, dealing with specific teachers you don't like, completing homework, and collaborating with classmates. Adjust your view about the bad way you think you are being treated or any other way you think you are being slighted. Consider what you can do to get over it and move on so you can win the game. Focus on winning the game.

Focus is what motivated me to produce my first rap video when I was an independent candidate for Fairfax County Chairman of the Board of Supervisors in 2010. I was mad when as an official ballot candidate and a small business person for an elected office I was excluded from participating in the candidate forum that was sponsored by the Fairfax County Chamber of Commerce. I was nobody and I had no rights with which I could argue that they had to let me participate in the forum. In the end I figured it wouldn't matter anyway.

I thought about why I was being excluded and finally realized that the Chamber was doing its part to reduce and negate my platform and that they were playing up to either of the other two candidates affiliated with the two major political parties who were much more likely to win the election than I. Putting me on the stage with them would give me credibility.

As an alternative to the speech, I decided that if they weren't going to let me have five minutes for my speech at the forum that I would convert it to lyrics and rap the lyrics in a video to be posted on YouTube. Then even better — it would live forever. And that is exactly what I did and that is how I became a rapper. I went on to produce five more candidate rap videos about fighting corruption and in the process I even discovered the legal means of how Sheriffs, working together, have the legal obligation to their constituents to arrest corrupted governance.

Think creatively in a similar manner so you are not penalized and so you can get ahead without jeopardizing your future. The school system is there to help you so there is no reason to resist it. Embrace it. If you are uncomfortable don't make enemies, just adjust your thinking like I did so you can make the best of the situation and still come out a winner.

I didn't win the election and I probably never will, but I'm still in the game. Now I even have my own book with a place for my personal comments in Chapters 5, 6, and 7. Pretty cool.

And all of my rap videos are posted on my channel CDRapper1. My kids want me to make another and they want to be in it.

Books
**Reading is the only way you can unlock the
real power of your brain.**

Make time for it.

**Books provide a lot more in depth knowledge
then you will ever find online.**

Phases of Life

Books are a great deal because they cost so little relative to the amount of information they contain. Reading them exercises your brain and they can even be borrowed for free from the library or bought used online from many different sources.

Books are a great source of knowledge and insight into life and other topics. Reading is also a great exercise for your brain so you get two benefits from one activity. And best of all without you even realizing it, reading develops your critical thinking skills.

Reading is great food for your brain.
Feed it.

Extra curricular activities

These are very important because they expose you to other subjects or help you specialize in subjects of interest. They also help you to explore and develop other skills including working with other people in a volunteer environment.

Don't go to school to just see how little you can get by on or to isolate yourself.

"Just enough, just in time," is not a good mantra.

A big part of going to school is to be able to engage with so many people. School is the biggest environment you will ever be in that offers so many opportunities for you to get out, explore, and make so many friends.

Grades

The grades you receive are very important because they are a reflection of some of your character traits and your ability to perform. They are part of your permanent record. Work hard to get them as high as possible and be proud of your accomplishments.

You have so many teaching resources online that there is no reason you shouldn't be able to master every one of your subjects in school. You just have to have the initiative, discipline to avoid the distractions, and mental stamina to learn the material.

Smart boards make you dumb because they diminish the human element of presenting and actively processing information. It is easy to display, but since it is so easy to display, you are getting overloaded with information for information's sake.

It has become a case of quantity versus quality and we all have our saturation point.

Handwriting

Schools are doing a big disservice to students by not teaching cursive. Your signature says a lot about you and it is unfortunate that schools have dropped cursive handwriting in elementary education. If there is one thing you need to fix about your handwriting it is your signature.

The loss of handwriting class is another example of detrimental changes that are occurring in school systems and what did you get instead of a nice signature and an ability to write quickly, you got more standardized testing practice, and a lot of good that did you. You need to know how to write in cursive so you can take notes by hand which also helps your brain develop its critical thinking skills. Take a moment to lookup the number of articles on the benefits of cursive writing's processing skills. Laptops for note taking don't work as well because your brain is not as engaged in trying to synthesize the information when typing versus writing. When you take notes by writing you are getting two benefits from one activity, good notes that are imprinted in your memory and a mental workout. Many students now say they cannot read cursive writing, pointing out another loss to basic functions of language.

This change is a good example for a show or song titled, "School Boards Gone Wild."

Resources - Educational

You have so many resources available to you to help you learn and grow. Unprecedented quantities of educational resources are available to you instantly.

Phases of Life

Gaming does not qualify as a beneficial resource and is counterproductive in helping you to achieve your goals.

Schools

Schools are the institution which you are very familiar and they are made up of many components. The rapid introduction of technology and the push for efficiency has dramatically and detrimentally changed teaching methods, priorities, and your physical environment from when I was in school.

You may feel like these changes and school in general are inhibiting your educational opportunities, but regardless, there is no excuse for you not to be able to perform; it isn't that hard. You just have to think more maturely and accept the fact that you need to work harder in recognizing and working around the problems you encounter. The sooner you step up and apply yourself the better off you will be. All of which will help empower you to create your own better future. No one can do that for you.

I am going to give you some suggestions as to what you can do to try and survive in this new educational battlefield. I am going to try and explain some of the reasons why it has gotten to be such a mess compared to how it was when I was in school. Not that it was perfect when I was in school, but it was very different. We did not seem to have all the problems that you are faced with today. We only had one computer in the whole school and we didn't even have air conditioning. Most of us seem to have turned out OK.

Maybe, in the end, it was better that we had less.

To help set the tone for then versus now, I would like to point out that my son's high school newspaper, the *W. T. Woodson Cavalcade, April 1, 2019*, did a feature article on some of the teachers, with a then versus now photo, and their answer to the question:

What is your biggest high school regret?

The answers for the featured teachers are
PE, "Not working harder in foreign language."
US History, "Not playing basketball senior year."
Calculus, "I stayed in my click and didn't get to know everybody."-
Physics, "Not working harder senior year."
Biology, "Not learning how to study. I was very good at taking a test and not doing homework. It wasn't until organic chem in college I bombed the first test."
English, "I failed to speak out against discrimination by many members of one of my athletic teams against a teammate who I now figure must have had autism."

Moving on to today's concerns for you;
First, making excuses now isn't going to help you succeed in life because you are missing opportunities each day when you don't put out your maximum effort to succeed in your school work. Without the activity of school work, how else can you condition yourself to learn problem solving skills and to practice persistence?

Learn how to look up and pay attention to what is going on around you, stop complaining, and recognize that you are in school to improve your critical thinking and problem solving skills so you can have an improved future. No, you are probably not going to use algebra in your job, but solving complex math problem are exercising your brain and teaching you how to solve problems; those are things you are doing today and will be doing for the rest of your life. And, you don't want to be making bad decisions, do you?

Most of all, stop worrying about what everybody else is doing and what they may think about you because you are not going to see

Phases of Life

most of your classmates ever again except for the few that come to your reunions, if you even go. You are not in school to get likes, take selfies, keep Snapchat streaks going or to see how poplar you can be.

Only you can stand up for yourself when it comes to self-improvement. Don't miss out because your education, for the most part, is a once in a lifetime event.

You can start to correct any problems or difficulties you are having in school by examining how schools have evolved over the last 40 years and what negative effects the evolution may be having on you. Then, try to work around the problems.

There will never be a perfect educational system but you always have to strive to make the best of your situation whatever it is. Things will work out for you if you stop blaming others for your problems and accept responsibility for yourself and your choices in this quickly changing and competitive world.

It is also helpful to consider the real value of your education in dollars. On average, your community is funding your education at a cost of about $15,000 per year or $75 per day based on a 185-day school calendar. So, for every day you miss school you give up $75 of free education. If you were in school for 13 years and attended kindergarten through twelfth grade, your community spent $195,000 for your primary education.

Use your allocated $75 as wisely as possible each day. Get the most for the money that has been budgeted for you. Don't let it go to waste.

It is easy to make excuses as to why you can't be a successful student, but often, instead of wasting all that mental effort and energy making excuses, redirect your thinking. A bad attitude and a lack of effort does no honor to your intelligence.

Second, instead of excuses, focus your efforts on how to improvise, adapt, and overcome the distraction of social media and other school impediments. Social media is the real barrier to your success. It is not your classmates, teachers, administration, or school. For the most part, they all sincerely do care about you and are trying to help you succeed.

**Social media is your real enemy because
it has a detrimental affect on your brain's natural ability
to process information and reason.**

Social media overloads your brain and causes it to lock up.

I know that school can feel like a scholastic and social battleground in many ways, so play the game just like Gunnery Sergeant Highway would train you as one of his Marine recon recruits. Improvise, adapt, and overcome.

I know it isn't easy, but try adjusting your attitude for school by seeing it for what it really is, a place for your long term benefit. Do reconnaissance on how much it has changed from the time when I was in school and the possible affects those changes could be having on you. Also, consider some of the physical changes that could be making the environment uncomfortable and less conducive to learning.

Slippery chairs, white boards, fluorescent lighting, watered down lunches, longer class times, less natural light, no smoking, micromanaged teachers, standardized testing, and online text books to name a few could be issues. Moreover, don't forget the affect of Snapchat, Google notes, laptops, and Instagram on you and your fellow students. These changes are where most of the problems lie, not with your classmates, teachers, or the school and its administration. Teens are still teens; it is just a different environment with different influences.

And, even with the challenges these things cause, you have to admit that you couldn't ask for any better.

Be that as it may, you need to be able to cope in this re-engineered world that has become overwhelmed with technology. To cope, think of school as a game and pretend that you are mentally and physically prepared for whatever happens to get thrown at you. Get up with a positive attitude, a better understanding of why your world seems so difficult, and know that you are trained and ready to

Phases of Life

use your wits to improve yourself. And remember to be thankful for all the opportunities that are available to you. You are part of today's modern educational environment.

If you need help with your storyline, look to James Thurber's short story from 1939 for inspiration. *The Short Secret Life of Walter Mitty.* It is one of my favorite short stories.

You are still young and you have lots of energy and potential. You can easily teach yourself how to improvise, adapt, and overcome whatever obstacles you encounter.

You have the ability to put forth a maximum effort all the time and if you do, I am sure that you will surprise yourself with what you can accomplish just like the raw recruits did in saving the American college students in Grenada as depicted in the movie *Heartbreak Ridge*, with Gunnery Sergeant Highway.

Yes, "It's like a jungle sometimes, I wonder how I keep from goin under," just like it was rapped as the chorus of the rap *The Message* by Grandmaster Flash and the Furious Five in 1982. And if the chorus was a representation of the world in 1982, you know the jungle is a lot denser and more dangerous now.

Be that as it may be, I am confident that you can handle any situation and survive, just like Walter Mitty does, if you focus and put your mind to it.

Third, to understand the analogy of a battlefield of education further, it is also helpful to recognize that the current downfall in education not only comes from the distracted apathy of other students, but from the loss of trust in the qualifications of the leadership of the institution itself. Don't let them take you down with them.

Many changes are created in a bureaucratic and political environment where these changes take on a life of their own since there is no direct accountability and then they are impossible to get rid of once enacted.

The leadership has enacted so many changes in the name of progress, efficiency, cost savings, and political necessity without a complete understanding as to the detrimental effects each of the changes are having on the ability and motivation to learn.

The problems are compounded because the leadership doesn't participate in the environment they control. They are not teens in a classroom anymore so they don't have first hand experience of what it is like. They can't possibly know. If they were teens again, I am sure that they would feel the same real stresses that you are feeling and they would be just as distracted.

A big part of the problem today is that the educational leadership is conducting itself in a vacuum of real life experience because so much has changed since they were in high school. Survey answers can't possibly know what it is like to be a teenager today. Yet, they keep making changes and setting policy and wondering why they are not getting the results they are seeking.

They get hung up with elitist type thinking that they can keep tweaking regulations to fix the recurring problems. Or they get so side tracked trying to appease a special interest group that they totally miss the human element. And worse of all they act with a herd mentality as they run circles in their politically driven corral to nowhere.

Teachers - Part I

These are people who have been specially trained to help you learn about a particular subject and are in the classroom to help you improve your critical thinking skills, but they are fighting a losing battle.

Cursive handwriting has been eliminated creating the most gruesome signatures known.

Technology has been adopted as the mantra to save the world when it is actually destroying the personal learning experience by making it is so easy to detach.

The teachers are caught in the middle as computerization has increased the complexity of trying to provide an education while standards have been lowered so as to give everyone an equal opportunity to be mediocre. All this while special programs have been de-

Phases of Life

veloped for accelerated learners so they can hang out with the other accelerated learners with increasing dysfunctional social skills.

The educational environment is further complicated because the students are happily distracted by the nonsense on their phones and don't have to put out too much effort because there is always an option for a retest while teachers are held accountable if their students fail. Not to mention that text books have been all but banned as too expensive or (non-sensibly) as too irrelevant or too hard for today's young readers.

And to make it even worse, at the beginning of each school year, teachers have to learn the latest and greatest teaching method not taking into account all the handouts that have to be copied since there are no text books to go home with the students.

Where is the logic in all these decisions?

What is a teacher to do?

Teachers are not supposed to be baby sitters, but today's schools are a lot different from when I was in school. I did see a glimmer of hope last fall when my twelfth grade son had to write out his answers on a piece of paper for his government assignment just like I used to have to do because his government teacher said, "I'm tired of all the copy and paste learning."

Of course, writing out his answers was a struggle for him because he had to print all the letters because he didn't spend any time on cursive in elementary school. Suddenly, the home assignments stopped and so did the writing and the learning.

Education is a system that is slowly imploding on itself.

What will your career ladder look like?
Can you find it?

Your Career

Careers don't happen on their own.
You will need help and lots of it.

Generally

It is rare that someone stays on the same career track their whole adult life because there is so much that you can't and don't know until you get there and then you decide to make changes based on what you find and the opportunities that present themselves. There is no easy answer to what lies ahead but you can prepare yourself as best as possible.

The best thing to do is layout some goals and possible directions for yourself as best you can. Write them down. Then you can look back and have a better understanding of how you got where you are and whether it aligned with what you were thinking before or not.

Focus on gaining the best set of hard and soft skills possible so you can seize the opportunities when they arise. And remember that timing is everything.

Keep your act together and you have a very good chance of great success because so many of your peers are being sucked into the digital quicksand which will make it easier for you to stand out in the crowd. Don't get trapped in the quicksand yourself.

When thinking about your choices for a career take as much into consideration as possible such as how your body and mind will hold up in the work environment now and after 30 years depending on the type of work and whether it is manual or professional.

Give your career path as well as your options a lot of thought because as you age and get more in depth and specialized in your career you can quickly become trapped. Trapped means that you reach a level of value and earnings whereby it becomes too risky and costly for you to change and you are stuck.

Plan carefully. Keep looking at what is going on around you and stay on your toes. Try to think it through. Ask a lot of questions to get a better idea of what your future might look like and keep trying to evaluate the risks of not being able to reach your goals with the different options you are considering. Always have a plan B.

Career ladders

The Workforce Development Department of the Northern Virginia Community College system has developed six career ladders for various career tracks based on labor market research for the Northern Virginia area. The specific career ladder information is available from the college's website for Business and Finance, Health Care, Information Technology, Public Administration, STEM, and Tourism, Hospitality and Food Service.

You will be well served to review all these ladders to get a glimpse of where you are or could be headed. The ladders are current with estimates of applicable yearly wage ranges updated for 2018. As a resident of this area I can vouch for the proliferation of job opportunities and the yearly wage estimates. The opportunities are here.

The ladders are available at https://www.nvcc.edu/workforce/research/career-ladders.html

Competition for jobs

Competing for jobs and trying to increase your earnings will become your new sport. Getting a job is dependent on what you can demonstrate and show the recruiter. The recruiter is not going to give you a job just because you went to a prestigious school, that just means you went to a prestigious school. Maybe you can ride the reputation of the school as a door opener, but just because you attended a school with a name does not mean you are guaranteed a place or ride on Easy Street. You are not being hired to be a student, you are being hired to perform a job and how well you can perform it is all that will count in the end.

Today you do have less competition from your peers because they are all falling off the cliff of life as they keep staring at their cell phones. At the same time that businesses need more talent coming in to help with the complexity of the world or to make up for what is retiring there is less qualified talent for them to choose from because everyone your age is distracted by the nonsense on their phone.

Why is somebody going to give you a job? How are you going to be able to help them solve their problems? If there were no problems then there wouldn't be a need for any jobs.

You need to be able to sell yourself — how are you building your resume to be able to do that?

You need help with all of this because you don't have the experience and depth to be able to put it all together. Ask!

Doors

This is another word for opportunities and it usually refers to opportunities in your career. It implies that you hope to be able to find doors that you can open and move through so you can advance in your life journey such as when employers offer you a job they are opening a door for you, a door into their world.

You will be able to open more doors if you have the keys of innovation, creativity, and persistence.

Recently I was talking with a friend, Steve Barton from Virginia Beach, Virginia, who works for a company that supplies me with equipment that is used in propane distribution. Steve is about my age and we were talking about our unique career tracks. In talking with Steve I realized that his career serves as an excellent example about how one always needs to be aware of what is going on around them and looking for doors that might be present.

Steve said he was happy to have his story included in the book as an illustration of what is coming your way.

Steve explained, "I grew up in the Virginia Beach area and in high school I started working in the commissary at the local Navy

Phases of Life

base as a bagger where my mother was a manager. Baggers were supposed to wear a tie but I wouldn't so my mom fired me and told me that I needed to find my own job.

"I went to work at a Kmart store, eventually becoming an assistant manager. I worked a lot of hours which was fine because I was young, and while there I saw how much money the cleaning company was charging to clean the floors at night with floor buffers that were powered with propane fuel. The cleaning company seemed like a better career track so I decided to quit my job with Kmart and began working at night cleaning floors.

"I had been on a track to become a store manager for Kmart and my friends said I was crazy to quit what I had, but I wanted more than that. I admit that I thought I was hot shit carrying keys making $15,500 in the early 1980's but I took the risk to leave Kmart and was able to earn $20,000 with the cleaning company.

"The owner of the cleaning company got distracted and didn't manage the company very well. A few years after I started working for him he got into financial trouble so he sold the floor buffer equipment to me and financed the sale over two years. I ran the company for 10 years and I hustled to try and make it grow through expansion and diversification, but market conditions changed and the business began losing its appeal to me.

"Then one day I was talking to my propane gas supplier who needed a truck driver during the day. I got my commercial truck driving license and started driving a truck during the day delivering propane to homes and businesses for the national company, still able to clean floors at night.

"I eventually gave up on the cleaning company because the business model shifted with more competition which created lower margins. I had tried to diversify the business model and would have had to expand the business a lot more to make it work, but the frustration of having to hire and supervise so many people that didn't have any skills or morals wore on me so I closed the business.

"I started driving the propane delivery truck full-time and was promoted from being a driver to managing one location and then

122

later a second location which I did for 10 years. Then I was getting tired of managing the locations and one day Dicky, who was like a traveling sales representative for the company I am working for now, said he was retiring so I applied for his job. I was given it and have had his job of driving a circuit as a relationship manager for all my clients who run propane companies for 15 years. I enjoy being on the road during the week and seeing all my professional friends.

"My wife and I have been happily married for 31 years. It is interesting how we do more together now over the weekends when I am home than it seems we did before. Everything has worked out very well for both of us and our two children. Owning the cleaning company afforded us with enough income that she could stay home with the kids as they were growing up and both of them went to college even though I never did.

Steve said, "Tell your readers that I emphasize that, things will work out for you if you are willing to work and don't get caught in minimum wage jobs. Low paying jobs should just be a learning experience and a stepping stone to bigger and better. They aren't sustainable. You have to have aspirations to move on.

"There is stuff for everybody out there, you just have to be willing to look and work at it. Complacency is the hazard. Keep in mind that work is nonstop if you own your own company and there are no guarantees but that is what makes life interesting and fun.

"There is so much opportunity for everybody, you just have to be able to take some risk. That is why everyone wants to come to America. It is the land of opportunity.

"It worked for me and it will work for you if you put out the effort."

High tech today and tomorrow.

Today and for the foreseeable future there are a periphery of companies that develop and provide information and software services to the federal government as contractors. Approximately 50 percent of these contractors that work in the Washington, D.C., area need employees with a top secret security clearance to handle sen-

Phases of Life

sitive information related to the projects they work on. The combination of complexity of the work, the sensitivity of the information and government's huge need and demand to develop more and more applications is the major driver of employment and related opportunities in this region.

The United States government is funding and driving this development to improve operational efficiencies and to stay ahead of adversaries in defense which together has created tremendous opportunities for private companies and their employees to provide these services. This area is very unique and unless you are part of the culture here, very few people outside the area realize what is going on here and the opportunities all of it creates.

Trying to understand where all this technology is headed and projecting into the future I recently asked a recruiter at a university career fair, "Given the increasing complexity of these software systems and the need for them to be maintained and operated, how is the knowledge base of programmers going to be maintained to keep everything running?" She shook her head and said, "I don't know. It's a big problem and it keeps growing larger."

I talked to another recruiter at the fair who was recruiting for a small company and he explained that, "There is large negative supply," which means deficiency, "of people to provide these services." He also added that, "The saddest thing to see is a computer science or information technology senior ready to graduate that has not worked as an intern so they could have gotten a security clearance for their summer job before they became a senior. What were they doing? It takes a year to get a clearance and equates to earning an extra ten to twenty-thousand dollars per year after they graduate and now they will have to wait. What a waste!"

The same recruiter also explained that in the big picture of high tech that the name of the school that you attend is irrelevant and that grades are indicative of whether you work hard or not. After college, the big key to employment in this area with so much government contracting is to have passed various certification tests to gain credentials in different specializations. The specializations encompass many different job functions such as Human Resources or Help Desk or in Linux or Cisco Networking or other software or applications. These certifications are important because the government contracts are written for people with specific credentials, not whether they have a master's degree or a Ph.D. or that they got a B in chemistry.

The certificates are important because they provide a standardized way to evaluate a persons knowledge of a specific software application. To learn about and test for a specific application a person can either take a class that teaches the material or they can read a book and study online and on their own. It doesn't matter how someone learns the information, just that they can pass the test and earn the certification.

This is important because the government contracting officials write contracts when they procure services from private industry. The contracts identify the number of people and their requisite certifications that the government wants to procure to work on a specific project. The contract may also identify the pay ranges for those people and the length of time allowed for the contract to be completed. The contract might be for one Help Desk person, two Linux developers and one Graphic Designer who together will create an application that does something. If a person has the requisite certificate defined on the contract then they are qualified to fill the role identified.

In a contracting world that is being driven by certifications an actual college degree isn't as important as it used to be, but the degree does show that you can pull your weight and handle the load. And going to a community college is better than not continuing your education at all.

Community colleges are a great resource to get you started on a good path for success and then once you get your two-year associates degree you might decide that you want to move up to the four-year school and finish with a bachelors. And most of the state four-year schools have automatic acceptance for associate degree graduates as long as the student was initially enrolled in the program to start.

No one is going to think any less of you if you go the community college route in advancing your education. The important thing

Phases of Life

is to finish and graduate.

An analogy can be made by a successful comic book artist that I know who wanted to tell my daughter at Baltimore Comic-con how to be a successful comicer. As my daughter opened her notebook to make sure she got down all the details he stopped her and said, "Wait, you don't need all that. It's very simple. To be a successful comic book artist all you have to do is finish what you start." He went on to explain, "There was a girl in a high school art class with me who was a way better artist then me and probably the top artist at our school. At the time is was easy to see her talent and she was so much more talented than me.

"Then, many years later I happened to run into her when she was working at a fast food restaurant at the same time that I was having my book published by Scholastic. I was shocked that I had made it and that she had fallen behind. The thing that set us apart was my persistence."

Persistence is a term that was well developed in the movie about the history of the founder of McDonald's.

The same goes for your education. Don't stop after high school or part way through college. Keep plugging through it and keep your momentum going. Don't lose focus because once you stop or slow down it is going to be hard to get started again and you will be missing opportunities all the while. And remember that you can work on resilience in any situation.

A charge of "Possession of Narcotics" on your record is the quickest way you can destroy a lifetime of opportunities and high income working in the secure, high tech field. The second quickest way is to lie when you answer questions on the polygraph test. And, the third is to have a DUI. All three indicate a person of insufficient character to be trusted. Just be careful now, that you don't engage in anything that would cause you embarrassment and the need to lie and you should be good to go.

No security clearance, no high-paying and easier career path.

Another example of how high technology is evolving compared with other career paths comes from a conversation I had with a wom-

126

an who was recruiting for a consortium of banks called Swift. The group of banks maintain a very secure system for transferring funds between the banks around the world which, if penetrated, could create huge losses for the banks.

We were talking about the opportunities in high tech compared with other fields and she told me, "I have a friend who told her son many years ago that his choices for a career were either medicine or computers. For some reason he chose computers and now he realizes how lucky he was to make the choice he did because he has so many opportunities that pay really well."

Keep in mind that continuing education is a requirement for success in IT careers. Being a lifelong learner is a top requirement for successful high tech employment and with continuing education comes continuing rewards that include greater employability, career advancement and increasing compensation.

Continually expanding your knowledge base and skill set is especially necessary in IT or you will become out-dated. Just because you graduate from school doesn't mean you should stop learning. Change is what is creating the opportunities for you today and to keep reaping the opportunities, you also have to keep expanding your knowledge base so you will be current tomorrow.

Remember, complacency is your enemy.

Finding a job.

There are always lots of jobs, it just depends on what you are interested in, its future potential and how much you will be compensated for your effort or for performing the tasks.

**How much do you want to be paid
and how hard do you want to work?**

Military service

The military offers many opportunities so if you need more options or an escape from what you don't like about the world, the

Phases of Life

services will turn you into more than you are now. You just need to decide if you really need their help with training and discipline or if you think that you can do it on your own.

I highly recommend joining the military if your private sector options seem limited and you are open minded and want to join a really big organization. You will learn a lot about yourself and you will come out with a lot of benefits that will help to carry you along including educational benefits. It doesn't hurt to talk to a recruiter just to see what options are available but don't go and sign something on a whim.

You might want to do some research on the legal implications of the oath you will be required to take if you decide to join the military. See section titled Oaths.

You should also recognize how the military glorifies service and war which is anything but. Abraham Lincoln had a very serious problem in trying to recruit and then draft soldiers to fight against the South just as Johnson had a very serious problem trying to draft men to fight in Vietnam. Be careful that you are not played into thinking that military service is something that it isn't and what may seem acceptable at one point in time or phase of your life may not be so acceptable later.

**Military service does not come
with a "Get out of Jail Free" card.**

Oaths

You need to be very careful with oaths because they are administered to military recruits when they join the military and while the taking of the oath is approached in a very nonchalant manner as it happens, what is really occurring when you raise your hand and take it is that you are giving up some of your rights of protection that you received on birth.

This is a very serious issue that is never fully discussed in public and military officers are not even aware of this aspect of the oath, but as explained to me by a retired federal judge, "Once you take the oath to protect the Constitution, you are giving up your life so whatever happens to you while in military service doesn't really matter to the government because you willingly relinquished some of your rights when you agreed to defend the Constitution with your life."

Furthermore, by taking the oath to protect the Constitution, you are subjecting yourself to, a different set of laws regarding the Military Code of Justice and more so they are taking away some of your rights and replacing them with a different set of rules that you will have to adhere to.

The oath is the governments legal justification for why so many veterans feel they are under served by the VA health care benefit system. If the VA takes too long to provide adequate services the veterans eventually die and that problem is solved.

The oath is also the basis for your arrest and possible court martial if you fail to obey an order from a superior even if you feel uncomfortable with the order because it may put your life at risk. Recognize that the extensive training always comes with the risk of war.

So before you sign up think hard as to whether you want to be risking your life and your freedoms so you could be where you are today. It isn't an easy decision to make and it should not be taken lightly or made quickly.

I am not against the military per se because when I was your age I was very interested in going to the Air Force Academy and I worked hard to secure a Congressional Nomination and complete the process for qualification. I did not attend because I was ranked as an alternate.

My concern is that you are informed and not taken advantage of because I have learned that there are lots of instances where full disclosure isn't provided. In this case, once you agree to something like protecting the Constitution with your life, you might be caught having bargained for more than you care to chew later. Also take into consideration the conflict-of-interest that all recruiters have in that they have specific target goals for how many recruits they need to bring in each month so they can receive satisfactory performance

Phases of Life

reviews and stay on their path for promotion to a higher rank.

Remember what General George S. Patton said in his famous speech to the troops in his 3rd Army's 6th Armored Division in France on May 31, 1944,

"Now I want you to remember that no bastard ever won a war by dying for his country. You won it by making the other poor dumb bastard die for his country."

General George S. Patton

School Projects

Many school projects have lead to really big businesses.

Can you name some of them?

Hints, one has to do with an Internet search engine and another has to do with shoes.

Security Clearances

There is a lot of money and a lot of opportunity in jobs that require security clearances which are usually associated with nuclear energy, intelligence, data security, computers and the military. The clearances are not just for engineers or scientists with college degrees; they are for anyone that works in the office so even if college isn't in your plans, there are plenty of jobs such as just running wires in a data center or managing a contract that require a clearance so don't get dirt on your background.

At a recent George Mason University career fair, I was surprised to learn that the Federal government even has summer internships for rising college seniors that require a security clearance. The government will perform a background check for prequalified applicants which for the private sector costs about $10,000. I was even more surprised to learn that more than half of the applicants get washed out because they cannot pass the polygraph or the background check for many easily avoidable reasons. The reasons include that they have used drugs, have a problem with alcohol, owe a lot of money, are financially irresponsible, made inappropriate social media posts, have downloaded a lot of illegal or copyrighted files or games, or they lie about their past to the background investigators.

As told to me by a background investigator, "We always find out." It is unfortunate that so many young students would have already ruined their chances at such a young age because in this region a security clearance is the golden ticket to a career with solid employment and advancement opportunities.

This is especially true in today's political and technical environment where the problems related to security and complexity keep expanding and there are so many more jobs than there are qualified people to fill them.

Washington, D.C., is a unique area in many ways which also includes that there is a lot of money moving through this region. You wouldn't know it looking around my very normal looking neighborhood, but I happen to live in the Congressional District with the highest average household income. The high income is partly because of the high salaries government professionals earn and partly because of the high retirement income for all the former high salaried government professionals.

This area is also home to the fastest growth of data centers in the world which is being driven by the governments and the public's rapidly expanding need for information storage and retrieval. I also live in a unique cybersecurity corridor that runs between Washington, D.C., and Dulles Airport. Cybersecurity is a hot industry with the government even offering some full-ride scholarships at prestigious universities and even paying a stipend in exchange for an equivalent amount of time working for the Federal government in what I am sure is a high GS rating.

Opportunities like these are not going to discover you, you are going to have to discover them. Where I would have thought that there would be fewer employment opportunities because of technology induced efficiencies, it now appears that technology is creating even more employment opportunities because as everything becomes more and more complicated it is harder and harder for a few people to have all the knowledge they need to run the systems. This expanding complexity is never going to stop because as I learned at an

Phases of Life

Air Force Association seminar, mentioned on page 188, which ever country has the best technology wins the wars so your government has to stay ahead in technology, no matter the cost, to help insure its success and our survival.

Security clearances are so unique in this area that George Mason University even has a free program open to Freshman, Sophomores and Juniors called Clearance Ready. The program is designed to prepare students for the process of gaining a security clearance which includes topics about polygraphs and back ground checks. It appears that very few students are participating in the program which may be indicative of the extent that society has programmed the students to follow their passion instead of the money, especially since computers, programming, and the Internet are relatively simple disciplines once you learn about them.

A clearance is required for a lot of Department of Defense employees and the employees of companies that provide classified products and services to the Department of Defense. The acronym for this level of clearance is TS/SCI which stand for Top Secret/Sensitive Compartmented Information.

Many non-military career fields also require clearances due to the sensitivity of the information that is stored, processed and handled such as telecommunications, education, human resources, medicine and finance.

Basic information about security clearances:

1) They are much easier to get when you are young because you have not been an adult very long so there is less to verify and you had less time to make a detrimental mistake.

2) They are not hard to get if you have a clean slate and never lie.

3) Nobody will tell you that they have a security clearance because, as part of having a clearance, you are not allowed to tell anyone that you have the qualification.

4) They are very popular in the Washington, D.C., area because there is such a large military presence here that uses classified infor-

mation or information that came from classified sources.

5) You cannot request a clearance on your own. It is very expensive and you must have an employer that is willing to sponsor you for a position that requires a clearance as an employee of their company. The company or government agency that intends to hire you will pay the cost for processing the application for your clearance, which entails a very in-depth and extensive background check regarding your conduct and character. Before they initiate the process, they will perform their own due diligence to be as sure as possible that you will be a good fit in their organization and, by performing a preliminary review of your SF86 form, "Questionnaire for National Security Positions" that you are likely to pass the background check.

6) The approval process requires employment and education verification as well as an extensive review of your finances, personal contacts and a variety of other aspects. The background check will also investigate your character, mental stability, and trustworthiness. Depending on the organization and/or the level of clearance applied for, you may also have to take a polygraph which is a lie detector test. Drug use in the prior twelve months is automatic disqualification. And don't think you can lie about something and get away with it. You won't. The background investigators find out everything.

7) Top Secret clearances are valid for five years when another background check will be conducted if the person is still employed in a job that requires it. The initial clearance costs about $10,000 to process and the investigation can take six months to a year to complete. There are about 4.5 million people with clearances in the United States with about two-thirds in the military and one-third with private defense contractors.

8) Unfortunately, even after an initial screening, over 50 percent of the young adults who apply are denied a clearance.

In March of 2018, I attended a forty-five minute presentation by Alex Cooley, the Labor Market Intelligence Analyst for the Workforce Development Department of the Northern Virginia Community College. The presentation was very enlightening even for someone

Phases of Life

like me that is familiar with the area and has lived here all his life. It was my wife's idea to attend his presentation so she gets all the credit.

When it was over, I realized that it was the best presentation of the event. It was unfortunate that more parents and students were not there to hear what he had to say.

In particular, Mr. Cooley explained that in this area there are 1.3 million jobs broken out with 78,000 with the Federal Government, 123,000 in State and local governments, 1,000,000 in private business, and 73,000 self-employed. This area has very low unemployment, so low that it is very hard to find people to fill the jobs so the students can easily move into these jobs if they have the where-withal. Furthermore, local employers give preference to applicants that live here, especially those with family roots because they are less likely to leave the area.

Mr. Cooley said that this area has the highest percentage of Asians on the East Coast and that 10% of the workforce is employed in IT versus a national average of 3%. One third of all cyber jobs in the U.S. are here and he emphasized that for electives students should take as many classes as possible in the areas of professional writing and communication skills.

The most startling comment he made was, "A security clearance is the golden ticket, even more important than a degree." He continued by explaining that, "Degrees age themselves out."

Mr. Cooley had the one golden nugget of all the other presentations that day and I don't think there were more than 25 people in the room to hear it.

Wow!

Vocations

Vocations fall more under a category of trade related jobs versus professional jobs. Trade jobs typically involve the use of ones hands and back more than their minds and professional jobs typically involve more use of ones minds than their hands and back.

There are lots of vocations and professional jobs that you can enter and there is a lot of material regarding these so I am not going to discuss them in this handbook except for the ones related to computers, cybersecurity and technology.

Working

Don't complain, "I had too many bosses telling me what to do."

Did you do what they wanted you to do is the real question and did you got paid for your time and effort? If so, then what is the problem?

If it was all fun and games then they wouldn't have to pay you to do it, right?

If you are not happy where you work, don't get mad and give management an ultimatum because you will be setting yourself up to have to carry through on it. And don't start complaining to the other employees either. That won't get you anywhere.

When you are employed there is no X-box, you just have to work. Sleeping on the job is irresponsible and dishonest; so is playing video games or checking social media on company time.

Before you confront management with something that you don't like, consider their perspective by imagining what you are going to say and how they may respond. Know that what you probably want to say probably won't be well received either.

Be very, very careful not to burn any bridges.

Recognize that a lot of people in your industry may know each other very well and you don't want to get blacklisted or known as uncooperative or as a trouble maker. It always helps if you have good references when you go to apply for your next job otherwise interviewers are going to be skeptical of you at the start.

Be careful that you don't start telling other people how to run their companies.

If you don't want a boss telling you what to do then start your own company.

Phases of Life

When I was in school we didn't have a ton of information showing us that everybody else was happy when we were slogging it out and the world was not moving as fast.

Your College Education

I am trying to balance the presentation of this information so that I don't cause you a lot of stress in trying to over-think all of it. Still, I want to get all my thoughts out and aspects for analysis on the table for your consideration. This is an area that is subject to a lot of interpretations and unknowns.

I would like to add that if you question what I am writing versus what your parents are telling you that you should give a lot more weight to your parent's opinion over mine. I do not want to cause any conflicts between you and your parents. Always remember that they love you very much and that they are trying to guide and do the best they possibly can for you. Should you not be able to talk to your parents, find a mentor—the world is full of willing supporters for you.

Disclaimer

I would like to reinforce that my ideas and views are only that of a full-time college student from 40 years ago that did not graduate, a former and current part-time college student, an entrepreneur that successfully started and continues to operate a small business, and a parent of today, and that I am not trying to be or appear or act as an academic authority on the current state of higher education. I am just offering my experiences, observations, and perspectives. I am open to and welcome any insight provided as I try to be objective in my expectations and presentation while offering my impressions and analysis based on my life experiences and those of others I know.

Definitions and comparisons

Scientist vs engineer: a scientist is someone that does research where an engineer is someone that is trying to solve a problem.

College vs university: colleges only teach where universities teach and also seek funding for research projects.

Community college: a school with an open-door admissions policy and a requirement of a high school or equivalent degree. It offers two-year Associates Degrees and everyone that applies is usually accepted.

A couple of illustrative resources for reference

There are many factors and articles about how attending college changes lives and how hard it is to even measure the changes because there are so many variables. A recent representative article that illustrates some of the variables and difficulty in analysis associated with the information is explained in the recent article posted online at Marketwatch on December 4, 2018 titled,

"How Elite Schools Change the Lives of Male and Female Students in Dramatically Different Ways." https://www.marketwatch.com/story/elite-schools-steer-the-futures-of-male-and-female-students-in-starkly-different-ways-2018-12-03

Another source for information about what happens to students in the college environment is provided by a trade association in Herndon, Virginia, called National Student Clearing House that compiles information from all participating two and four year colleges by tracking each student and compiling the numbers regarding who transfers, drops-out, and who completes school along with a lot of additional information.

The results of the assessments are posted on their website and help to quantify the percentage of students that change schools or don't graduate and at what level in their pursuit of advanced learning the change occurs. This information should provide you with some guidance regarding the norms.

The question I would like to know and have answered but is never answered—is how everything worked out for everyone that

Phases of Life

ventured down the road of life and some of the reasons why? Is that is too much to ask?

Overview

The neat thing about college in America is that it is available to everyone at any time in one's life unlike in other countries such as in Europe where you have to pass a battery of tests your senior year to qualify to get in.

America's educational system and its opportunities for continuing education provide the foundation of America's resilience and strength.

It is all available to you, you just need to make the effort.

Colleges are waiting for you to come to them so they can help you succeed. Your parents have already paid taxes to the state and federal governments, a portion of which is returned as funds to subsidize some of the tuition costs at public institutions so they will be more affordable. The Foundation for Economic Education stated that in 2016, yearly spending for students "reached an all-time high of more that $9,000 per student." https://fee.org/articles/government-spending-on-education-is-higher-than-ever-and-for-what.

So why not take advantage of what has already been paid for you?

Also, today's schools have so many programs and support staff who are sensitive to your needs, ready to assist you in overcoming whatever obstacles you may be faced and goals you would like to achieve. They are all there to help you succeed but you have to be the one to initiate the conversation, ask questions, talk with them, attend class and show you are willing to perform. This is the real learning experience.

Two-year community colleges provide an excellent alternative and/or foundation to four-year schools and most have an open door acceptance policy for any person who holds a high school diploma or equivalent.

The community colleges have many vocational classes as well as two-year curriculum's. The vocational classes can encompass everything from auto mechanics, nursing and cosmetology to CAD drawing, computer networking and programming routers. The academic programs will provide you with a two-year Associates Degree and if you plan properly you can continue your education through automatic acceptance to a four-year college as long as you initially structured your classes for that contingency.

You need to take the time to talk with your community college guidance counselors so they can help guide you. They are ready, willing, and able but you still need to verify what they are telling you to reduce any possible confusion in the future. Remember to take notes, write things down, and keep your information organized.

It is your time, money, life, and future.

No matter who you are or where you come from you can't ask for any more options for success then you have here in America.

Aim high; you can always scale back later if you have to. Push yourself to see what you are capable of. You never know unless you try and nobody will fault you for trying. Remember the saying, "If at first you don't succeed, try, try again."

College, wherever you go, is scary as well as exciting. It was scary for me because it was a new environment with so many unknowns. I didn't have any friends when I began classes at Georgia Tech in Atlanta and none of us were sure we would be able to cut it.

To ease the transition to a four-year college you can always take a few classes at the local community college your senior year in high school and/or the summer before you go to college to get a taste of it, which is what I did.

You have a lot of freedom and responsibility for yourself when you enroll in college but the discipline to learn and do the class work is the biggest problem everyone has once they arrive at this phase of their life. I am sure that you are smart enough to learn the material

Phases of Life

if you study it carefully no matter how hard it is. As with everything new you have to pay attention to the details. You have to learn the terms and then learn how the terms are applied together into a process and then be able to use the process to solve problems.

It is the self-discipline and ability to manage yourself and your time that will make the difference in your success or failure, not the course work per se. Distractions are the enemy that will keep you from attaining your objectives. Self-discipline is such a key point for success.

Today you can find whatever help you need on whatever subject online. It is truly amazing to see all the resources available, but at the same time, you the student needs the self-discipline to stay on task.

Work has many meanings, some good, some bad depending on one's perspective. Just like reading this book is work, all of the subjects are part of your life. How you approach "work" depends on your perspective which is in your control. Your work ethic is also a controllable.

Be and stay focused and try to make all aspects of "work" fun, interesting, and enjoyable and take pride in your accomplishments no matter how small. Putting out the effort now will be the best investment you can make and it will pay returns to you for the rest of your life.

What is the purpose of a college?

The purpose of all schools is to create an environment for you to mature and improve your hard and soft skills.

Colleges, just like high schools, function to provide a "credential" or certificate that you met certain standards and were proficient in certain skills as defined by the school in a specific area of expertise. When you attend a school there are no guarantees except that if you complete the curricula accordingly you will be given a diploma that certifies that you completed the curricula.

What else you get from your attendance and what you can do with the experience after graduation is up to you.

College and you

Part A

Write down your five reasons of why you want to go to college.

1. _____ -_____

2. _____ -_____

3. _____ -_____

4. _____ -_____

5. _____ -_____

Now, to the right of each reason rank them in order of importance to you.

Part B

Write down the five reasons of why your parents want you to go to college. No guessing, ask them to learn what they think.

1. _____ -_____

2. _____ -_____

3. _____ -_____

4. _____ -_____

5. _____ -_____

Now, to the right of each reason rank them in order of importance to them. Make sure you are researching basic educational requirements.

Does attending college guarantee you a job and a higher paying job?   Yes   No

Phases of Life

Quantify in total dollars how much you and/or your parents are investing and/or borrowing for you to continue your education instead of starting to work and earn money? Estimate of the total budget for college. Include everything.

$_____,_____.

Estimate how much you could have earned with your time for the same time period working in a job if you didn't go to college?

$_____,_____

Add the two items for your total cost.

$_____,_____

Part C

List your traits that will help you to be successful in achieving each of your five objectives listed in Part A?

1. _____ -____

2. _____ -____

3. _____ -____

4. _____ -____

5. _____ -____

Now, to the right of each trait rank them in order of what is your strongest versus your weakest.

Part D   List your traits that will cause difficulty for you in achieving each of your five objectives listed in Part A?

1. _____ -____

2. _____ - _____

3. _____ - _____

4. _____ - _____

5. _____ - _____

Now, to the right of each trait rank them in order of what is your strongest difficulty versus your weakest. Think hard, this is a tough one but probably the most important.

You and your parents support and expectations

**Today you need to go to college "smart".
Do you think you have what it takes?**

You are who you are and your success in life is going to be based on your personality. The school you attend and the teachers and friends you have there will have some influence on your happiness and success, but in the end it all comes down to you and your personality. The school is the vehicle by which you can improve your skills and exercise and refine your personality.

College is a test in discipline and in keeping yourself motivated.

You and your parents expect that your continued education in an environment with achievers will help you to learn and achieve. They may not understand if you are apathetic and not motivated or if you feel that you are not good enough to keep up. When students get overwhelmed they can start to feel depressed and seek remedies for their depression which can take them into an ever growing hole of despair when what they really just need to do is to get a hold of themselves and do the work that is expected. Stay focused on the priorities.

If you find yourself in this situation of despair do not be afraid to talk with your parents or a counselor about how you feel and don't think that you are all alone. Failing is riskier than asking for help to succeed and as one of today's teens you need all the parental support and help you can get. Never cut yourself off from the guidance and influence that your parents or a counselor can provide at this critical point in your life or even later. It is OK to ask for help. I asked for help when I realized school was not working out for me the way I thought it should and my parents said it was OK if I didn't return after my Sophomore year. We knew that I had other educational options.

Choice Paradox

One of my concerns is that parents can have much higher expectations for their child and they may push to get them placed in a more prestigious and usually more rigorous school even if their student is not mentally or academically capable. Placing a good but not fully self-motivated student in such a competitive environment may put the student at risk even though some parents think that a miracle of maturity and independence will occur. This unbalanced set of expectations versus reality can put a lot of pressure on the student to perform with the risk for unexpected outcomes.

Parents need to realize that if their students have the wherewithal to apply themselves it often doesn't matter what college they attend, they will have the skills to sort things out and succeed in school and in life. For students that are borderline marginal academically, the risk in pushing them too hard into an environment that they can't handle is a possibility. A student may succumb to new academic and social pressures through alternative means of coping. In the end the parents as well as the student need to recognize that if the student doesn't have the maturity to independently apply and manage, then it doesn't matter how prestigious the school is. The student may end up feeling they failed in not being able to live up to one's own or parent's expectations. Trying to balance all these factors in choosing a college can create a challenging paradox for the parent as well as the student.

Expectations are the biggest change from when I was in college to today. When I was in school we didn't have a ton of information showing us that everybody else was happy when we were slogging it out and the world was not moving as fast.

When I was in school we didn't compare our self to everybody else because we couldn't and we took everything one day at a time. We established a small circle of friends, got our grades, went home over break and that was all that mattered.

As one of today's students you have to deal with the additional challenge of sorting through the fact and the fiction. Nobody posts photos of them being sad, stressed or depressed, they are all happy photos with smiles and cups raised like they don't have a care in the world. You, as today's students and your parents as parents of to-day's students, need to recognize the huge burden and risk this social information puts on you. Having the maturity to deal with this over-whelming amount of propaganda and distractive content is where it is important that you have the maturity and the constant, regular and continuous communication with your parents to help counter all of social media's negative influences.

Facing a continuous stream of false and misleading information can be very difficult for you, just as it would be for your parents if they were in your shoes. It affects your ability to keep everything in balance and in perspective while maintaining your inner confidence, work ethic, and persistence. The key is to be able to stay focused on what is important, which should not be the social scene, but that is easier said than done for all of us.

College acceptance rates and applying for acceptance
Take the pressure off yourself that you have to get into a school with a low acceptance rate to be successful in life. This in not true. And stop thinking that if you go to a school with a high acceptance

Phases of Life

rate that you are inferior. This is not true.

Just because a school does not accept you does not mean that you are a poor student or person. It just means that you didn't rank high enough in whatever selection criteria they are applying to their applicants.

I received a Congressional nomination to the Air Force Academy in 1976 but I was not ranked high enough for acceptance into the class. My current neighbor was denied to the Naval Academy and then someone who had been accepted decided to go to an Ivy League school instead and so my neighbor was accepted.

It is amazing how the abundance of information has skewed thinking, in particular, that the schools with the lowest acceptance rates are the best schools to go to for career and personal success.

A recent commentary by Jay Mathews of *The Washington Post*, March 25, 2019, destroyed the myth by analyzing his own college alma mater relative to other successful people as well as his managing editors who are responsible for running the paper.

Mr. Mathews explains that he graduated from Harvard which has an acceptance rate of 5%. He then raises the question, "So why have I spent my life being ordered around by people who attended less-selective schools?"

In the commentary he lists the many editors that have the power to fire him with their corresponding college and its acceptance rate. It is a surprising and interesting read.

The President of a college, whose daughter happens to attend Harvard, of which there are probably many, was recently asked the difference between Harvard students and those at his school. The answer was simply that the students at Harvard come from families with lots of money.

Furthermore, there seems to be a prevalent train of thought that being accepted by a better school will make it easier to get a better job because it will appear that being accepted by the school served as a prequalification and validation of your capabilities. Be careful of this train of thought.

In 2015 I was talking with an academic advisor for the English

146

Department at George Mason University when Mary Jane was still a senior in high school. The advisor was very friendly and seemed willing to enroll Mary Jane on the spot.

We were talking about all the job opportunities in the area when she made the off-the-cuff remark that recruiters preferred to recruit and work with George Mason students rather than the students from the more prestigious Georgetown and George Washington Universities. She explained that the recruiters had better experiences with the students from George Mason because they were more motivated, capable, and easier to work with than those from the more prestigious schools. She could have just been feeding me a line but I didn't take it that way and I felt that she was being sincere and honest.

Be careful that you don't get sucked into thinking that going to a prestigious school is going to make your life easier. You may find that it can easily work the other way around.

It is more important to go to a school that works best for you, something, unfortunately, that is very hard to try and figure out and know because you only really get one chance.

Hard and soft skills

Does the school make the person or does the person make the person or does the person make the school? Yes, it depends on every individual!

Even if the name of a prestigious school does help students get a supposed more prestigious or higher level initial job, if the students don't have the right skill set and right interpersonal abilities they will eventually crash and burn in their climb to the top.

Individual success is more about the soft skills than the hard skills, but you can't measure soft skills and it is hard to change personalities if the soft skills are deficient. While it is the hard skills that get measured and evaluated initially and get you in an employer's door, in the end it is the soft skills that allow you to get along, progress and move on and up.

Phases of Life

David Archer, a friend of mine from Cincinnati, Ohio, recently told me, "I am exactly where I wanted to be in life. Some people have lofty ambitions in life, I figured that if I could wind up in a job where I don't have my name on my shirt, I'm successful.

"When I was in the 4th grade and my mother was a single mother with three of us and I was the middle son, my teacher requested a conference with my mother. "Mrs. Archer," the teacher said, "your son has a mental block about his education and he is incapable of learning. He thinks that his purpose in life is interacting with the other students and making them laugh. She was concerned that I was going to become a juvenile delinquent.

"What I have always wanted to be was a stand-up comedian but that was not going over very well in the 4th grade.

"Today, my mother would like to find my 4th grade teacher so she can thank her for her concerns and to say that in the end I turned out alright."

I know David from when he worked as the Executive Vice President of Sales for a large trucking company. He now serves as the Midwest Sales Representative for ARCOSA Tank, a very large propane tank fabricator.

David's attitude and life are an example of someone who did not fit neatly into the educational mold but was still able to parlay the combination of his pleasant personality with a drive for success into a rewarding career for himself and his family.

I learned that David's childhood and life in general was way beyond more complicated than normal when he told me the story about his father.

"At the time when my brother was 9 and I was 6 years old, my father was stationed with the Army at Fort Sill in Oklahoma and we lived there off the base. Then one day my father went to work but didn't come home. And he never ever came home and the Army couldn't or wouldn't tell my mother, who was pregnant with my sister at the time, what happened to him.

"The Army would not declare my father AWOL and they would not say that he was killed. All they could imply was that, as far as they were concerned, that he had just disappeared which left my mother and us to find our way, for the rest of our lives, on our own."

David added that, "My father had mentioned something to my mother in passing about a theft ring that was operating and his knowledge about it might have been a factor in his disappearance. My only positive thought was that he was put in a witness protection program, but on the other hand I can't believe that he would have abandoned us and my mother like that."

David, after telling me the horrible story about the loss of his father, went back to the story about his career by recounting, "When I heard that companies would pay me to fly around, eat dinner at nice restaurants and stay in fancy hotels I raised my hand and said, Oh yea, sign me up baby."

David's personable and friendly personality won him over with all his clients and his employers and he has succeeded with persistence in applying his talents, just as he wasn't expected to do in the 4th grade, of trying to make people happy and laugh. And he was able to accomplish it all in spite of the unusual circumstances surrounding the sudden disappearance of his father and the stress it placed on his family growing up.

School transparency and priorities

My biggest fear is that both the K-12 educational system and the college institutions are promoting the agenda that works for them and their staffs in the short term, not for the true long term benefit of the students.

K-12 educational systems are doing a disservice to their students by pushing so much technology on the students that students think technology is the norm and it is most beneficial for learning. Colleges are doing a disservice to their students by not being more transparent and realistic in describing what happens to their students during and from the college experience at their institution.

Getting mentally prepared for college

College was very hard for me and I would work on my home-

Phases of Life

work in the library almost every night during the week until it closed at 11 p.m. It was the only place I could concentrate to study. I know first hand how uncomfortable it is to sleep with your head on a desk.

I was very homesick which I knew was normal and I tried to deal with it as best I could. One day I discovered that the school library had one day old copies of *The Washington Post* newspaper and I found that reading my hometown paper made me feel more connected to home and less homesick.

I might talk with my parents on the phone every couple of weeks because long distance calls cost money and you had to pay by the minute so we kept our calls short. My parents and my grandparents would send me letters in the mail. I did have a girl friend at home who was very thoughtful and she sent me a lot of supportive letters and cards which was very helpful, especially my first year. I saved all of her cards and letters and still have them in a box today. Maybe someday I can thank her again for all she did for me.

There were no such thing as suicides at college as far as I knew. It was unheard of. We all just did the best we could and tried to find out what worked best for each of us.

I am sure that you have what it takes to succeed at school just as I did for the two years I was there. You even have the ability to communicate with your parents and old friends instantly. On the other hand, you have the new problem of having too much communication and information with the consequence being that you miss out on establishing and nurturing relationships with those around you and getting more in touch with who you are and what you are capable of. The distraction and propaganda from the constant barrage of social media is the biggest hazard you face so try to keep it checked.

We had to make friends to survive and it is very healthy to have in-person relationships. We all needed and continue to need each other to get through it all.

Today you carry your friends and family in your pocket. If you start talking with someone you don't know, that person may think you are odd because nobody does that anymore but that is the best thing to be able to do. Communicate in-person and learn how to make friends by talking with them instead of trying to slide into somebody's DMs.

The best way to stay sane is to slow down and make friends. We had a clinic at school, but there were very few if any issues with depression. It is as if the Internet and cell phones have manifested depression in the minds of students causing them to trip their mental circuit breakers.

Mentally, what would happen to you if you did not have a phone? Would you be more attentive to what is going on around you? Would you become more in touch with yourself? How would it affect you and who you are? Try it and see how it feels.

Your relationship with your parents

Parents may be doing a disservice to themselves and their children by turning them lose in the college environment without more oversight and close supervision. Some teens can handle it and some will go berserk in the vacuum of discipline.

One of the hardest things to understand is that it isn't a specific college that is so important for your success in life, but how much effort you are willing to invest in yourself and if you have the mental and moral fortitude to stay on track while you are at school. To complicate matters you might find that you want to switch schools or tracks.

Don't think that you can do it all on your own. College was hard for me as it is for everyone and it is much harder today than when I was in school. The stakes for your future are much higher than they were for me because everything is moving so quickly but that doesn't mean you have to get caught up in the quick pace. You just have to be able to set your own pace and have persistence. Think strategically.

Communicate with your parents as much as possible especially when you are at school and ask them for help or advice because they know you the best and have more experience. Many times, just

Phases of Life

talking about problems helps put them in perspective or find solutions and your parents are the best one's to talk with. They know you and they have a lot of experience.

You will find that most times just talking with someone you are close to will help you cope and see things more clearly even if they don't say anything. Don't feel like you have to prove anything to anybody and even if you think your parents seem distant they will and do miss you when you go away to school. In a lot of ways, going to college is as hard on your parents as it is on you. Always remember that your parents are your best resource and the best way to succeed is to keep communicating with them as much as possible.

Some parents may not express their concerns or they don't recognize the risks of sending their child to college thinking their child can learn from their mistakes. The problem is that today's mistakes have much larger consequences than mistakes of 10 or 50 years ago because the world wasn't as complex as it is today and the disparity was not as great. Your time is of the essence and hopefully it won't be wasted on frivolous and detrimental activities. Students should try to avoid going down the wrong tracks and getting caught up in self-made detours. There are lots of opportunities for you out there but to uncover the best ones it helps when you can keep building on what you have learned and moving on the right track.

We all have our stories and "Time gives good advice." Your challenge, in spite of all the what-ifs that are coming your way is assembling the right parts for you so you can live as well and as rewarding a life as possible.

Comparing schools in general

All schools are all good for general disciplines and they all teach and test the same standard subject material from a variety of text books. Schools don't make the student a better person, you are who you are. The schools just provide the environment for students to mature and gain more skills and abilities and find opportunities.

Research universities offer opportunities for the very motivated and directed students who are interested in research within their career fields.

You and your choice school

As you decide which school you would like to attend from the one or one's that you applied to and were accepted, how are you and your parents going to rank them on the basis of what it will cost you in terms of time and money versus all the intangibles you hope to gain in return?

What will the final reasons be that drive you to attend one school over another now that you have the insight from all of your research about each school and their acceptance or rejection?

Some of the criteria that you may consider and rank could be;

1. Financial resources - amount of money available for education.
2. Personal contacts to be made at the school.
3. Professional opportunities made through the school.
4. Proximity or distance from home.
5. Close friends who are or are not attending the school.
6. Interest in going on a big adventure and proving you can handle it.
7. Interest in having fun at school.
8. Quest for the best education possible for me.
9. Like the brand message of the school.
10. Ability for courses to or not to transfer to another school if you decide to change. (Refer to section on school transfers.)
11. Cost of attending the school.
12. Need to borrow money to attend school and how much?
13. How much money you may need to borrow to attend each school.
14. Scholarships offered by the school.
15. Geographic location of the campus.
16. Rural versus urban campus environment.
17. Research opportunities.
18. Parents or siblings attended the school.

19. Specific clubs or Greek life.
20. Other _____
21. Other _____
22. Other _____

Benefits of attending college - generally stated

College isn't required for success but it helps a lot and the credentials will show that you can perform and that you have the critical thinking skills to finish tasks.

College is similar to high school but more serious. You fail a required class, you will pay to retake it and poor performance can cause you to be put on academic probation which can lead to suspension.

Apply and use your time extra wisely because you will be launching your career next and now that you are becoming an adult you are going to be given less flexibility. You will need to adhere to more of the rules and strive to meet the higher expectations. With the right level of maturity you will succeed in college and walk away with the confidence that you can run with the pack and keep up. I did.

Warning: Something is amiss in college

As a recently reincarnated college student, I have been very surprised to find that the college environment today is very different from the college environment I attended. I am concerned that so few parents are aware of how different it is and the possible affect of the changes on their child.

This is my investigative assessment of a very complicated and difficult subject with many different institutions, participants, and aspects for interpretation.

My sense is that there has been a big detrimental shift within the college scene from when I was in school forty years ago. Now that

I am on campus again as an official student with current classroom experiences, I have some preliminary theories that I am developing as well as some inside information that I am trying to confirm.

As a parent of prospective students my family visited many schools. As would be expected, we quickly realized that there was a simple standard message in all the presentations. The schools are all saying to the parents, trust us with your child. To the students, the colleges are saying this is the place for you, we will help you grow and succeed.

There are several problems hidden behind these boilerplate messages.

First, the parents are the check and balance in the continued growth and development of the student but, in actuality, the colleges are pushing to exclude participation of the parents in helping to guide their children. After all, in most cases, a college freshman is not any different than a high school senior. This leaves students left to fend for themselves without proper and adequate supervision and/or guidance.

Second, colleges are preaching that the students have reached a point where they need to take responsibility for themselves and many parents willingly agree and let their children strike out on their own just as they did. This is the same situation I was placed in when I went to college at 17 years old. It was challenging then but it was a different challenge compared to now because there are so many more detrimental distractions and influences that make the freedom to venture out more complicated and risky. The standards have been raised also so there is less room for error.

Third, compared with when I went to school in the '70's, there is larger element of risk now because there are a lot more opportunities and the investment in time and money is substantially greater. There are more opportunities now but they change faster because connectivity and the rapid dissemination of information has created a much more competitive environment. Students need to be tuned in to more things all the time to stay in the competition.

Phases of Life

Fourth, the most disturbing part of the college equation is that higher education and the subsequent career paths that a graduate can pursue are a different and more complex game now than when I was in school. Now there are more, and bigger opportunities, as well as correspondingly more, and bigger consequences.

Yes, it is important to find yourself when you go to college, but the stakes are higher now because going to school costs so much more than it did before; cellphones have provided a false sense of security and a distraction for the students, and there are a lot of financial distinction and opportunities between one career path or another.

Academics are further complicated because the schools are telling the students not to give their user ids and passwords to their parents, as if the advisors and the rest of the faculty are qualified, ready, willing, and able to establish relationships with, and provide individual guidance to each individual student based on each one's unique level of experience and maturity.

The schools have made a ton of information available to the students via the Internet and the student's user id. How can they be expected to process all of it and keep their sanity? (Class schedules, career information, special events and their future to just name a few.) But, parents cannot gain access to most of the information because it is proprietary for the student so with user ids the parents are excluded and that is what the schools are recommending to the students. As a registered student with a user id, I was able to open doors and get access to a lot of information without having to negotiate with my child for access.

Maybe part of the difference, then to now, was that generally our lack of technology made us more mature compared with today's students, but I don't think that is fair to say. It's impossible to know. The difference comes from the combination of all the changes.

Maybe we were more mature and independent and less coddled than the students of today, but I also think that things were much simpler. There weren't the myriad of majors, clubs, internships, workshops, volunteer and scholarship opportunities, etc., that there are today. It's really overwhelming.

156

Even if a child is a very focused type A personality, he/she will probably need guidance to know where to look and what applies to them. The advent of the Internet and social media opened so many more opportunities but also provided a powerful source of distraction.

Regardless of maturity, today's environment is one where the parents are left to trust the institution for the care and guidance of their child but in reality the students are left to their own devices which can have a detrimental effect on them. And, all of this occurs with overwhelming financial risks where most parents are footing the bill or will be on the hook when the loans can't be repaid and/or their child is not happy and unable to find meaningful and financially adequate employment and life fulfillment.

The bottom line is that the schools should not be trying to distance the students from their parents and the information, guidance, and responsibility the parents have and can continue to provide. Your parents are in the best position possible to help you and the schools should be reinforcing that relationship instead of trying to become a fake substitute for it.

Granted these are generalizations, but they are valid perceptions because I am part of the educational environment as a parent as well as a student. I have been experiencing and seeing how everything is shaking out at my local college where I am enrolled as a student in two classes and on campus engaging with other students, and am familiar with many of the current college stories regarding the children for many families in my neighborhood and the friends of my children.

Today, you need to go to college "smart."

The only people that are really in the know with inside information about this subject can't discuss how college has changed and what is really happening for fear of losing their job and/or being blacklisted by the industry.

My best explanation for how and why college has changed

Phases of Life

came recently from an inside, on campus source, who I confided my concerns to. Hesitantly, they explained that the college scene is different now than when we were in school because public institutions have adopted a for-profit educational business model.

This for-profit educational model has created a class structure in school administrations to the detriment of the faculty and students whereby money rules. The administration is rewarded handsomely for their efforts to attract it.

As further explained to me, the problem with this model is that the priority has shifted from providing a quality education to the students to one of attracting more money for the administrators and the school in general. The pursuit of money has modified the goals of the leadership and created a class structure within the school.

The administration's disconnect with the staff and students is a result of the change in how college budgets used to be heavily supported by public funds from state legislatures that were concerned about, and wanted to promote, education. Public funding allowed tuitions to be very low compared with today. Lower tuition costs promoted higher education that was justified as being good for society. I believe that student development and achievement were the primary goal and focus of the institution when I attended college.

Then, in the 1980's, as legislatures began cutting back on funding for higher education, tuition rates had to increase and the student loan industry began to blossom as part of the new funding mechanism to fill the void. The other funding mechanism that started to kick in was the behind the scenes solicitation of private donations which can have an affect on who is admitted and can come with caveats and special acceptance consideration for families of wealth. This morphed into an acceptance driver with the hope that the more wealthy families would become large donors in the future.

All of this seems to have created a shifting of priorities where today's college administrators are selling out their students as the administrators strive to justify their very high salaries to their Boards of Regents who control and set the standards for the supposed "public institution."

It appears that the leadership in higher education has shifted its focus from excellence in education at and across all levels to a class structure for those at the top that rewards those who can bring in the dollars.

Priorities are further distorted and complicated because each college department needs tuition dollars to justify the salaries of its faculty.

No students in a program, no jobs for the teachers.

Strict revenue and expense analysis and budgeting for each department is part of the way that schools have had to adjust their priorities and justification in their shift to the for-profit business model to survive.

The saddest part is that with the shift, college personnel have a job protection bias in what they do and say which is not disclosed to the students. No professor is going to tell their students that the career path they are on is bleak even though that is probably why the full-time professor is teaching the class. IRONIC BUT TRUE.

This lack of transparency is not fair to the students who look to their professors as role models and for guidance.

Knowledgeable parents; the real threat to colleges

All of this brings this section back around to the real answer of what I may be sensing on campus and in class and how and why colleges are trying to distance the parents from the students. The real answer might be hidden in the excuse that schools want the students to grow and mature on their own. In actuality, this mantra may be promoted because the colleges don't want the intrusion of the parents or to expose their modified for-profit gig.

By distancing the parents from the students the colleges are able to avoid the scrutiny that a parent's experience and involvement can provide. Granted, parents can't and shouldn't be involved in all the minutia of their child's college education, but, on the other hand, they shouldn't be completely excluded either. It's complicated both ways.

My impression, though, is that it is better and more important for the parents to be involved than to be excluded. But from the schools perspective, the less the parents know about the school, its academic operations and priorities and how the students are or are not being led, taught, or performing, the better off for the school.

The school's greatest fear has become knowledgeable parents who might start to see through what the schools are saying and promoting as a ruse to what they are actually engaged in and their real objectives. The million dollar questions I ask, and in this case they might be worth an easy million, are, "Are the students getting their money's worth from their education?"

"Where is the check and balance in the process?"

The students can't be the check and balance because they don't know or have any experience. The school can't be the check and balance because they have a conflict of interest. The check and balance should be the parents but they are being excluded.

In addition, the schools go a step further, by encouraging the students and almost trying to inflict guilt upon the parents during orientation for wanting to be able to see their students' grades even though in most cases, the parents are paying at least some portion of the tuition. Why? So that the parent doesn't pull the plug sooner when the student in not performing?

As it stands, if the student, and indirectly the parents, reach the end of the road and come to feel that they were short changed by the institution, its process, and staff, the standard institutional response will be, "Sorry, it's too late now," or "It's not our fault," or "You should have known." Or, "I guess you'll need to stay another year."

Cults at college

We are all gullible. As young students you are extra naive because you don't have as many life experiences on which to base your perceptions, conclusions, and choices.

It is unfortunate that schools and their faculties are not more forthcoming about their priorities so you need to be extra careful that you do not get sucked into one of the many cult mentalities at school.

It is important to be and stay focused, not so much on what you enjoy, but more so on what is the best investment for you at this point or phase of your life.

**Keep long term practicality in mind as you
construct your short term building blocks.**

As a student you need to be able to make the distinction between how teachers and/or the school and/or fellow students might be leading you and trying to imply what is best for you. It is easy to get caught up in the pursuit of a lifestyle or particular subject or discipline that is enjoyable to you. At the same time your activities might come at a substantial expense to your future.

In economics, these different options are called opportunity costs. Opportunity costs are the loss from pursuing one opportunity versus another.

You are the best person to make the decisions about what is best for you. But to do it with maturity, you need to be able to recognize the emotional component as well as the practical component for your decisions.

Don't think that just because you can master a subject that you will be financially successful. Expertise and success are two different things and even though expertise does improve the chances of success, there is no guarantee.

Examples of this can be seen in how English departments will feature guests and give them quasi-celebrity status even though they might have had to endure and are still enduring sustenance living for a decade or longer, no matter how perfect their writing may be or what company published their manuscript. Why don't they feature successful writers who are able to make a living in the profession?

Or how sports management departments can feed off the glory and hype of the sports industry where, in reality, only a very se-

Phases of Life

lect few that pursue this discipline will be financially successful and many won't be included as one of the few regardless of the stellar grades they may earn. Or how the truth about what happens to the careers of the majority of art, theatre, history, political science, or music majors is never mentioned or discussed.

Hang tough and keep researching

Recently I was talking with a student in my sports management class about why he was studying sports management.

He explained that his real preference was statistics which shocked me because statistics is such a math heavy discipline compared to sports management. He explained that he was a junior and that he had recently decided to change majors to sports management because his first two years of math were so hard. I sympathized with him because two years of calculus took its toll on me.

I was surprised to hear that he changed majors to sports management though, because in today's new environment of data sciences, statistics is a great field to pursue with graduates guaranteed a strong job market. I explained that he must have done well to survive the two years of calculus and he said yes, but it was tough and part of the reason he decided to bail on statistics overall. Statistics, though, was his real passion.

I suggested that he might want to give statistics another look because the opportunities there were going to be much more lucrative than where he was headed in sports management. I added that if he got a security clearance in conjunction with a degree in math or data sciences that he would be in high cotton. He was not aware of the opportunities that come with security clearances.

That weekend I met a woman, at my son's basketball game, who works for the Army as a data analyst and I mentioned the student's story. As a person familiar with a trajectory for statistics and math graduates, she said that he was through the worst of the math and that now he was positioned to get into the fun stuff and yes, it was a field with lots of opportunities. Who was advising this student? Where was his guidance coming from?

162

The statistics student was a case of a student who was on the right career track and then got overwhelmed and discouraged.

If the going gets real tough, see if you can hang in there and keep doing your research to make sure you are on the right track. It is always a good idea to keep yourself motivated by talking to people in the career center and/or the industry who can reinforce the opportunities that are waiting for you after you graduate.

Refer back to the beginning of this section often about continually planning and working towards your next phase.

Fantasy world versus reality of life

At this phase of your life it is important that you are able to balance any projected fantasy world with the more realistic one of probable reality. Be very careful in the steps that you take in weighing your options.

Be careful that you are not a student who is hoping things will work out on a whim as you chase dreams with low probability for major success. (Here is more talk about statistics.) If your direction is leaning towards this, you might find that it would be more prudent to keep the risky fantasy world as a minor side gig while keeping yourself focused and on track for what is more probable and more realistic in helping you to earn a living and support yourself in the future. Try to choose a major that will provide multiple career opportunities that have growth potential and are well-paying. Any kind of passion can be explored later.

Once the money is accrued, the passions can be pursued!

As you already well know, your life and the environment around you will never be perfect. Accept it for what it is, try to be aware of what is occurring, and keep positioning yourself accordingly. It isn't easy but you can do it.

Be careful not to put all your eggs in one flimsy basket because you might wake up one morning and find that they're all broken. Make sure you have a strong basket.

Phases of Life

I guess that is why basket-weaving used to be a college elective, even though I never understood its relevance. The class must have been a metaphor for taking care of one's life.

Strong and important advice about relationships with parents

Be careful in how you modify and adjust your relationship with your parents. I think it is better to err on the side of caution and stay extra connected and involved with them than to use school and its possible distance from home as an excuse to try and blaze new trails on your own that might lead to nowhere.

Keep texting and talking to them all the time and encouraging their input, and you will reap the benefits many times over as you navigate the maze of college. Don't discount their ability to support and help guide you through all the twists, turns and dead ends that lay in front of you. Talk to them about what you are thinking and what you are learning about your environment. They, as always, are your best resource.

Researching, Comparing, and Deciding

Questions for research and consideration

The problem with researching colleges is there are so many intangibles, variables and unknowns and it is hard to sort fact from fiction. Average class size, projected graduating pay, percent of graduation are all numbers but they don't tell you much about the school and its student body. This is where you have to put on your investigative hat. And your opportunities for research are going to be complicated for the schools that are distant from your home because, assuming you visit them ahead of time, you are only going to have a small window of time in which to try and collect your information.

What questions are you trying to answer? Write them down.

Is it something like, "How do I get the best idea of what it will be like for me to attend xxxx school and what will or won't I get from the experience?"

If so, try to come up with some creative ways to uncover the real heart of the school. You can do it discreetly or indiscreetly.

One way is to ask students what they really like and dislike about the school? If they were the president of the school what would they change if they could?

A discreet way is sit yourself somewhere, like next to some tables where other people are sitting and eavesdrop on their conversation to try and get an inside track on what their life there is like. What is the topic of conversation, what are their priorities?

Do the students walking around look happy? Are they engaging and talking with each other while waiting for a bus or in the cafeteria or are they withdrawn and looking at their phone?

What range of departments does the school have which can offer the opportunity for socializing with people interested in other subjects? Engineering, nursing, teaching, art and rank their popularity at the school by how many students are in each program if you can find the information.

Look at the job recruitment board in the career center, if they still even have a board, or online to see who is posting jobs or who is coming on campus for interviews. Maybe you can get access to the career placement system at the career office. Visit it.

One problem is that a lot of the information may only be accessible online and you may need to be a student to access the information.

Talk to some parents that you might meet while on campus tours to compare notes and impressions. See what insights they may have about the school, what major they are considering and why?

What percentage of the students are international or out-of-state?

Does the school have a strong athletic program and is that good or bad?

What seems to be important to you now and what may become important to you tomorrow?

As you consider what you will actually be learning in classes at

Phases of Life

a school, one way to approach the question of which schools curriculum are better or worse is to look at the class text books. And if two schools use similar textbooks, are the classes any better or worse at one school versus another?

Unfortunately, a new problem with this approach is that many school book stores don't have the text books out where you can peruse them like when I was in school. Now all the books seem to be kept at the bookstore behind a counter and you have to ask for each based on the class you're enrolled in. I am not even sure you can learn what text books each class will use because that information might only be available online to students able to register for class but if you can uncover the title(s) some of the text books might be available for review at the library.

Do you have any idea what percentage of undergraduate classes for your major will be taught by graduate students with no teaching training and experience, or by tenured professors whose focus is teaching and what are the pros and cons of each?

And what are the teacher's salaries at the school relative to other schools?

Is there any way to try and understand the real interest and motivation of teachers and if they are happy with what they are doing? Their attitude can make a big difference in the class and how they interact with students and how the students interact with each other.

The big question that is never discussed is what is being taught in the classes and how? What is the composition of the other students, who are they and who are the teachers? Which graduates get the better jobs and why?

The paradox seems to be that the schools are making a lot of efforts to build their brand and attract students but the schools don't provide much detailed tangible substance as to why the students should attend. None of the schools seem to be saying or selling themselves on the basis of hard information that supports how their school is the best because of these specific tangible aspects of how they are going to make you the best you can be and it seems like a lot of the negatives and the risks are completely avoided and dismissed as in any sales pitch. It would be nice if the system was more transparent.

If the school can't be more transparent in how they can help me strategically when I am considering enrollment than how can I expect them to be able to help me strategically once I am there? I guess to a large degree schools don't have a specific sales force trying to recruit and sell the school as a product. The school is what it is and you have to dig through a lot of fluff to see if it can provide what you think you are looking for and what will be the best fit for you. It is not a business per se, but each department and the school as a whole is dependent on recruitment in order to survive.

I am raising a lot of questions here not to make you feel that you have to answer them, but more to give you a perspective on how to look at what your are considering from different and unique perspectives. Use the experience of choosing a college as another opportunity for learning and applying your problem solving skills. The experience alone is a good one to go through and it is your life so it is kind of important and worth the effort. Then when you arrive at school you will be that much more in tune with an understanding of how to look at where you are and where you are trying to go. I am not trying to get you to over think it now, but by the time you are ready to graduate you will have, so I am just trying to push you ahead a little quicker.

Choosing a school

This is a subject worthy of its own handbook which I will save for the future. My short comment is that with your smarts, the help of your parents, all the information that is out there and the information in this handbook, you are qualified to make that choice and to succeed.

The short answer and the bottom line is that you are going to be the one in control of your success or failure more than any school. You will either rise to the occasion or you won't.

Researching and Investigating your schools of interest

I highly recommend that when you visit colleges or other

schools that you eat all your meals in the on campus dining halls. What better place to experience a prospective school? Why would you eat anywhere else? You can just pay at the entrance and it costs about $10 per person for all you can eat buffets and the food is so much better than what was available to me in the '70's. Assuming that school is in session when you visit the campus, the dining halls give you the best possible opportunity to observe the culture of the school in many ways.

Eating with the students will give you the chance to sample the food, mingle with the students, and get a better representation of the student body. The dining hall is a great place to pickup on the vibe of the school and to observe the students and how they do or do not integrate with each other and their overall demeanor, dress, behavior and attitude. Sit and relax and watch the students on parade. They are the heart of the school, not the architecture of the buildings or the scenic views of the vista.

You can also use the dining experience to start conversations with students to learn about their inside perspective of the school. You will be surprised to find that even though the students may seem preoccupied or bashful, they will all be happy to talk with you and answer any questions you may have about their school or their experience there.

We used a Spring Break to visit six Virginia schools in seven days and it went very well especially since we visited the schools back-to-back and that way all the impressions stayed fresh in our mind as we transitioned from school-to-school. It was a lot of fun and a great adventure.

One of the most interesting sights we saw occurred as we were driving into the campus at Virginia Tech from a rural and scenic route. It was a route that brought us into the back of the campus where there are several student apartment complexes adjacent to the road which comes down from a mountain. As we entered the residential community at about 3 p.m. the first person we saw was walking on the sidewalk towards us carrying a package of beer. We laughed at the coincidence and as we continued another 200 feet we passed another person who was carrying an even larger package of beer.

We hadn't even gotten on the campus and we already had a pretty accurate idea of some student priorities at the school and it wasn't books.

My eldest daughter Mary Jane was interested in attending an art college in New York City so we made a family trip out of it and we went to Manhattan to see what we could learn about the school and its physical environment in downtown New York City. School was in-session and I was not all that impressed with the school or the students during the tour. Being a small specialized art school in such an urban environment meant that the school was composed of separate buildings located in different places and there was no central campus. For a school that branded itself as being so prestigious, we were surprised at the minimal investment in computer equipment and the classes seemed over crowded and cramped. Then when our group was walking through the dining hall one of the students with a very goth appearance said with a slight sinister inflection, "Don't worry moms and dads, we'll take real good care of your child."

The comment helped solidify our feeling of concern for the school. First, I probably wasn't going to be able to afford to send Mary Jane to the school even with a scholarship which is just a discount, second it wasn't a good fit for us, third it did not have a very pleasant feel to it, but fourth the students comment definitely helped us cross it off the list.

It was a good experience for us to go to the art school and all the other schools we visited because each one helped us to understand what was out there and become better able to recognize, understand, compare, and analyze all the pro's and con's. Moreover, it helped to ease Mary Jane's concerns as to what she might be missing when she got to see and experience each school in-person instead of what was being portrayed online, or through the comments of her friends and teachers, or being portrayed via the schools branding strategy.

Phases of Life

College majors

Choosing a major is a tough job, but part of going to college is to try and see what works for you. How much money you are going to be paid in your future employment is one component. Your passion and an interests are another. And yes, you are most happy when you are involved with X but if it is hard to find a job doing X or the jobs don't pay very well, maybe you should be thinking of something else like Y or Z.

Try not to limit yourself. Keep an open mind as to what careers you could pursue. Talk to people to learn what industries are hot and where the action is so maybe you will be recruited before you even graduate. It is a rare case, but I recently heard that some law firms in New York City were paying a very select group of students $30,000 for a summer internship. These jobs, which will probably pay $150,000 plus starting are going to be a strenuous work environment, but it can also be strenuous to try and find a job when nobody wants your skills and you don't have any money. Which part of the strenuous would you prefer to be on?

I am not saying that you should only focus on money, I am just saying that you need to keep your options open and try to put yourself on the right track to start. Then, if and when you make a lot of money for a few years and you get tired of it you can always quit and find the job you really like, but this will not work in reverse because you will have missed the opportunities.

**Go for the gold now and you can always adjust
or scale back or play more later.**

College intangibles

Status.
Effect on your aspirations and expectations.
Friends you will meet.

Do the research - be a detective.

Before you are going to commit a possible four-years of your life and thousands of dollars to the purchase of an education, do as much research as possible before you make the purchase.

Some of the research can include questions like;

How does the school brand itself?

What is the message the college is promoting to prospective students?

Does the brand message seem credible?

What did you learn from conversations with other students?

What did you learn from conversations with faculty members?

What did you learn from conversations with any police officers you happened to talk to? They know all the dirt but probably can't tell you.

Write up your notes each evening after your visits so you can get it down while everything is still fresh in your mind.

Compile your research into a matrix to see how it sorts out.

Student Body and its composition

Why does it appear that the students are here? Is there a consistent theme? What is the disposition of the other students? Do they seem like achievers or party people? Are they more interested in finding the next party or being serious in achieving their goals? Does the school have a strong Greek community and what might that indicate, bad or good? What kinds of clubs are active at the school and what is the demeanor of the participants?

Then versus now.

Your parents college experience then versus today's expected college experience for you.

What is the same and what has changed and why?

Analyzing Information and Making Comparisons

Writing Out Your Strategic Plan

Write out what you expect to get from your education and write out the factors for the basis for your decision. Explain the method and reasons why you are choosing your school just as you might prepare a research paper for your English class. Explain why you why you are not choosing the other schools.

In-state vs. out-of-state.

Some states offer strong in-state school options so you can save your parent's money, and it is beneficial to be closer to home. There isn't anything to be gained by going to an out-of-state school that you probably can't get in-state except to get farther from home and the influence of your parents. For some, that may be needed to succeed. However, be realistic and focus on the real purpose of going to college.

College vs. university

Keep in mind that the difference between a college and a university is that a college only teaches where a university teaches like a college but it also engages in research and professors have heavier publishing demands so the university can keep attracting more funding for more research.

Finding, writing proposals for, and getting grants for performing research is a never ending process for universities and they are dependent on performing the research as a means of providing more funding. I am not saying one type of school is better than the other it is just another aspect to consider and I never knew the difference until we started going down this road and asking questions as we were looking at college options for our first child.

Local college versus a school farther away

Be careful that you don't overlook your local college because it seems "too local" or you feel it would be degrading to go there or because you want to get away from your parents and live on your own so you can experience more of what you think life has to offer. I do not recommend emphasizing this factor too much in your decision unless there are some really strong academic reasons that draw you to school that is more remote from home. Having an attraction to a school's football or basketball team is not a good basis for choosing a school. To choose a school based on their sports program is to fall in the propaganda trap that they have set for you.

Why else do you think that large schools pay their football and basketball coaches more than their school president or other astronomical salaries and bonuses? The disparity in salaries doesn't make sense to me. Is the school saying that the coaches are more important than the president and if so, what is the real purpose of the school? Is it sports entertainment, student bonding, the pursuit of academic excellence, your future career or your growth and maturity?

Check the salaries of the coaches and the president before you enroll at a school to get some sense of its priorities. Research student, alumni and faculty accomplishments to see what you can learn. A pattern of accomplishments might indicate the fields where alumni have been successful which could provide you with a guide of which programs are more in demand and/or where the graduates have been successful. Keep in mind that your money is going to be helping to support the faculty salaries and the programs that you attend.

Keep your college choice objectives in perspective relative to your future goals.

I went away to school forty years ago because it was the best engineering school that I was accepted and it didn't cost that much more relative to an in-state school.

The one way you can get in-state tuition at an out-of-state school is if you are interested in a program of study that is not offered in your state. There are some reciprocity agreements between states regarding this. As an example, one daughter of a client wanted to

Phases of Life

attend West Virginia University so she decided to major in Museum Administration which is not offered in Virginia. It worked and for the most part, her thinking was that administration is administration whether it has to do with a business or with a museum.

I also heard the President of George Mason University sympathizing with the local students in the new freshman class for having to attend his school and why they should not be disappointed. He provided 10 easy reasons why they are actually very lucky to be attending George Mason, even if they have to live near home. See if you can find these 10 reasons for each school you are interested in attending and see how they compare. Ask questions.

I chose Georgia Tech in 1976 because I thought it was the best school I could get into for my interest in studying electrical engineering. There were no schools that offered engineering in Northern Virginia and I never even visited the Georgia Tech campus before showing up to register my freshman year. I could have attended Virginia Tech instead but I thought Georgia Tech was a better school, for whatever I knew at the time, which wasn't much more than whatever I had heard and in looking at the college handbook I received in the mail which couldn't have meant much to me. And relatively, Georgia Tech didn't cost that much more than an in-state school and my thought was that if I didn't like it there my contingency plan was I shouldn't have a problem transferring to another school. If I started off at what I thought was the best school I could get into then I could always transfer down to another school. So I was up for the adventure and off I went which is probably the thought process of today's high school graduates.

I was miserable the whole time I was there and was so relieved toward the end of my sophomore year when I finally realized I didn't have to continue. I consider my experience there to be the worst two years of my life but I didn't know any better. I figured that was how it needed to be. Others probably had opposite experiences.

I finished my sophomore year with a 3.2 gpa overall but it came with an emotional price and I survived and I guess I became stronger from the experience. I can't quite remember, but we might have had a grading scale back then where A's were 94% and higher, not the 90% of today.

By comparison, George Mason University which was just a very small school in the 70's with no stature in academia has grown and expanded tremendously in the forty-three years since I graduated from high school. Knowing everything I know now and living here today it would be the school for me.

The funniest thing is that I can go there for free now because in Virginia once a person turns sixty-years they have free tuition to audit up to three classes at any Virginia school as long as the classes have not be filled by paying students.

Pretty neat. Now I can go to college with my children. That is one of the funniest things I could ever think of. My going to college with my children for free. I never would have thought of this possibility 40 years ago.

I am attending two classes this Spring of 2019 and it is a really neat experience to be back in college again. When I am on campus it is as if I am a time traveler that has gone back in time and I can put all my responsibilities away for a few hours. It is very refreshing.

One class is in creative writing because I am trying to write a novel about a sheriff, played by me of course, who is going to fight political corruption by trying to arrest elected officials that accept campaign contributions. The second class is in Sports Communication so I can have a better understanding of the sports industry because I would like to start a new semi-pro national basketball league that will use moving basketball goals for which I have received several patents.

Financial aspects and student loans

These can be a trap. You need to be very careful with borrowing money. The loans can lead you down the wrong road.

Just because you qualify does not mean that you should accept all the funds. Exercise prudence and don't take the easy street just because it is available. Easy money is a lure that is being put out to you to offset the high cost that secondary education has become.

Phases of Life

Realize that higher education didn't cost much before. My mother's college tuition and room and board in 1950 was $508 per year at Danbury State Teachers College. Mine, in 1976, was $1,000 per year at an out-of-state school. So why is in-state tuition with student fees and room and board $30,000 per year for an in-state school? Have the costs of running the school and faculty salaries increased that much since when my mother and I were in school or have states reduced how much they are willing to subsidize education?

How can community colleges offer many of the same classes but only cost 35% of the tuition and mandatory student fees of a public four-year college? Where does the rest of the money at four-year schools go? Why can't tuition at the four-year colleges be priced closer to the community college rate? Are the professors at four-year schools earning triple what community college professors are being paid?

Are the extra benefits and services of a four-year school that much more valuable and are the students able to utilize them and get that value back?

Benefits versus Cost and Cost versus Debt

It isn't a good idea to accumulate debt while in school if you can avoid it. If you have to borrow money for school, stay in-state at a minimum and be thrifty. It is really hard to pay back student debt and just because you qualify doesn't mean that you should accept the funds. The interest fees are not discounted and you will be paying full price for using the money.

Student loans are special in that the funds are available to you because you are using them for education. The funds are being given to you even though you don't have any sources of income to repay them, which in normal circumstances would disqualify you from the money. The repayment terms are special because you don't have to start paying the loans back right away. Otherwise, the loans are standard loans and having them will reduce your future borrowing ability.

In-state tuition for a full 18 credit hours for each of my children at George Mason University in 2018 is about $15,000 per year. Access to a specific number of meals at the dining hall is about $800 per year each, and one upgraded parking pass that they have to share is $800 per year. If they were to live on campus their housing would be an additional $7,000 per year for each of them.

As a reference, tuition at a Virginia community college is about $6,700/year or 46%. So if finances are a concern or if you want to try treading water before you swim, be sure to consider the community college route which may not be as prestigious but it does offer a lot of benefits. As one community college professor told me, "It so inexpensive that you can pay for the tuition with a credit card." Keep in mind, that this was just a figure of speech and not a recommendation on their or my part.

Savannah, a 19-year old classmate in my creative writing class, told me that she started accumulating college credit at her local community college when she was sixteen and still in high school. She was able to do this because her high school had dual enrollment classes and because you can start attending classes at community colleges when you are sixteen.

Dual enrollment classes are those given at high schools and are certified as community college equivalent. So between Savannah's dual enrollment classes at her high school and the ones she attend her community college during the summer and online, by the time Savannah graduated from high school she had also earned her Associates Degree from the community college.

Wow! That is pretty neat.

She entered her four-year college as a Junior and saved herself two years worth of tuition and housing and a ton of money. She is a very practical, industrious, and forward looking woman.

Money for tuition - then vs. now

My out-of-state tuition, room and board at Georgia Tech was under $1,000 per academic year in 1976. Today the same out-of-state tuition and room and board would cost $50,000 per year. Attendance at the school had good value then but as an out-of-state student having to pay $50,000 per year I don't think the value in going out-of-state is present today compared to the 1970's. Especially since Virginia Tech or George Mason or the University of Virginia are competitive in-state priced alternatives for half the cost if one stays on campus and half of that if one is able to commute from home.

The reason for such a big disparity between then and now is that before, back in the 50's, 60's and 70's, state legislatures were subsidizing more of the college budget as a means to promote higher education. Now, with the development of the student loan industry, , states have reduced their financial support for higher education and that is part of the reason why the costs are so much higher today versus before and the burden has been shifted from the taxpayers to you via the new student loan industry. The federal government has guaranteed that the lenders would be paid and so with all the extra money available for education colleges realized they could start raising their prices and passing the cost on to you. And that is what they did.

Contingency plans

You should have a strategic educational and life plan that includes how you will handle changes such as if you decide to change majors or transfer to a different college.

It is best to keep as many options open as possible as you blaze your trails while keeping in mind the possible consequences for each of your decisions.

Two simple illustrations of this aspect are regarding an understanding of what courses will transfer to other majors if you decide to change majors and what courses will transfer to other schools if you decide to transfer to a different school.

You will be better served if you can attend the better school as your first choice even if it is closer to home than attending a school whose courses won't transfer to many other schools but you like the school that is farther away because being as far away from home is your primary goal.

This is being very short sighted and shows that you probably don't have your priorities in order. Do the research and ask the questions before you make commitments that come with limited options and flexibility.

Community college versus four-year college

My experience with community college classes has been nothing but fantastic. I think the faculty is as good and probably even better than at a four-year colleges and the students are down-to-earth. And sometimes you will get professors for night classes that work in industry and they will bring a perspective to class that no four-year college professor can bring because the industry professor is going to be able to relate current real-life examples of the subject matter.

Life at College

Dormitory living and roommates

Another life experience from college is having roommates. I had three my Freshman year, one each quarter and they were all horrible and I almost got into a fist fight with one of them because he was so nasty. I would spend most of my time in the library usually until 11 at night because dorm life and the accommodations were so bad. I would stay out of my room as much as possible even though I considered myself lucky that I was in the newest dorms that were not next to the interstate and they had air conditioning.

In general, dorm life isn't much different today except at a lot of schools girls and guys are living on the same floor. I got an apartment off-campus my sophomore year with some guys from my floor and it was much better and a lot more livable.

Dining Halls and Food

The food quality and selection at college dining halls today is beyond comparison to what was available for me and my dining hall was only open limited hours for breakfast, lunch and dinner, not 24 hours like on most big college campus'.

Phases of Life

Friends

You will not have as many close friends in college as you did in high school because most of your friends went off to pursue employment opportunities or to different colleges. And the friends you do make won't be as deep as those in high school because you will just be meeting them and you won't be in class with them as consistently as you were in high school.

Social pressure

Don't worry about the perpetual problem of comparing yourself and your life to what your friends are doing or where they are going to for school. You don't have to prove anything to them except your own happiness and success. You can always keep in touch with social media and visit them on breaks or vacations if what they are doing seems so important. Live your life, not theirs.

Classes that all students should take at least one of

Accounting - double entry bookkeeping

Computer programming

Creative writing - It is very helpful and therapeutic to get your ideas out of your head and down on paper.

Finance

Psychology

Real Estate - You will need to take this class at your community college or at a real estate licensing school. This is a very worthwhile activity so you will be much more in the know when you go to rent an apartment or buy your first house. And if you decide to get your real estate license you may end up with a career in real estate.

Speed reading

Touch Typing - This means that you can type through muscle memory and without looking at the keys. Very easy and important.

Child development

How to thrive and get the most from my education at "insert your school name here," is another good class to take. Check to see if your school offers this type of one credit class. You can't go wrong.

What do you have to lose and you will make some new friends.

Classes that are not offered at school

How to make lots of money. This is the one class everyone would like to take but none of the schools offer. Why? I guess it falls under the category of "Individualized Future Studies."

Life after college

Beyond the college experience

All careers are not created equal.

What you are going to do after college is the reason you are going to college, but colleges seem to sidestep this issue as a priority until you are getting close to graduation and you start to realize you need a job. It seems to me that this process is all backwards.

I think that one of the first places to visit when you go to a college is the career services office to see who is interviewing and what the hot careers are.

Your career is where you are going to end up, so why not start there at the beginning of your research and planning so you have a better idea of what you are going to find at the end of your Yellow Brick Road. Is it going to be Oz or a witch from the West?

Why does everyone stay out of the career services office until it's finally time to graduate? Why don't the colleges present career options first?

I think the reason the career center is overlooked is because some departments might lose their students if they look at career opportunities first. But this is the best thing new students should be doing because, for example, if you like sculpture, but there are no jobs in sculpting but lots of jobs in graphic design, then maybe you should focus on graphic design and just keep sculpting on the side. Or if you like sports and are considering a career in sports management but it seems like the only jobs are dead end jobs and only a few people

Phases of Life

end up in prestigious coaching positions then maybe you should find something that has more demand and you can always coach on the side.

This concept of anticipating where you are headed was best illustrated five years ago when John, my eldest son, was a freshman in high school. At the time when he was preparing to register for his sophomore classes Kathleen and I thought it would be a good idea for him to start taking some computer science classes, so we went and talked with one of the computer science teachers. When asked about the computer science curriculum, all the help his counselor could provide was to hand us a piece of paper that described the class, which even we had difficulty understanding, and then she directed us to a faculty member. The counselors lack of knowledge of the computer science field surprised us given that we live in a very tech heavy community. It also showed us that you have to be able to think for yourself and that you can't always depend on the counselor or advisor to be able to elaborate what is best for you.

The computer science teacher quickly set us straight by showing us with her thumb and fingers far apart to represent how many people get a liberal arts education and then she made a little distance between her thumb and fingers to illustrate the quantity of jobs for liberal arts majors. Then keeping her thumb close to her fingers she said, "This is how many people are studying computer science and" as she spread her thumb and fingers apart, "this is how many jobs there are in computer science."

My advice is to give serious consideration to as many aspects as possible before you choose your major so when you graduate you will be on the path that you hoped you would be on. And, hopefully you will have multiple job offers to choose from because everybody will want you. As a side note, depending on how you put your educational plan, job, and employer together, your future employer may even be willing to pay for your advanced degree.

Yes, colleges don't present the full picture as to what happens to their students but that doesn't mean you have to fall into their trap. It would be interesting to know how many don't return and how many transfer in each semester and more importantly what happens after they graduate because the end results are what matter the most let alone how these statistics compare for the different majors and the different schools.

Unfortunately, these detailed metrics are not made available on a school by school basis but they are available in aggregate from the National Student Clearing House in Herndon, Virginia, except for the graduating salary information. When researching specific schools, look for any information they do provide regarding student retention and graduation reports. This information may be also be broken down into other classifications such as local domicile, gender, academic unit, and financial aid status.

The National Student Clearing House collects information from most colleges and tracks what happens to the students as to whether they drop out of college, transfer to another school, continue to graduate school, or graduate or drop out altogether. It collects information from four-year schools as well as community colleges. The charts are interesting to review and are available to the public on its website.

I am sure that part of the industry thinking is that if you are studying something that you are interested in that you will be more inclined to continue with your studies and graduate. This thinking might be too institutionalized and outdated.

It seems that the students would be better served if the colleges were more upfront with the career options their graduates are going to be faced with after graduation. I don't think it is right for the schools to imply that if you do your best, and are the best, that you will get the best.

Life doesn't work like that and I don't think the schools, as well as society should be propagating the myth to follow your passion so strongly. Yes, it is nice to follow your passion but that might not be the best course of action for you. There is a lot more that goes into the "Happy Life" equation then just being the best artist or the best mathematician or engineer or singer and I think that colleges should be driving that point home a lot more than they are which isn't much

Phases of Life

at all.

Maybe it is a way to separate the men from the boys, or the women from the girls, at the end of the day or a way to keep their enrollment up. It doesn't seem right when the students and their parents are putting their faith in; that the school has their best interests at heart when there might be other aspects to the story that are not being disclosed.

Be that as it may, keep in mind that the best place a college student can probably get the best sense of where the career action is happening is by working part-time in the career services center. Another place to gain insight and more detailed career information is by attending career presentations and panel discussions that are held at your school. All of these options are an excellent way to have personal access to a broad array of recruiter activity as well as general information about employers and industries. Your interest and participation can help to put you at the front of the line when the opportunities come along.

My mother was able to parlay her part-time employment at American University in 1969 in the office for the Education Department when she was in graduate school. While and through helping in the office she learned about fellowship grants for education students and she applied and received one which allowed her to go to graduate school for free.

It is important that you really research your career path and have some contingency plans because you don't want to invest a lot of time and money into a skill set if you are going to find that there are limited employment opportunities for it. It is important to talk to some people that are actively employed in the industry you are interested as you are considering your major so you can get their inside perspective of what is and isn't happening, where the industry is going and how best to position yourself so you have the right skill set when you graduate.

A college curriculum provides the basis for your education in that specific field but knowing what other more specialized skills would also be helpful is beneficial to know. Naturally, you need to be as prepared as possible with some contingency plans for whatever paths you choose. And don't forget that the Boy Scout motto, "Always be prepared," still holds true today.

In 2017 I met a student from George Mason University who had graduated a year earlier with a degree in automotive engineering who had only been able to get work as a car mechanic. He had given up being a car mechanic because it wasn't going anywhere and now his career was in limbo. He had chosen automotive engineering because he liked high performance cars. In hindsight, it seems like his priorities were skewed too far to what he was interested in.

I recently met a graduate from a Virginia College who was 27 years old and digging test holes for soil samples with a hand auger. It didn't seem like he made the right choice in pursuing a degree in History because he had not been able to parlay what he studied into a related career. He had chosen to major in history because he liked history but that did not translate well into providing an income because there are very few job opportunities in the field and even fewer that pay very well for a skill set trained in history.

Yes, you need to choose a major that fits with your interests but you also need to choose a major that will make you feel good about yourself after you graduate.

Keep your eyes, ears and options open.

I also talked to a family with two college graduated male children. The first, about 35, was a doctor performing kidney and liver transplants, and the second, about 28, has studied computer science. Evidently, the doctor career path was not that rewarding for their son because the parents told me, "Don't let your kids go into medicine." They also implied that the younger child was earning more money and had what seemed to be a much better life style than his older brother.

As a programmer, the younger brother worked all around the world depending on his client's needs or his interest at the time. He was traveling, staying in different places and better yet, he even had a female companion that he had met in Asia while on a project who was also a programmer and she was from Minnesota.

Phases of Life

The two of them were reportedly earning substantial sums of money and it sounded like they were living a great life style all because they had pursued and applied themselves in a career that was in demand and growing. They had established themselves in the network of people related to the specialized services they can provide.

He had received very high scores on his certifications and she had inside developmental knowledge on how a specific software application was developed so she is qualified to modify the program as changes were needed. I am sure that they continue their education by expanding their certifications in different programming applications and languages so they can stay competitive in the ever changing field.

Oh, if I was only young again...

Notes

Initiative and interpersonal skills in college and life

In the summer of 2018 I attended an excellent one day presentation of government, military, and industry panelists sponsored by the Air Force Association at George Mason University and it was unfortunate that only about 70 students attended.

The presentation was designed to help students understand some of the opportunities that lay before them and where the critical needs were and how to fill them but relative to the size of the school, very few students attended. Many more students should have attended, if nothing else just to see what the panelists were talking about, because you want to go where the action is so you have the best opportunities for advancement and that was what the panelists were there to explain.

The university also has a once a month evening event called Clearance Ready to serve as precursor to getting a security clearance which in this area near Washington, D. C. is a golden ticket. Unfortunately it is not very well attended either.

It appears to me that there is a serious lack of student interest in at least seeing or trying to understand what the educational environment offers and where the action is or the schools are not providing comprehensive guidance to the students. This apathy indicates that students are not developing an ability to think for themselves and seek out opportunities. It appears that students are becoming trapped in the tracks that society has placed them in and they are following the steps that they are told to follow in their quest for the supposed Holy Grail or golden ring. The golden ring is an old analogy that came from riding a Merry-Go-Round and trying to stretch to reach a ring with your hand each time the Merry-Go-Round made a revolution.

But the real world doesn't function in a box and you can't succeed if you get stuck or stay in it. The real world is more like a never ending chess game where you keep moving your pieces to stay in the game and you have to be creative and strategic to avoid checkmate.

Yes, it is easy for schools to layout and provide the programs for the students and then graduate them once they have fulfilled the program's requirements. It is unfortunate that schools are not addressing my biggest concern which is that I am seeing a lack of initiative by the students to put out the extra effort with curiosity and the initiative to explore.

I am sure that this has always been an issue but now I suspect that it is a lot worse. Too many students have become lackadaisical and distracted by their phones which not only create a distraction from what is important, but create the illusion that when the time comes they will be discovered and live happily ever after. And the educational system along with all of its newly adopted technologically based teaching methods are only reinforcing the students belief that just because they fulfill the schools graduation requirements that they will have everything they need to enter the workforce, have a successful career and a happy family for the rest of their life. Very few people post comments or photos of when they are depressed or miserable or feel like a failure so why would today's students think that anything other than success is waiting at the end for them?

Phases of Life

Unfortunately, schools are indiscreetly perpetuating this myth. The schools know the reality that graduation is only a validation that the graduate was in a specific program and studied certain subjects and met the academic expectations for graduation, many of which have become watered down. The schools as well as the employers are fully aware that a degree doesn't convey anything more about the student's personality, initiative or unique skills and unfortunately the point is not being sufficiently driven home to the students soon enough.

Getting along with people and having initiative are critical skills that the educational system glosses over because they can't be easily measured and evaluated. It is hard to predict someone's personality or ability to get along with others or to measure their initiative but it is easy to evaluate how well students can regurgitate facts and figures. By comparison getting along with others and having discipline and initiative are probably more important than grades on tests because people can always gain hard skills but you can't change their interpersonal skills or their personalities. So schools are missing the point and have skewed the priorities.

My report cards from Cedar Lane Elementary School in the 1960's did have a section to rank students regarding "Gets Along Well With Others" and another section titled "Shares Well." Unfortunately concern for these critical personality skills has been replaced with concern for standardized testing of one's ability to absorb and remember a multitude of facts and figures that don't measure anything except one's memory skills which is only important to professional quiz show participants.

It does help to be able to remember facts and figures but creativity and critical thinking skills and an ability to get along and work with people are of the utmost importance in one's future. Unfortunately, these skills are intangible so they are the hardest for schools to measure and don't fit nicely into standardized testing. Solving a math or physics problem provides a finite tangible result whereas analyzing a story doesn't have a specific answer like in math so the answer is subject to a range of interpretations which are hard to quantify and score.

You need to figure out what is important to you, where you fit best now and more importantly where you will fit best in the future. A simple example is how someone told me a long time ago, when we were discussing different types of careers, that they liked accounting because once the debits and credits balanced you knew it was right. It was simple, no questions or interpretations, problem solved. Move on.

A lack of initiative and an inability to get along with coworkers were problems that my father had and he missed many opportunities for success according to my mother. She explained that in spite of however smart he was or was not, as a scientist he was dependent on grants for funding research and his continued employment, but he resisted putting out the effort to find more contracting research work. Then, when he did write a professional research paper with two other scientists to be published he wanted all the credit for himself and he wouldn't share the glory.

Once the other scientists realized how difficult he was to work with they found a way to give him a contract from a different company so they could get him out of their group. Then once that contract was finished my father was out of a job.

In hind sight my mother realized that she was played. He wasn't the ambitious, hard working person she thought he was when they were dating in high school and through college. It wasn't until after she was married that she recognized my father's true personality which was that he was lazy and that he thought he was so important that somebody was going to discover him.

It never happened.

Chapter three
Soul Deep - Relationships

Topics listed alphabetically

Aging

Don't get old before your time. Stay young in body and spirit as long as you can. None of us can imagine ourselves as a very old person, but hopefully each of us continues heading in that direction each and every day.

Behavior

Kathleen, my spouse, has taught me a lot about looking at the behaviors of people regarding whether they practice acceptable or unacceptable behaviors. She believes that one's behavior tells a lot about a person's character and whether they have respect for others.

The challenge in getting to know and work with people is trying to understand who you can and cannot trust and who has honor and is honorable. Behaviors are an indicator of trust worthiness but not a guarantee. You can have someone who acts very trustworthy but they would stab you in the back if the opportunity presented itself. And you can have somebody that is crass but would do anything to help you when in need.

More often the best display of a person's true behavior occurs when they don't think anybody is watching. These kind of situations will tell you more about people — and to see how they treat others. What they say about others is also another indicator of a person's character.

Sit back and watch people when they are with someone and see what you observe. It is a good skill to have especially when you are looking for your special person. Don't talk as much and just observe and listen to see what you can learn.

Church

You don't have to believe or adhere to everything they tell you but churches, mosques, synagogues and temples do offer a good environment for children and for promoting positive living.

Cool - The secret to being cool

Recently, Kate, my seventh grade daughter came home with the answer to the question of how you are cool as told to her by the dad of one of her cool friends. The dad reveled that his daughter was just as nervous about starting junior high school as Kate but that his daughter's secret to dealing with her nerves was to just pretend that she had confidence.

Co-workers

These are the people that you are going to spend most of your time with when you are earning a living. Some of these people you are going to like and some you are not going to like. Hopefully you will be able to find employment with a group of people who you mostly enjoy being with.

You are quickly going to learn how many of your co-workers are going to try and shift their work to you or someone else. Don't complain; look at it as a challenge and you will get noticed and advance more quickly. If not, go find another job somewhere else.

Empathy

This is another of those terms that is never mentioned. It is an

Soul Deep - Relationships

important emotional feeling and different than sympathy.

It is an essential component of successful relationships.

Family

You can never write enough about the topic of family but here goes...

"Family" is the nucleus of society.

Your relationship with your family is the most important relationship you have. It provides you a sense of who you are and where you came from. It gives you a unique bond with a small group of people that are together because of similar heritage and genetic makeup. It is your tribe.

Together you are bound to try and learn from and help each other and to enjoy the common experiences that you have together, the good and the bad. You help and encourage members of your family in each persons unique way caring for each other as a system of mutual support for the survival and benefit of the group.

As you get older the family supports you in different ways and you support your family in different ways. Families, just like their members, are always evolving.

Your family is the second most important aspect to your life. You are the first. Your family provides you with your initial training ground where you learn many aspects about yourself and the world.

Family means those people with which you have a common ancestry. The ancestry is directly connected by those who are connected by blood, which means from the birth of a child or more loosely by marriage. All your brothers and sisters are considered blood relatives whereas someone that marries into the family is not.

You are here because you have a mother and father and they had mothers and fathers and so on, so you have little bits from everyone that came before you.

Your family is your everything. It feeds, clothes, and protects you and will continue to support and help you in whatever way it can at least until you are eighteen years old and become an adult, except in unusual family circumstances. In return, you need to help your family in whatever way you can because together you are much stronger than if you were all separate. Even in dysfunctional families, you will have your advocates.

As you get older, with luck, you will probably find someone that you are compatible, and the two of you will decide to make your relationship official and binding by getting married. Marriage will mark the start of your new family. The two of you will be responsible for your decisions as a couple and together you will probably create some children and with the birth of the first, the cycle will have repeated itself and all of a sudden you will be walking in your parents footsteps.

As I age I like to consider my life with that of my parents and ancestors when they were my age. Adolfo was sixty years old when I was born in 1958. Now I am sixty years old. What did his life look like at that point and how does it compare to mine today? Or for my father, where was he when he turned sixty and what was he doing at that time in his life?

There are no perfect families just as there are no perfect people. A lot of your ancestors as well as your parents worked hard and made sacrifices so you could be where you are today. They and your family today provide the foundation from which you can find your own opportunities and start your own family. Be happy with whatever you have and make the best of it especially if you were adopted.

My great, great grandfather Domenico Maghett-Cunibertii, in Italy, was adopted. His parents of the Maghetti family could not take care of him so they put him up for adoption and he was adopted by the Cuniberti family when he was five years old. He married Vincenza Berta and they had five children. His first child was born on July 18, 1877 in San Martino, Alfiere, Italy, and was named Antonio. Antonio eventually met and married Maria Aliberti who was five years older than him and they had two children. The first girl was my grandmother Vincenza and a second child died in infancy. The three of them had a difficult life in Italy because Antonio never acquired

Soul Deep - Relationships

any special skills so he was always looking for work as a laborer and the same went for Maria and they lived in very crude accommodations in Savona, Italy, barely making ends meet.

When Maria's father died she received an inheritance from his estate and they decided to immigrate to New York City. They decided to leave Italy because even though life was predictable in Italy, there were no opportunities to have a better life like there seemed to be in America where Antonio's two younger brothers, had already emigrated, Vincent (Pino) and Pietro. Antonio, Maria and Vincenza arrived at Ellis Island in June 1911 when my grandmother was nine years old. Her parents were 33 and 38 years old.

They lived in a flat in an area known as Hell's Kitchen in New York City and my grandmother Vincenza, who naturally didn't speak any English when she arrived, became a student in New York City Public Schools. Maria, who did the best she could under the circumstances, found work mostly in laundries washing clothes. She emphasized school with Vincenza as her way to achievement. Fortunately, Vincenza, who called herself Clara because it was easier to say in English, thrived in school and her teachers took an interest in her because they saw that she applied herself and was ambitious.

Vincenza attended school in New York City for five years until 1916 when they moved to Newark, New Jersey, because Antonio had found employment working for a priest at a church. Vincenza continued her high school education in Newark, where she attended four years at East Side Commercial and Manual Training High School. There were 25 students in her graduating class on January 7, 1920. As a graduate, Vincenza had several business skills such as typing and she found a job working at Mutual Insurance Company.

Vincenza's real passion was to be an opera singer so after working for a while at the insurance company she started looking for employment in New York City so she could be closer to the best place for her to pursue her passion. She went to an employment agency for a possible job referral which was the practice at the time.

The way she told the story was, "The placement man sent me

to apply for a position in the purchasing department of a company called Schumacher because they imported a lot of fabric from France and Italy and they needed someone that could communicate in French and Italian as well as English. It was one of the toughest placements the agency had been trying to fill because the job requirements were unique and the manager was very particular.

"I had grown up speaking an Italian dialect that was similar to French because I grew up in an area of Italy near the French border. I had also studied French in school. I got the job and eventually I became the head of the purchasing department.

"The job paid me good money and it kept me working during the Depression. I was even able to start saving enough money so that I was able to buy a produce store with your grandfather, Adolfo after we were married. Then your mother was born in 1932."

The big difference between Vincenza and my other grandparents was that she had the ambition to go to school and learn. Unlike Vincenza, Adolfo didn't receive much of an education in Italy. He started working on ships when he turned sixteen until he arrived in America so he didn't have any skills except to be a common laborer when he jumped ship in New York City in 1924.

Vincenza and Adolfo met when Vincenza was visiting her cousin and Adolfo was doing odd jobs painting her cousin's house in Wanaque, New Jersey at what is now a restaurant known as Berta's Chateau. Vincenza's grandmother's maiden name was Vincenza Berta.

They dated for awhile and when Vincenza had an opportunity to pursue her passion for opera and go on the road with an opera company, she never went because Adolfo said that he wouldn't marry her if she did.

They got married in 1928 and with her by his side she provided the opportunity for him to learn skills that would carry him for the rest of his life. They worked, saved their money, and bought the produce store in 1931.

The former owner of the store was Italian and as part of deal for the sale he taught Adolfo what he needed to know to run the business which included how and where to buy the produce at the Central Market in New York City which would opened at 4 a.m., as well as the other aspects of being a successful business person. At first, Vincenza continued to work at Schumacher but she eventually had to join Adolfo in the store once her daughter MaryAnne was born. Together they made a good team especially considering that Adolfo did not speak any English. Adolfo had found his Guardian Angel in Vincenza.

My father's grandmother immigrated from Italy with two of her sons, Francesco (Frank) and Vito arriving in New York City on July 10, 1922. Francesco was to become my grandfather. About the same time my father's future mother Josephine landed in Boston, Massachusetts with her mother on August 5, 1923.

In contrast to Vincenza, my father's parents, Frank and Josephine didn't have much if any formal education. I do not know what grade Frank completed or if he even went to school in America, but without any marketable skills he was destined for a life of labor. They could barely write in Italian let alone in English.

Josephine was supposed to go to school in Bridgeport, Connecticut where her mother settled with her older brother Jimmy who eventually became a successful barber, but Josephine didn't want to go to school and her mother thought it was more important for her to go to work. So Josephine missed out on an education even though the school was trying to get her to attend.

Josephine told me, "When the schools came looking for me my mother, who didn't speak any English kept saying "Italy, Italy" so the school official thought my mother was trying to say that we were going to return to Italy soon and they eventually lost interest in me."

Despite her skill at avoiding school, Josephine paid the price with lifelong employment working as a seamstress since that was the only skill she knew which was taught to her by her mother. Later in life Josephine always complained about pain in her feet because she had to use them to power the treadle sewing machines.

Frank was as industrious and hard working as he could be given his education, but he always needed some direction since he didn't have any unique marketable skills either. He worked as a longshoreman man carrying cargo on his back unloading ships when he was young and later he worked for Steinway pianos in Astoria, New York as a polisher. He tried growing vegetables in Homestead, Florida, but an early frost killed most of the plants and that dream. He ended his career as a yard man and truck driver for a lumber company called Getman and Judd that was located in Darien, Connecticut.

Josephine and Frank were married in a civil ceremony in New York City on 1928 and their first child was a girl who died in infancy. My father was born on October 1931 followed by a sister. My father got his first job working at a coat factory in Stamford, Connecticut, when he was fifteen by using a doctored birth certificate of his deceased sister to appear of legal age.

Josephine learned her lesson of what happens when one skips education the hard way. She was determined that her children wouldn't make the same mistake, so she pushed both of them to go to and finish college so they could enter the workforce as professionals. My father got his Ph.D. as a chemist and his sister received her Bachelors degree in education to become a school teacher. Relatively speaking, they both went on to have successful careers that would not have been possible otherwise.

Vincenza carried on the need for education with her one and only child, MaryAnne who attended Danbury Teachers College in Danbury, Connecticut, graduating with a teaching degree in 1954. MaryAnne had met my father while a student at Stamford High School in Stamford, Connecticut, and they were married in Stamford in 1956. My mother dropped "Anne" from her name after she was married.

I was born in 1958 in Greenwich, while my father was a graduate student at Fairfield University. And then the three of us moved to Washington, D.C., in 1959. My sister Susan was born in 1960 and in 1961 we moved to Vienna, Virginia, when my father got a job as a scientist at a research laboratory.

Soul Deep - Relationships

My father was well positioned for job opportunities with his education as a scientist because the launching of Sputnik by the Russians in October, 1957, had put the United States in the position of playing catchup in technology with the Soviets. The United States suddenly had a need for all the scientists it could get its hands on.

My mother was an elementary school teacher in the D.C. public schools and later taught elementary education at a private school near our Virginia neighborhood because my sister could have free tuition. My mother began thinking that she wanted to get out of the elementary school classroom so she decided to go back to graduate school to get her Master's degree in 1967.

She explained, "I decided that I wanted to do more than teach primary education so I decided to go back to school. I had the thought to transition out of primary education into the field of social work when I was working as a teacher at Grant School in Washington, D.C., which was located across the street from George Washington University. It was 1960 and I made an appointment to talk with the department head for the Department of Sociology at GW. I met with him about attending GW. He was very arrogant and impolite and he told me that to get a degree in Sociology I would have to make up all the introductory classes in sociology which wasn't practical for me so I decided to forget the sociology idea. I went back to thinking about staying in the field of education.

"Toward the end of 1966, I went back to the idea that I wanted to do more then work in elementary education. I had picked up a brochure about a selective assistantship program with the Department of Education at American University so I filled out the application and mailed it in with my college transcripts.

"I got notification from American University that I had been accepted into their Assistantship Program on my birthday in the spring of 1968. The program paid for five courses each semester for one year and included the cost of books and even provided a stipend that I could use to pay for child care for you and Susie. The ten classes fulfilled the requirement of a Master's Degree in Education which I received in 1969.

Chris DeCarlo

"At American University, I worked part-time in the Department of Education Office while attending classes for my Master's Degree. My presence in the office led me to meet the people that worked there which led to my finding more educational opportunities because one professor in particular, Professor Gotenberg, had personal contacts in the Federal Government at the Department of Education. Her contacts allowed her to secure five fellowships for graduate students in Education. The fellowships would lead to a Ph.D.

"I was able to receive one of the fellowships but it was only because I had been involved in the office and helping with stapling and other odds and ends such that I could hear what was going on and learn about opportunities as they were being explored or coming in the door.

"The fellowship was similar to the assistantship I was just completing and it provided me classes and a stipend so I could do the necessary research to be awarded a Ph.D. For the Ph.D., I would have to demonstrate capability in research so I needed a major professor for whom I could perform the research. I found a professor that I could help in the counseling center named David Sandsberry because he was interested in doing research on the incoming freshman class. He already had some of the data, he just needed help putting it all together.

"The question he was researching was whether students would change philosophically after their first year in college. He had an elaborate formula that he had used, and then after I processed the data using key punch cards he realized that his formula was wrong. Unfortunately, I had to remake the punch cards with the corrected data from his revised formula. Then I had to write up the results with notations in the form of a dissertation which is like a little book. The professor helped me learn how to construct the dissertation and the result of the study was that during the first year of school the students didn't change their perspectives but actually showed that their time at school reinforced their attitudes."

"The fellowship provided funds for two years so I was able to keep taking classes as long as I was entitled to them. I started taking classes in Public Administration and then once I had received my

Soul Deep - Relationships

Ph.D. I could audit any classes I was interested in for free so I continued auditing classes to expand my base of knowledge.

"I owe all my opportunities to the assistantship and fellowship grants, the second of which would have been impossible for me to learn about if I hadn't been working in the Department of Eduction Office at the time it became available. And, it was also important that there were people in the office that had faith in me that I could succeed. I think they saw that I had always worked hard and been ambitious like my mother who had immigrated into New York City when she was nine years old as an Italian immigrant. She had innate ambition, determination, and a desire to achieve, all of which her teachers saw so they kept giving her chances to do more things. So my hard work paid off in the form of people giving me opportunities just like others did for my mother sixty years earlier.

"In many ways my mother was my role model and she provided me with mentoring that I was able to emulate in my life. As an Italian immigrant she was able to integrate with others—particularly non—immigrant WASP people during her summer's at an acting camp in Brookfield, Connecticut, and when she married her your grandfather, Adolfo, another Italian immigrant, she was essentially living her life trying to juggle the two cultures which is very hard to do."

Now, as the author looking back, my family's story has helped me write this handbook for you and your future family.

Fathers

The traditional role of the father in a family is to provide the financial support as well as to be the person that gives real world guidance and helps with practical skills. It isn't an easy job for fathers who are trying to balance their own needs and expectations with everything else, especially when family members resist.

While my father had good intentions, he did not understand that his perspective on the real world was less developed due to narcissism.

My father was a disappointment to me in the end. I always looked up to him and thought he was very smart and I could trust him as all children do with their parents. Unfortunately, as I got older, I realized that either he changed or I got wiser. I realized that he had not been as upfront with me as I had always tried to be with him.

It was really hard for me when he broke the trust that I had placed in him because I had thought we were a team.

I had always tried to be a good and honorable son.

Friends

Having a good circle of friends is critical to your success. Always try to make at least one new friend in each class which will make the class more enjoyable and expand your friendship circle.

Make time for friends. Don't act so busy and important that people think that you don't want to be their friend.

Stop what you are doing and look at people if they approach you and listen. Try to be focused and interested in what they are saying. Don't be impatient with them. When you are around people try to engage with them instead of trying to look important by looking at nothing on your phone.

On the campus of George Mason University you can look anywhere and see so many students looking at their phones and some with their ear buds in also. Phones and ear buds are the new accessory. These students are missing out on the opportunity to increase their circle of friends because they don't know how to look up and invite friendship. The sad part is that good friends are more important than the trivial conversations that they are trying to keep up with on their phone. Engage with others and then text when you are alone.

Remember that to have a good friend you have to be a good friend. Don't try to be the popular person with so many acquaintances that none are really friends.

Grandparents

Don't neglect your grandparents. Call them and talk with them as much as possible. Spend time with your grandparents and ask them about what it was like when they were growing up. Listen to them. They are very proud of you and love you very much.

Soul Deep - Relationships

**Grandparents won't be around forever
and they have many life lessons to offer for free.**

Guardian Angel

Your absolute best friend who is always trying to look out for your well being and keep you pointed in the right direction is your Guardian Angel. Always listen to your Guardian Angel(s). You might not like what they say but they won't steer you wrong.

Help

Never be afraid to ask your parents for help if you need it. They won't be disappointed in you for asking but don't make asking for help an excuse for not doing something that you don't want to do.

People are not going to be inclined to help you if you don't have the initiative to help yourself.

Insecurities, maturity, and relationships

It is very difficult to establish a successful relationship before you are comfortable with who you are. We all grow up with insecurities buried in our psyche. The challenge for each of us is in being able to recognize them and mature beyond the emotional boundaries they create.

**Neither guys nor girls should expect their prospective
mate to be a crutch or solution to one's own insecurities.**

Doing so creates imbalance in the relationship which puts it at risk.

A large part of maturity is reconciling these inner emotions in a way that they don't interfere and become a burden to the other person and the developing relationship. Creating a hostile or manipulative environment is not fair to the other person that is investing their emotions, energy and resources in the relationship with you.

Part of maturing is reconciling the human factors and variables so two people can create a mutually supportive relationship together.

A relationship that will grow in depth with the resilience to adjust to all the unexpected and natural life changes that occur.

The dilemma in finding one's special life partner is being able to recognize and understand the true visceral attitudes and feelings of the other person and their level of maturity relative to one's own.

Gaining one's maturity is the first step, recognizing immaturity in others is the second. It is difficult to accomplish either without adequate and trained observational and critical thinking skills.

How are you working to improve yours?

Intimacy

Everyone thinks of intimacy as being physical but it is more emotional and occurs and grows deeper as you start to share more of your personal feelings and then the physical part comes into play.

Mothers

Your mom is your guidance counselor, career counselor, tutor, editor, traditions keeper, nurse, shuttle service, maid, housekeeper, cook, procurement, quartermaster, advocate, relationship advisor and therapist, stylist, nutritionist, secretary, and scheduler. She also makes sure that all your credentials are kept current and in order.
As my mother-in-law Jane says to my wife Kathleen, "It is a lifelong job and just because they turn eighteen it doesn't stop."

Growing up, my mother had a card tacked to our kitchen bulletin board that further elaborated her role as "mother."

In bold type the card read, "Around here I have a very responsible position. If anything goes wrong it is my fault."

Parents

The mom and dad that hold and support the highest dreams for their children do so with the trepidation that they won't become their biggest disappointment.

Listen to your parents: What do you have to lose?

We all want our parents to be happy in their lives and their relationship with each other, but as we get older we see that nobody can be or is perfect, ourselves included.

Appreciate your parents for who they are even if you don't agree with them or are disappointed because they don't seem perfect. Set a goal of trying to be more _____ and _____ to or with your parents.

Parents - appreciate them

Remember, instructions are not included with newborns.

No matter what they did or didn't do for you, they are your parents and they always will be.

It is wise to accept whatever they do for you and to accept them for who they are. Whatever love and support they provide, be gracious in whatever quantity they provide it. They are not perfect and were a teenager with similar peer and family issues growing up just as you are a teenager with peer and family issues growing up today. Don't blame them for whatever you think you missed out on because maybe they were restrictive or because they didn't or couldn't provide you what you thought you deserved.

Growing up is hard for all of us and growing up we all want to believe that our parents are the smartest people in the world. The reality is that they are human just like us and all of us have flaws. Part of growing up is learning that nobody is perfect and also, more importantly, how to stick together and to help each other get through difficulties which is part of the maturing process.

There is no perfect formula for raising children or families and there is no perfect life or family. Growing up in too perfect a family could create unrealistic expectations and lead to hasty and rash decisions in a spouse. A broken family can create ambivalence in the institution of marriage.

Whatever your experiences with your family you are the person that has to reconcile them with your own thoughts, feelings and personality. You will probably have a chance to walk the same path your parents are walking so begin preparing yourself now so hopefully you can do a better job or at least as good a job managing your future responsibilities as they did for you. Remember the saying, "What goes around comes around."

The key to your success, no matter what environment you are raised, is be in touch with who you are, do what you think is the right thing to do, and not engage in risky behaviors to prove something to your peers or your parents or to try and get attention. Part of the maturing process comes from learning about who you are and what you think is right and wrong, one of the best ways to explore this is to write down your ideas so you can reflect on them as events occur and your perspectives change.

There is no way you can accurately remember everything that happens to you and your thoughts at that time, but writing it down as it occurs will provide you with a good record for you to see how you became the person that you are becoming and where you are trying to go. It will also help you to remember events better so you can analyze them in the future and see patterns that will help you discover subtle things that may be influencing you in positive and negative ways.

I remember when my father's mother, Josephine, was having one of her holiday tirades and I was about 15. It happened in the basement of her house which had a big area that was a kitchen as well as an area for us to all gather around the table. I happened to be there as the stress unfolded and the theatrics played out. Somebody finally said that maybe I should leave but instead someone else said, "No, he can stay." I think the thought was that my presence would help defuse the controversy but it didn't. That was probably the first time I saw the really serious tension in the family.

I remember watching my grandmother carrying on probably about her children not showing her enough love or something to that effect. My grandfather Frank was trying to console her along with my father and his sister. I could see how my grandfather was trapped with this hysterical woman for a wife. I didn't understand how my grandfather, who always had a very friendly and easy disposition got himself into such a situation with her so after she finally tired and went upstairs I asked, "Grandpa, didn't you know that grandma was going to act this way before you married her?" I remember that I didn't get an answer, just a look of despair.

At home in Virginia other stressful times occurred in my early teens after my parents would have a dinner party with their friends. First, we had all the stress associated with having to get ready for the party whether it was cleaning the house and putting everything away, or the cooperation and planning by and with my parents. After everyone went home at 1 a.m., my mother would cry and my father would yell at her. I never completely understood what caused them to argue but I could tell that my mother had too much to drink and she was probably upset because my father was flirting with the women and my mother didn't like his behavior. One time I remember that I was ready to go and defend her if things got anymore out of hand but they finally settled down. I hated it when they would have the parties.

There was always an undertone of stress in our house that I sensed but didn't understand because I was young. As youth, we don't have any way to evaluate what is normal and abnormal and like all children in families all we can do is do our part to make the best of the situation. I remember several times when I would hear my father talking secretly on the phone to another woman and he had a routine of going out at night on the weekends by himself.

At the time I sensed that my father's behaviors and actions were not appropriate for a married man but as a teenager we are trapped in the environment we live and we don't have any basis or authority to parent our parent(s) when we think they are out of line. My mother seemed to accept everything for what it was and make the best of it so my thinking at the time was, "If mom isn't worried about it than I guess I don't need to be worried about it either." And, of course, there was the futility of trying to address ones' parents in that they are not going to listen to their children and any confrontation will probably just make our relationship with them worse and add to the overall stress.

I remember that my father's nightly weekend adventures peaked in 1975 when at sixteen years old I had just gotten my driver's license and with it access to the other family car. My mother always went to bed early and I realized that I had the opportunity to be a detective and I could follow him to see where he was going. I asked my sister if she thought we should go together but she wasn't very interested in being a detective with me and I didn't want to take the risk on my own so I never did find out where he took off to at night.

It wasn't until my father left my mother in 1989 and I had to help her reconcile the separation that everything became more clear and I saw that my impressions as a teen and more recently in my 20's had been correct. Fortunately, while growing up I had an alternative family with my next door neighbors the Eisenschmidts, where I would go after dinner and watch TV and engage with them because it was more calming and welcoming than in my house. Karl, the father of the family, and I would talk shop about cars and machines and about all the other aspects of life.

My mother realized that her life began anew when my father left her in 1989 and that she realized that she was finally free of his passive-aggressive behaviors which were very emotionally destructive. One of the fears that my mother had after my father left was that she was going to have to tell her father Adolfo that they were separated and that he was going to say "I told you so." However he didn't say that and he was very supportive of her in her new situation. She worked hard to put the pieces of her life back together. She went to counseling and started looking for a job at 59 years old which isn't easy but her credentials came through for her again and she was offered a job for $40,000/year as a grant administrator at the State Justice Institute in Alexandria, Virginia. At her new home she made a lot of new friends and was able to enjoy the final phase of her career for next ten years.

Power

What people will try to have over you is power and you will probably try to have it over others. It is part of life, and relationships, and being human. The key is to find the right people to associate and

Soul Deep - Relationships

to stop fighting the power your parents have over you. They are only exerting their power to try and make sure that you don't make bad choices.

Parents don't have anything to gain by making you think you are miserable.

Relationships

As humans we crave relationships and that is why solitary confinement is the worst punishment in jail. Being alone is no fun. So, talk to people and have lots of relationships and fun and don't voluntarily put yourself in solitary.

We are all connected together like a big puzzle — a puzzle of life that keeps changing shape and appearance.

Relationships are the special keys to linking all the pieces.

Reputation

Take good care of your reputation because it takes a lifetime to build but can be destroyed quickly.

Responsibility

Don't run from responsibility; it's coming whether you like it or not, so take it on and test yourself. You can handle it if you have the disciple and try hard enough. Stop worrying about what everybody else might think. They don't matter because they will not be living your life or dealing with the consequences.

Respect

Which people or friends do you have respect for and why?

How does someone earn respect? Is there anything else that you can be doing to earn the respect of others?

Siblings

Brothers and sisters teach you a lot about many things — good and bad — but mostly good. They are your closest buddies because all of you experienced growing up together and know each other very well from that perspective. They will tell you straight what you need to hear and more. It is usually a good idea to listen to what they are saying even though you might not like it.

The most important aspect about having siblings of the opposite sex is that they give you a perspective on the other sex which is very important when you start considering candidates for marriage because of the impressions that you have from your sibling(s). As an example, my theory is that if you are a guy and you had nice sisters and a nice mother you would be more likely to think that most women are nice and considerate like you experienced. You would not be as suspect to more closely consider or recognize any hidden tendencies that may come out in your prospective mate that could come out and make you uncomfortable if the relationship is formalized and vice versa for girls that have nice brothers and a nice father might not be as suspecting that guys can have serious negative hidden character traits that may come out that change the relationship once the relationship is formalized with a marriage license and vows.

I met Kathleen when I was 27 and she was 24 years old. We met at a Christmas/Holiday party on Saturday, December 29, 1985 at the house of my godfather, Bob Fallon. My family was invited because Bob was my godfather and he had gone to school with and worked with my father. Kathleen was invited with her family because her mother was roommates with Bob's wife Pat in Georgetown before they were married. Kathleen arrived at the party late and I had talked with her younger sister Christina and her younger brother Matt before she arrived. Kathleen showed up with her short blonde hair, blue eyes and a big smile and dimples wearing a white fluffy sweater and I think it was love at first sight for me.

Then when I talked to her and learned that she had backpacked in Europe during the summer when she wasn't working for Fairfax County Public Schools as an Occupational Therapist, I was impressed and hooked. She was too good to be true. The thing that impressed me the most was that even though it was talked about I had never met anyone that had the wherewithal to backpack Europe which told me that she was a woman who could take care of herself. Remember, this is a time where the only resources you had when traveling were your own smarts and a book called "Let's Go."

I never asked her for her phone number when we left the party because I didn't want to seem too forward and I knew that I could always call Bob for it, which I did a couple of weeks later, and then we talked on the phone some evenings. I really wanted to go on a date with her and I wanted to make a good first impression.

I asked her to go out on a Saturday night but when I asked her she said that she couldn't go on Saturday for a few months until March because she had a part-time job commitment working at a junior high school teen center on Saturday nights through March. She said that she was free on Fridays. I stuck with my idea for a Saturday first date and told her I would wait and we would go out after the winter teen centers closed. Our first date was on Saturday, March 23rd. We went to dinner at a nice Italian restaurant in Alexandria, and then dancing at a place called P.J. Skidoo's in Fairfax. We got along really well together and the rest became history.

Spouse

The most important decision you will make.

Everything for the rest of your life hinges on this decision.

Is your prospective spouse a team player?

Is the person a team player or do they like to be in charge?

Are you better off with a wealthy banker that verbally abuses you or an auto mechanic that is happy with himself and admires you?

Are you better off with a trophy wife that has high expectations for you to take care of her or with more of a plain Jane with a big heart and lots of compassion and love for you?

And obviously, how do you know? These are some of the questions of life.

So work on your interpersonal skills now so you don't get played and so you can make the best decisions possible and your life won't end up in court and increase the statistics for divorces.

Strategic Plan

Your plan for yourself and your life and how you are going to try and accomplish your goals can be viewed as a strategic plan.

Do you have a strategic plan and if so what is it?

Social Media - Part II

Don't be paranoid about what somebody might say about you if you are always careful and don't do anything wrong. If somebody says something that isn't true, your real friends will know the other person is lying, which will make them look bad. If it is true then you shouldn't have allowed it to happen in the first place so don't make the same mistake again.

Another way to reduce you concerns about negative or critical social media postings is to realize that all your friends are consuming so many small bits of information that they can't possibly see everything, assimilate all of it and remember all the little pieces. You and your friends are consuming so much nonsense that it all just becomes a big blur anyway so don't worry about it.

Just be yourself and be happy.

Teachers - Part II

The best resource you have going for you other than your parents are teachers. The teachers are there to help you but you have to have initiative, effort and work ethic. They are going to guide and help those that want to help themselves. They are not there to give you a free ride. You will pay the cost of today's free ride many times over in the future.

We never had the option for retakes of tests. We took the test once so we needed to get it right the first time and move on. Life rarely gives retakes.

Retests give you an excuse to not work as hard up front and make more work for the teachers. Ultimately, its more work for you.

Teens

I have found that hanging out with my teens is probably going

Soul Deep - Relationships

to be the highlight of my life. As they move into their twenty's I will not be able to interact with them as much because they will be more independent which will take a lot of the fun out of our relationships.

Their growing up is a double edged sword because on one side parents work hard to help them mature and succeed, and, on the other hand, you know that in doing so they won't be looking for your help as much in the future and you will miss them when they grow up and become independent.

My challenge to you is for you to project ahead and imagine that you have teenage children and to imagine what it will feel like. You are the parent in some different place in a far off time.

What do you think having teenage children will be like for you?

What will be the same?

What will be different?

What kind of parent will you be to them?

Women

Guys, always be very nice to women. They are remarkable individuals, deserve the utmost respect, and have bodies that can create amazing things.

Women can be just as practical and entrepreneurial as men, if not better, and they are the backbone of most successful children, individual achievements, and successful men.

Give them the credit they deserve.

Your Marriage

Pay attention to this section because it is very important.

Men think that the women won't change and the women think they can change the men and they're both wrong.

When I was your age I thought that the following sections on marriage and children should definitely be in the next section titled Pitfalls, Risks and Dungeons, but now that I have experienced both they're the best part of your life if you are prepared and approach them properly.

Happy wife, happy life.

Realize that once you have a spouse the dynamics change with your family (hopefully for the better). Where before you only had to take yourself into consideration and your family members knew that, marriage introduces another person with their personality into your family's dynamics and you are in the middle because now there is someone outside of your immediate family that can and will be influencing you.

Nobody wants to marry a loser.
The load will be unbalanced.

The sooner you get your act together, the better, because then you can impress somebody when you meet them and maybe keep someone you like a lot from being distracted by someone else.

This is the second most important topic and it is extra important because statistics show that almost 50% of marriages end in divorce and the average length of marriage is eight years. You do not want to marry someone if there is a good probability that you are not going

Soul Deep - Relationships

to be compatible in the future. And the divorce rate for second marriages is even higher at 60% so you need to do everything possible to make sure you get it right the first time. There is not much to be gained by rushing it so take your time. If they are not willing to wait for you to be comfortable with the arrangement than they are probably not right for you. Don't let someone push you. And vice-versa, if someone doesn't seem able to commit to you in a reasonable amount of time, baring extenuating circumstances, then it is time for you to move on.

I only learned of the high divorce statistic recently when Kathleen was shocked to learn that another couple in the neighborhood, with children the same age as some of ours, was splitting.
Marriage is the most important decision you will make because this is someone that you are supposed to want and be able to live with for the rest of your life, that you can trust, that you can work with to create wealth and a family, and that you admire and they admire you.

I didn't really understand the sacrament of marriage until, as my official fiancée, Kathleen showed me some books published by the Catholic Church that discussed the institution (of marriage) in more depth so I had a better understanding of what it was supposed to be about instead of what I had experienced in my family or seen in other families. I was really worried about making the commitment and it was extremely hard for me to make because I had not been exposed to many happy marriages and I didn't see any driving reason why I would want to subject myself to the pain and anguish that I had seen or heard others experience.

My grandfather Frank, on my father's side, seemed to be tormented by my grandmother Josephine every holiday or summer vacation when we would visit their house in Stamford, Connecticut. My other grandparents, on my mother's side, seemed to be pretty content with each other, but Josephine really scared me because I don't think Frank had any idea what he was marrying and he had such a nice disposition. He didn't deserve the treatment she dished out at him.

I grew up on Bowling Green Drive in Vienna, Virginia, and my

German next door neighbors, Margrit and Karl Eisenschmidt seemed to have a nice marriage that worked and they had mutual respect for each other. Their house with their three children was my second family so I knew them real well and everyone seemed happy and content.

The Watkins family lived on the other side of our house and they had two sons that were older than me. Charles was the husband and he was tormented by his wife Delores. He was tormented so bad in his house that the only way he could get any peace on Sunday morning was to take the newspaper and read it in his car parked in the driveway. We didn't have garages.

His wife, Delores, would be so angry with him on the weekends, I never knew why, but we all felt real sorry for Mr. Watkins.

Delores would open the front door and yell at him for a few minutes while he was sitting in the car with the windows rolled up and then she would slam the door as hard as possible. Mr. Watkins's experience with his wife taught me a lot about how I needed to be careful about who I married so I wouldn't have to seek refuge in my car on Sunday mornings. I think Mr. Watkins always found his most enjoyment every Fall season when he would rake the leaves while listening to the Penn State football game on the radio.

Every family has its story just as yours does, but you want to do everything possible so you and your family-to-be can have as nice a story as possible. No family is perfect regardless of how they seem or present themselves.

Dysfunctional families are actually the norm and no family is perfect, but if the two of you are mature and properly prepared you should be successful in achieving your family goals and establishing a comfortable and happy home. Seriously dysfunctional families are usually due to serious personality disorders and problematic matches.

My own parents seemed to have a difficult relationship in that my father seemed to create a lot of stress in the family while my mother tried hard to please him and to keep everything as normal as possible for my sister and me. I once asked my mother why she

Soul Deep - Relationships

didn't have any more children and she said that it would be too difficult because my father wouldn't accept and help with the responsibilities of raising my sister and me and that he was more interested in chasing other women than in being in the marriage and having responsibility for a family.

I asked her why she stayed with him and she explained that it was better than the alternative of leaving Washington, D.C., in 1960 and going home to her parents in Stamford, Connecticut, where she had just used marriage as a means of escaping, what she thought were, her overbearing parents. So instead, she stuck it out with my father and his passive-aggressive behaviors and his shenanigans of dressing himself up and going out on his own on Friday and Saturday nights and having difficulty getting up the following morning.

My sister and I never quite understood what was going on but my thinking was that if my mother didn't seem bothered by what he was doing than I figured it was OK. Who was I to question my father's behavior?

I was further afraid of the institution of marriage because I was very close to my girlfriend in high school. She was very smart and attractive but things didn't quite work out and while the relationship was exciting and fun, at times, it was also difficult.

My experience in the relationship added to my concerns about making a commitment to someone for what was supposed to be for the rest of my life. It is a tough decision for all of us.

Kathleen was different, in a good way, more than any of the other women I had ever met or dated, but it still took me seven years before I could ask her to marry me. She gave me so many ultimatums and said, "We need to do something here, I can't keep waiting," so many times that when I finally got down on my knee in 1993 and proposed to her, she didn't think I was serious even though I had my grandmothers wedding ring for her.

We probably would have gotten married much sooner but I didn't want to bail out on my mother after my father left her in 1988, which my mother finally recognized was the best thing that could have happened to her because she got her life back, or when her father Adolfo was aging and I was living with him to keep him company, until he died in 1993.

I can't complain too much about my parents' marriage because if they hadn't gotten together I wouldn't be here to write this story but after my first-generation Italian father left my mother, my mother explained to me, "Grandma and Grandpa did not want me to marry your father."

I was confused so she explained how before she got married they had told her, "Why are you marrying an Italian when there are all these nice young American boys to choose from and, even worse, you are marrying a Southern Italian?"

My mother explained that part of the reason that she married my father (they met in High School) was because she thought my father had more ambition and was of better caliber than most of the other boys she knew. My mother felt that her parents, Adolfo and Vincenza, were very overbearing, especially because she was a girl and an only child, so she thought marriage was the best means of escaping from her difficult overbearing situation. Furthermore, she told me, "I got the sense that your father's family was close and friendly which provided a comforting feeling," even though later on she would feel that her mother-in-law valued a glamorous wife for her son more than the substance my mother was trying to provide to the marriage for the future well being of the family.

Marriage is also important because it is what society is based on. I remember when I was sixteen how I told my mother that I wasn't getting married because relationships are so complicated and difficult. Even though she was unhappy in her marriage, she said, "And just think what would happen if nobody ever got married?"

I had to ponder that one.

I later visited the parents of my high school sweetheart after she had married her boyfriend after dating me, and I told them that I was sorry that it didn't work out for us. Her mother was very nice in her reply of, "Oh we knew it wasn't going to work."

Puzzled I asked, "How did you know that?"

"Well, because you are Catholic and we are Protestant."

Soul Deep - Relationships

I was stunned and never saw it coming. The thought had never even crossed my mind. I think that the young man their daughter had married was Catholic though, just like me, and they had two children together. Unfortunately, they got divorced and they each got remarried to someone else and each had more children.

There are some other aspects to marriage that you need to consider such as realizing that you are not just marrying the person, you are marrying their family so if you couldn't live with their family for two weeks for whatever reason than take that as a big cautionary sign and vice versa. If your family couldn't live with your prospective spouse for two weeks then you might want to reconsider because it might not be a good fit. You are bringing them into your family just as they are bringing you into theirs and if the two families don't appear to get along, be careful because that can add to stress in the marriage where it always helps to have support. You don't want your parents saying, "I told you so."

Even though I have never been a big proponent of going to church, the process the Catholic Church follows for couples interested in getting married is good and before we got married Kathleen bought some books from the "Catholic Store," as we called it, about what the sacrament of marriage meant. I was comfortable with how the church explained the sacrament which helped me to put everything into perspective, probably much more so than my grandparents or parents did considering that all my grandparents had civil weddings. However, I guess the teachings didn't work that well for my parents because they were married in a Catholic Church.

Being of the same faith or of different faiths is another factor to consider before getting married and it might not seem that important when you are dating or engaged. Being from different faiths can become a bigger issue once you have children. My mother gave up trying to take us to church after I was 13 because my father would not participate but Kathleen's discipline in continuing to keep us involved in our church has been a good thing for the family. With Kathleen's persistence and guidance I understand the Church's importance now much more than I did when I was a teenager. I kind of wish I could have continued with my church experience as a teen as my children are doing now because now I see it as a great place for making more friends and getting some spiritual development.

Despite all of its risks and problems, marriage is a healthy institution for children, young adults and families.

About ten years after I was married I stopped by to visit Karl and Margrit Eisenschmidt and I was telling them how marriage and children seemed to agree with me after all my procrastination and they told me that they have a saying in German that translates to,

"You want to marry someone that you can steal horses with."
German proverb.

I was very confused as to what stealing horses had to do with marriage and they explained, "What the saying means is that you want to marry someone that will stay with you no matter how bad things get, even if things are so bad for the two of you that you have to steal horses to survive."

"Oh, I see," I replied.

"Ja, we can see that you made a good choice," Margrit said.

The big question in who you marry is who do you want to share responsibility for your life and the lives of any of your children and whose life do you want to have responsibility for?

**Who are you going to trust with your
emotions, money, life, and children?**

You can tell a lot about a person in how they treat their parents such as how a son treats his mother is an indicator of his perspective on woman and how he will probably treat his wife and, vice versa, how nice and caring a daughter is to her father will probably translate to how nice she is to her husband. So pay attention when you meet prospective in-laws because the family and personality dynamics are very important in understanding people's behaviors and character traits. They will serve as a good indicator of what kind of emotional and mental environment lies ahead.

You probably won't talk about it with your prospective spouse because, like me, I couldn't get past the marriage part, let alone even consider children and the responsibility they entail. Bringing up the subject of possible children can scare a lot of prospective mates when either of you are on the fence and having difficulty with the marriage commitment part and what it all means.

I was so scared to get married that the words wouldn't come out of my mouth for the vows when we were practicing the ceremony at the rehearsal the evening before the wedding. I was so nervous that I was speechless. I had to pause and try to relax so I could continue. It took a lot of effort for me to say the words and afterwards my wife's aunt told me, "Don't worry, tomorrow you can take all the time you need, we will wait." One of my groomsman told me they were going to chain the doors.

Remember as you consider getting married that your offspring will carry your spouse's genetics which will be mixed with yours regarding family traits and characteristics so keep your eyes open as to what you are marrying, not just in the physical sense but also in terms of their parents, grandparents and siblings. Consider spouse's genetics because between the two of your families you can get some idea of the possible predisposition of your children. As your children get older you will be able to see connections between the behaviors of your children and the behaviors of other family members.

Can your selected spouse take care of herself or himself or is that person needy?

You don't want to marry needy.

Your Children

Pregnancy

As I just explained, I was never interested in having children and never gave it any thought because I couldn't get past the marriage part first. I did know, that no matter what, that I didn't want to get saddled with a child out of wedlock so I was very careful to not get myself into that type of situation because I knew that there was a good chance it would ruin my life. I will admit that there were many women who were seductive but I was always able to manage the relationship and mitigate those risks.

Children were so far removed from my and Kathleen's thoughts that Kathleen and I never even mentioned the concept for the eight years we dated, and for probably a couple years after we were married, even though Kathleen was working in the public schools in child development where she was around children all day, every day.

Then, once we were married and the subject of children finally came up, Kathleen thought it was too risky because she was afraid that she would get a child who had special needs. She knew what to do with them because those were the kids that she saw every day and because she has an older sister who is mentally retarded even though her disability isn't genetic. I was more the risk taker when it came to children, especially compared to how I was with marriage and marriage seemed to be working out well. I felt that we were going to have to give it a try sooner or later and since time was not moving backwards, the sooner was better—and so Kathleen was surprised to find herself pregnant in September of 1996 with our first child Mary Jane.

I am telling this story because as teenagers you need to recognize the serious physical and emotional risks that having sex can and do create. Having sex with someone for the sake of having sex is very risky and can ruin you and your relationship in many ways. First, as you know there are a lot of serious diseases that are transmitted sexually. These diseases can effect one's ability to get pregnant

Soul Deep - Relationships

and exposure to them is not worth the risk they pose, as well as the risk of an unexpected pregnancy, and the emotional changes that occur in relationships that engage in such intimate activities.

It is much better to err on the side of caution than to take the plunge—no matter what precautions are taken—because sex changes relationships and expectations in very serious and usually detrimental ways. Usually the best way to ruin a good friendship is to have sex with the person. The sex will then get in the way of your trying to understand who the person really is and what they are made of and whether you want to get married to them forever. Realize that once you get married you can have all the sex that the two of you want so later you can make up for any lack of it now and you can do it without all the stress, risk and baggage that comes with having it out of wedlock.

Children are a big responsibility and they cause big changes in your life so it is best to have as much in place as possible before you go down this road of making them.

Child birth

Children come from child birth which for me was an experience I compare to going on military maneuvers. It is similar in that it is a very stressful moment in life, it can happen at any time. You are in new surroundings, you don't know what is going on and you have to work with people that you don't know. You're not sure how it is going to turn out and it will effect you for the rest of your life.

My one suggestion to first time dads is to make sure that you get something to eat at the hospital cafeteria to keep your stamina up because I was so tired and hungry that I almost passed out when they gave Kathleen an epidural with the birth of our first, Mary Jane. And I have found that the food is really good too.

Kathleen's water broke with our first child when we were home at about 11 p.m. and when that happens you have to go to the hospital for delivery to avoid the possibility of an infection. There, I had to sleep on a short couch for two so I didn't get any sleep at all and I was too worried to eat and the delivery dragged out for a long time because Mary Jane was stubborn and didn't want to come out until 6 p.m. the next evening.

There isn't anything for the father to do during the ordeal except to be supportive and worry. It is very stressful. In anticipation of the downtime I brought a hardback notebook in which I could record all the blow by blow events that occurred during child birth so we would have a permanent record of everything that transpired since it is very confusing when you are in the middle of it and how our child, whatever it was, was born. I wrote all the details down regarding the time and who said what and what was occurring so we had a record of the life changing event as it occurred. Fortunately all the child births had happy endings.

Children - Creating Part I

Some years ago my sister Susie said to me, "You are the last person in the world that I would have thought would have had five children."

"Yes, I am," I said. "I can only thank Kathleen for making it so much fun. Her training in child development brought skills and insight to having children that I was completely unaware of."

I have always been interested in business, mechanics, and building things and always thought that children would be a bother and a pain kind of like how a wife can be considered a "ball-and-chain." But unbeknown to me when I married her, as an occupational therapist, Kathleen had a unique and special skill set regarding the natural child development process and she saw and explained it to me as it was happening with our first child, Mary Jane. It was fascinating for us to watch and experience her development as it was occurring little by little.

Kathleen was just as thrilled to watch it unfold with Mary Jane as I was. She would explain each aspect of normal development that we all take for granted. The markers included very simple things such as how to hold a spoon or a crayon or whether they could use scissors properly, jump or bounce a ball. These were all indicators of development that are supposed to occur at certain stages of human development. Then, after she observed the normal development of our first child, she started to look at her role in special education with a different perspective.

Mary Jane is named after my mother who is Mary and Kathleen's mother who is Jane. We couldn't resist.

Mary Jane became Kathleen's private laboratory experiment and Kathleen, because of her education and training, was such a prepared mother, that I felt very comfortable with the aspect of trying to make and raise more children with her. Everything seemed to work well with Mary Jane so why not? I suggested we go for two even though Kathleen still had her misgivings.

Success prevailed and our second child John was born in 1999 and then we were on a roll and had Mike in 2001 and Vincent in 2005 and Kate popped out in 2007 when Kathleen was 45 years old. We were very lucky and I tell everyone, "We waited to rush."

Kathleen's concerns of having a child that needed special education were unfounded, and we were blessed with five wonderful children and knowing what I know now I would have started sooner and probably had ten children with her but that would have changed everything so I would prefer to just keep what I have. They are all really neat and fun and unbelievable.

And if someone asks me, "What about having enough money for college?"

I respond, "Who would not want to have been born because their parents were worried about providing their college tuition?

"I'm sure you can figure something out when the time comes because when it works it is just amazing at how a little up front fun can so easily create something so complex, beautiful and unique."

Children - Creating Part II

I quickly realized after my first child was born that if there were any big projects that I had wanted to do in my life that they were now on hold for at least twenty years. Once you have a child your life changes and there's nothing you can do about it. To be more accurate, your life starts to change once someone gets pregnant.

You will probably not remember that you read this here once it happens to you, and it took me many years to realize it, but with the birth of your first child you will automatically join a very special club. It is called the "Parents Club." Your child is your membership card and as long as you have your membership card with you all of a sudden you can talk to any other club members without any introduction whether it is in the grocery store, a swimming pool or parking lot, at a school or just standing there watching your child at a park.

You can talk to non-club members also and you won't appear odd for just starting a conversation. Of course, you may appear odd in public when you are trying to deal with your child's behavior, but only to the people that have never had a child. Everyone else will just be endeared to you and your situation.

It is kind of like when you join the "Marriage Club" when you get married, but the Parents Club is a much tighter group. The "Singles Club" is always the Singles Club unless somebody from the Singles Club borrows a child and then they can have a temporary membership in the Parents Club but not really.

Knowing what I know now I would have gotten married sooner so I could have had even more children with Kathleen, but of course then that would have changed the equation and I'd rather just keep the ones that I have. To Kathleen and I, they are perfect in every way.

The catch-22 about having children is that you go along for your lifetime up to that point worried that you are going to get pregnant and then you cross a line and all of a sudden you want to get pregnant. It is an interesting quantum shift.

The big question is whether all the equipment will work or not and if the two of you can really make one or not and what you can make. And there is only one way to find out.

A couple ages 29-33 with a normal functioning reproductive system has a 20-25% chance of conceiving in any given month (National Women's Health Resource Center). After six months of trying,

Soul Deep - Relationships

60% of couples will conceive without medical assistance.

Reproduction is such a funny thing because at first it is so risky and problematic and then it is good and you want to hurry up so you don't have to worry. Then once you get pregnant you worry because you don't know what you are going to get. And then you worry about your child for eternity.

Take your time and relax, there's no hurry and everything will work out OK. The best part is that when everything works it is remarkable at how little effort created something so unbelievably complex. Of course, you have to nurture and work with it for the rest of your life but that's part of being in the Parents Club.

Keep in mind that there are many factors that can impact fertility. They include body weight, exercise, caffeine intake, alcohol consumption, smoking, recreational drugs, sports injuries and even, possibly, the radio-frequency electromagnetic radiation from cell phones.

When working with my mother on the family history, I saw that she had a relative named Giovanni Robotti who was born in Italy in 1890 and immigrated from Alessandria, Italy, to New York City in October, 1912. Giovanni married Clotilde, my mother's cousin and who I met several times, one year later when he was 23-years-old in 1913. Together, they had their first and only child, Maria, within ten months of when they were married. Then they didn't have anymore children.

"That's odd, why didn't they have more children? What happened?" I asked.

I didn't understand why if they were so young when they got married, that they didn't have more children since everything worked really easily to make their first.

My mother explained, "Giovanni decided to take up professional wrestling sometime after they got married and it was rumored that, probably through no fault of his own, his reproductive organs were damaged."

Giovanni Robotti had a very friendly demeanor and was very outgoing. He worked hard for a bakery delivering Italian bread to stores and restaurants in New York City. One morning he had an accident with the delivery truck that almost killed him so he decided to start his own bakery in Stamford, Connecticut. Somehow he was able to buy a place to live and start the bakery at 15 St. Mary's Street, Stamford, Connecticut.

Giovanni Robotti didn't know it at the time, but his life was put at risk by marrying Clotilde because she believed in the Seventh son of a seventh son, a folklore type of witchdoctor. In 1938, Giovanni was sick with a gall bladder infection. Clotilde preferred to trust her friend with his diagnosis and recovery instead of an educated doctor. Giovanni's condition continued to worsen and by the time she did take him to the doctor, who immediately admitted him to the hospital, it was too late. He died at 48 years old. His son-in-law continued with the business. A few years later Clotilde remarried to a man named Freddie.

My mother explained, "After we sold the grocery store in the Bronx in 1944, we went to live in the duplex apartment above Clotilde and Freddie. I was in the 7th grade.

"Your grandfather helped out by trying to fix up around the house and by working in the bakery to help make bread each morning. This arrangement worked for about a year until Clotilde started accusing us of doing things that we didn't do. We decided it was time to leave so we bought our own house on Plymouth Road in Stamford and moved out."

Marriage, fertility, pregnancy, family making, and your future illnesses and death are probably at the very bottom of your list of concerns at this phase of your life, but from the story above and the ones following in the next chapter you can see how some of the actions and habits that you form now have the potential to create new and unexpected problems for you, your mate, and your as yet unborn children in the next phase of your life.

Chapter four
Pitfalls, Risks and Dungeons

Accidents/Crashes

Auto accidents make you pay in several ways. Higher insurance premiums, loss of use of your car, feelings of remorse especially if someone was injured or killed, embarrassment, attendance in traffic court, points on your drivers license and lots of expense and wasted effort are consequences of accidents.

So slow down and drive to avoid problems. It isn't that hard. You just have to think about what you are doing, what is going on around you, anticipate, and stay focused.

Advertisements

Another word for propaganda that is trying to get you to think or buy something.

Alcohol

Biggest killer of young adults.

Destroys livers.

Is not necessary.

Listen to your Guardian Angel, not the Gremlin that tells you to drink.

YouTube: "How I overcame alcoholism - Claudia Christian - TEDx-LondonBusinessSchool.

Arrest

This is something you want to avoid and you can avoid it by making sure that you do not do anything that would subject you to such an extreme police action.

The police officer is an officer of the law, and that means he has been given the authority to uphold the law. It is their duty to enforce the laws and protect people and property. Police Officers are trained in the rules and procedures that they have to follow in order to balance the keeping of the peace and likewise not violating people's constitutional rights. It is not an easy job and keep in mind that the final say rests with a judge, but you don't want to get to that point in the first place.

People are placed under arrest because they are suspected of committing a crime and the crime is severe enough that they need to go before a judge.

When a police officer makes an arrest, they are not saying that the person is guilty, but that there is "probable cause" to suspect that the person violated a specific section of criminal law.

When a police officer turns on the blue lights or summons you, technically you are under arrest and need to respond to them responsibly. How you respond can determine your fate. If a more official arrest occurs, you are physically restrained and read your rights. At that time you will be considered a prisoner, are probably going to see a magistrate, the inside of a jail, and a judge who will tell you when you need to appear before the Court.

Once physically restrained, the arresting officer will transport you to the courthouse where you will be taken before a citizen magistrate who is an employee of the court but neither a judge or a police officer. The magistrate is supposed to be an impartial person to help insure that your rights are not being violated and that the police officer is not exceeding his authority in placing you under arrest and charging you with a crime. If the magistrate agrees that there reasonable suspicion that the arrested person did commit a crime then you will be placed in jail and brought before a judge.

Pitfalls, Risks, and Dungeons

Most community police departments have ride-a-long programs that students can participate in once they are 18-years old. These programs are deigned to promote police transparency and provide participants with an excellent opportunity to see many hidden aspects of society. I participated in about six ride-alongs and they were always very educational, whether it was just getting to know the officer or to see the mired of problems they were faced or to see how policing actually works. They even have these programs on college campuses if you ask and participating is a lot more beneficial then just hanging out in a dorm room watching videos or gaming.

Another educational activity is to be able to visit the courthouse and attend some criminal or traffic courtrooms while they are in session with a nice feeling that you didn't have to be there because of an infraction.

Bullies

Stay away from them because they are sinister.

Watch out for them so they don't pull your chair out from under you. Read the story of my concussion in the Concussions topic of this chapter.

I have had many experiences with bullies in and out of school so I know about their deviant behaviors. One ruined my Boy Scout experience.

I joined the Boy Scouts and was a Tenderfoot when I was in elementary school and then I continued as a Webelos when I was in middle school. I liked the troop in middle school but I had a problem with an eighth grade bully in the group named Todd. This was a time when very few dads participated with their sons like they do today.

Todd was always picking on me or other seventh graders. He was older than us and would prey on younger scouts. It got so bad that I eventually reported him to the scout master but in the end even the scout master couldn't control him. Todd was so nasty that he infected the whole troop and took all the fun out of the group so I had to quit.

There was another bully in high school that would pick on one of my friends named Bob while we were waiting in the cafeteria in the morning for school to start. There was no reason to pick on Bob because Bob was a nice guy. Bob just took it. Eventually the bully was so intolerable in terms of always wanting to exert his power over others that I found a group of girls to sit with in the morning. They were much nicer than the boys that were always trying to exercise their masculinity and bravado. The girls were much cuter, too.

Beware of people that make fun of others for their amusement or the amusement of others. And if someone talks badly about others to you, then know that they also could be talking badly about you to others.

Just stay clear of bullies because you don't want them for friends no matter how popular or funny they may seem and associating with them will make you complicit in their taunts.

My son Mike says that if someone bullies him that he is going to DM their mom on Facebook to tell her that her child is using drugs.

Cheating

Cheating now cheats you out of a lot more later.

My son John complained to me about how he worked hard to get good grades in computer science his junior year but that a lot of the students in its different classes were cheating on the tests and it bothered him because his grade did not appropriately reflect his knowledge compared to their knowledge because they cheated.

We discussed telling the teacher but decided against it. I told him to not let their dishonesty get to him and to just ignore them and that it would all catch up with them in the end. They were only cheating themselves.

College experience

There are many options for defining the term "college experi-

Pitfalls, Risks, and Dungeons

ence," which can be best represented by the many choices of Holy Grails as depicted in the cave and protected by the Knight in the movie, *Raiders of the Lost Ark*.

Now, imagine that the Knight is talking to you as you choose how you are going to define your "college experience." The Knight says to you, "But choose wisely, for while the true Grail will bring you life, the false Grail will take it from you."

How you define your college experience, if you attend, is up to you. If you must choose, please choose wisely.

Will you define your college experience about doing things that you shouldn't be doing such as gaming, drinking alcohol, and being irresponsible or will it be about getting school work done and pushing yourself on academics?

What do you think college is for or should be for?

Why are you there or going there?

Take the time to write some of your thoughts below because this is the million dollar question that you need to answer. The sooner that you can answer it correctly and stick to the right answer, the better off you and your college experience will be.

_____

_____

_____

_____

_____

Hint, the partying experience can always be postponed until after you graduate.

Benjamin Franklin wrote of Harvard students, "Most of the students who attended "this famous Place," he wrote, "were little better than Dunces and Blockheads." This was not surprising, since the main qualification for entry, he said, was having money. Once admitted, the students "learn little more than how to carry themselves handsomely, and enter a room genteely, (which might as well be acquire'd at a Dancing-School,) and from whence they return, after

Abundance of Trouble and Charge, as great Blockheads as ever, only more proud and self-conceited" *"The Americanization of Benjamin Franklin, Gordon S. Wood, Penguin, 2005, p.21*

Collisions

As described in physics, "A collision occurs when two objects try to occupy the same space at the same time."

This also holds true for people walking in a hallway or when crossing a street or for two cars traveling on a road or when parking your car.

Take your time and pay attention to try and avoid collisions which can be painful and costly.

Avoid jay-walking as it is unfair to drivers who have enough to pay attention to and who do not deserve your laziness. Cross at corners to be safe.

Concussions

Concussions are damage to your brain which may or may not be able to repair itself. Concussions are serious injuries because they can create a lot of problems for you now and later in life. The spooky part of concussions is that after a concussion you never can know the full extent of the injury or the full extent of the recovery. And it is even spookier because your brain controls your emotions and energy so a concussion can cause abnormal and extreme changes in how you feel and react.

The scariest part is that if you have a concussion you'll never know if it modified you because the brain is not a simple machine.

I had a concussion once when two of, what I thought were my friends, played a trick on me in my 8th grade shop class. Bill was sitting across from me and he took my pen so I had to reach for it and then my other so called friend moved my stool so after I reached to grab my pen and went to sit back down I crashed on the floor. When I went down I hit my head on the lower steel edge of the steel table behind me. They obviously didn't think through what was going to happen and I never understood why they picked on me.

Pitfalls, Risks, and Dungeons

I ended up with a gash in my head and a big lump, and after a couple of hours I noticed I had a temporary blind spot whereby students who were walking across my field of view would disappear and then reappear as they walked. I went home when school ended. My father was home because he was unemployed at the time. He called the doctor and they said to just wait and see if I got better which I did and my sight recovered by the next morning. It could have been much more severe of a concussion and their antics could have caused me to break my tail bone when I landed on the concrete floor. It hurt me physically and emotionally that they did that to me.

What they did was really mean and they probably didn't think their prank through well enough to realize the danger they were placing me in. Bill's mother did call my mother to check on me that evening and say how sorry she was.

The experience taught me that just because someone seems like they are your friend you still have to be careful of whom you think you can trust. For the two of them to gang up on me like that for their entertainment was sinister and I never trusted either of them again.

Choices, Actions, and Consequences

Consequences: the results, which are usually negative, from doing something or taking a specific action, from our own, or someone else's, choice.

Not putting out your best effort all the time, even when you think you can relax and take it easy, can have negative consequences and create big trouble for you and others.

An excellent, real life example to illustrate this topic, is a story that involved my good friend and former Staff Sargent Marty Braithwaite of Charles Town, West Virginia, who works at a propane rail terminal I frequent every few days in Stephens City, Virginia.

The incident he was involved in occurred one morning when his 2nd Platoon of Alpha Company, 1st Battalion, 46th Infantry was on patrol in Quang Tin Province, Vietnam, January 1971. Marty was

234

Chris DeCarlo

21 years old.

"Sarge, we got some activity over there," Wilson breathlessly said as he took a knee next to me and leaned on his M16 trying to catch his breath. "You need to check this out, man. I think there's some big shit gettin' ready to go down just past that ridge."

"Damn," I said as I got a sick feeling in my stomach. Wilson and Moose, had just gotten back from checking our right flank while we were taking a break. We were getting ready to cross some open rice paddies. "What d'ya think it is?" I asked, not looking forward to the answer and thinking I was glad he didn't use his radio.

"It's a couple of hooches. Strange lookin'." Moose added. "Out in the middle of nowhere. It's definitely Charlie. They're up to something, sir."

"How far out did you go?"

Wilson replied, "It's just odd. A little farther than normal. We found what looked like an active trail and followed it, kept goin'. Maybe a 150 to 200 yards since it was pretty open and easy to move. They're just past that ridge," pointing to where he had just come from. "Surprised the shit out of me Sarge. We could even hear 'em talking. They didn't know we were there though. Thank God for that."

"Uh oh," I said, "I guess we got company."

Moose added, "Yea, and I guess they're pretty confident that they are far enough off this trail that we wouldn't bump into them. Few people moving around, no outposts. Man, I've never seen anything like it. To be able to sneak up on them like that and all. We're lucky they didn't see us. We'd be toast by now."

"Good thinkin' not to use the radio." Looking over at Smith, I said, "Go tell the Capt'n to sit tight, we're gonna run a recon to check out some hooches. Redmond and Phillips and the rest of Bravo squad, huddle up and get the lieutenant up here so he can be in on this."

The five other members of 2nd squad got up from their break on the trail and circled around. "Everyone here? Good." I said, "This is what I think we've got."

Pitfalls, Risks, and Dungeons

I started to draw a map in the dirt with the seven guys from our squad except for Lieutenant Raymond. "Wilson said Charlie's on our flank about here over this ridge and we need to check it out. Grab your magazines. Let's go see if we can surprise him. Pass it down the column to be ready if we get into trouble."

The lieutenant, who had joined the company to get his CIB (Combat Infantry Badge) came up to the huddle curious as to what was going on. I repeated what recon had learned and explained how we were going to go toward the ridge to check it out.

"I'm in," the lieutenant said excitedly even though he had never seen much combat. He'd been sent to the Company a handful of days ago so he could get some live action experience and earn his badge. He needed 30 days to qualify. When he arrived, the Captain told him to stay in my hip pocket, pay attention, and, if he did as I said, that he'd be all right and make it home alive.

"Calm down, we don't like lookin' for trouble. Enough seems to find us on its own. Hopefully we can take 'em by surprise if we're quiet. We will move to the base of the ridge and stay low. I'll take a look and then we'll blow our mags, reload and make an advance. Stay down, don't make any noise, and be patient so we don't give ourselves away.

"I think we got an invitation for lunch. Right?"

"Yes, sir." everyone said.

"Wilson you lead the way. When we get there, Redmond you go right, Moose, you're on the left. Get rid of anything that'll make a sound. When we get there spread out about 50 feet. Let's go crash the party."

Gheez, I guess it isn't going to be a stroll in the park today. Maybe a stroll around the rice paddies? I guess the quiet from the past week and last night was too good to last.

It was about 1100 hrs, January, 1971, and here I was walking around rice paddies trying to keep my feet dry or from bumping into a booby trap or stepping on a land mine. I'd much rather be back in Charles Town, but now I'm stuck in this God damn war. All I can do is hope I make it back alive and with all my parts. 182 days left to go.

My platoon, part of Alpha company, came to Fire Support Base (FSB) Rawhide two months ago and we've been sent out on two to three week patrols ever since. Here I am trying to sleep on the open ground in the jungle every night, if you want to call it sleep, for $282 a month including combat pay. A big $3,600 a year.

Then, trying to stay awake during the day is the next challenge and the bad dreams just keep repeating. Minimum wage in the States is $1.60/hour and I'm not even getting that. I'll bet this place becomes some vacation paradise in 50 years. I feel like a walking zombie trying to live on five minute naps. I'm getting the short end of this deal.

"Shake it off," I tell myself, "You're better off not to think about it right now."

There were three platoons in the company, three squads per platoon. Each squad was supposed to have ten men but our squads only had about six each. Total, there were about 60 to 70 of us in the company. We were supposed to have more.

I've been in country since July last year and I'd already been in more fire fights than I could keep track of. We would make a contact every couple of weeks.

My platoon of three squads, 18 men in this case, was usually on point when on patrol. It was nice of Capt'n to give us a break this morning. Said we could fall back into the middle of the column. I don't know why he took us off point, unless he felt sorry for us taking all the heat of being the lead platoon all the time, we weren't complaining.

Every minute counts when you're on patrol because you don't know if it is going to be your last. Trip wires, Punjabi sticks, ambushes, claymores, snakes, chiggers, ambushes, and sleeping on the ground every night were my new life. Even in the rain.

Now that we are in the middle of the column we're responsible for keepin' an eye on the flanks so Charlie doesn't surprise us from the center and cut us up. Delta platoon is on point and Able platoon is in on the rear.

Pitfalls, Risks, and Dungeons

We'd spent the night on a ridge and been resupplied by choppers 'bout four hours ago. Then we'd hoofed it down the mountain about half a click into a valley filled with rice paddies. The Captain called for a 30 minute break for recognizance before we ventured out into the open toward the hills about one click on the other side of the rice paddies.

So far, so good. Not being on point made for easier breathing when we walked. Charlie is always full of surprises. You quickly learn to always be paying attention because you never know what surprises he will throw at you. Well, maybe we were gonna get some action after all.

We got to the ridge with the hooches on the other side pretty quickly with Wilson leading the way. I looked where Wilson was pointing and could see what looked like three hooches with some men in black standing around. They sure didn't look like farmers to me, especially since they were carrying AK-47's. I could hear their voices too.

Shit, I thought as I surveyed the situation. I don't have a clue as to what we're up against here. There could be three or 30. At least they didn't surprise us. That would have been ugly. The rest of the company is right behind us if this turns out to be bigger than it looks.

Wilson's extra effort paid off this time. This whole ordeal of fighting a war in a jungle wasn't for me. My father taught me how to take care of myself in the mountains of West Virginia, I could handle that, but these rice paddies and jungles were no fun. Complete exposure in the open or completely hidden in the jungle.

Sweat was soaking me from the humidity. I waited a minute to catch my breath, not only from running but from the adrenaline of what we were getting ready to do. I never did like it when my mother made rice and here I am risking my life to protect it. If Charlie wants these rice paddies than I say let him have 'em and I can go home.

Let's hope we get through this one. Here we go.

Laying next to the ridge for cover, I looked to my left and right and made sure everyone was in position and ready. They knew the drill. At least this time we had the element of surprise working for us.

238

I just hoped that once we lit the place up that the rest of the Company would show up quickly if we were in over our heads. Then, as per Army procedure, I yelled "Surrender, put down your weapons," in Vietnamese, knowing they would never give us the same courtesy.

All of a sudden one VC came running around the side of the hooch with his AK-47 blazing. All five of us opened up on him and the hooches not knowing what we were dealing with but they weren't friendlies. I can't imagine what the VC was thinking, to take us on? Better to fire first and ask questions later, I guess?

We emptied our first mag, loaded another, and slowly started advancing on what was left. I saw one of them run off towards a hill behind the hooches and then he went down face first. The fire fight lasted about five minutes.

I checked that everyone was OK, which they were, and then we checked to see what we had run into. Good thing there weren't thirty of 'em.

Wilson came up to me and said, "Sarge, there's an officer, I think, he's hit. Behind the hooch, part way up the hill," motioning toward the biggest of the three. "It looks like he took a round in the back when he was trying to run away. He's conscious but it looks pretty bad from where it went in."

"Send someone back for the medic," I said as I started moving where he pointed. I knew to be careful to not give the man a chance at trying to take me with him to get even. You never know.

I found him laying on his front, arms extended over his head. He was an officer I figured because he had a 9mm side arm pistol which was always a give away. He was in pain, scared, and starting to go into shock. He wasn't going anywhere in his condition. I reached down and took his pistol.

"What's your name?" I asked in Vietnamese.

"Go home, Americans, Go home, Americans" he said in broken English.

"Your English is pretty good." I responded surprised.

I asked, "Where did you learn English? Yea, I was just thinkin' I'd like to go home. I don't want to be here. You know, your English

Pitfalls, Risks, and Dungeons

is a lot better than my Vietnamese."

Well, if he could talk his lungs were still intact and he wasn't sucking blood. That was a good sign for him. The bullet must have just missed the lower part of his lung. He was in critical condition but he might make it if we medevac him out quick enough. It's hard to survive a body hit from 5.56mm round.

I told him, "I called a medic for you," but he just glared at me.

Wilson came back over to me and said, "Sarge, it looks like he had one of our PRC-25 radios in the hooch. I checked and it was even tuned to our frequency."

"Smart and resourceful," I said, "But not smart enough that we didn't find him first. Let's find the one that ran away and then we can figure out what to do with this one."

We searched around and couldn't find the runaway. We concluded that he was hiding in a tunnel. It was the only place left.

"God dammit. That guy thinks he's going to escape because we're too afraid to go in after him." I said as I started taking my bandoleer off. This one isn't getting off that easy. I'm going in after him."

"Sarge, we need you more than him. Let's think this through."

"I'm cool, I'll be alright." I said.

I crouched down and went into the tunnel in the hill with my flashlight. About 50 feet in I found him. He was scared because he thought I was going to kill him. I said, "I got you now, get your ass out of here," as I grabbed him by the collar and dragged him out.

Later I realized that going into that tunnel was probably not the smartest thing for me to do, but then Charlie probably knew that if he killed me then he would be as good as dead too. Turned out he was a lieutenant. A smart lieutenant that wanted to live more than he wanted to die. He had a grenade.

When I pulled him out into the light and we took a look at him Wilson said, "Sarge it looks like we got ourselves two officers today."

Epilogue

There were three KIA's and three captured including the lieu-

240

tenant and captain who was critically injured but survived. The Captain, who it turned out, was the Vietcong Deputy Province Commander of Quang Tin Province, had been taking part in a briefing with other VC officers in a small hooch area southeast of Tam Ky when they were surprised by 2nd squad.

Several days later it was learned that the VC Captain's name was Le Noi, and that he had set up an ambush with 40 of his men for Sergeant Braithwaite's company on the other side of the rice paddies. Obviously, Captain Noi never expected the Americans to find or get so close to his command post.

Shortly after he was shot, Captain Noi, was medevaced to a field hospital where they saved his life. Five days after the fire fight, Captain Noi happened to meet Sergeant Braithwaite's Company Commander, Captain Spilberg in the hospital when Captain Spilberg was visiting some of his wounded. Captain Noi commended the Commander, from Lexington, Kentucky. Captain Noi shook his hand and said, "You have a well disciplined, well coordinated unit, otherwise, you never would have captured me."

Captain Noi ranked second in command over an area in Military Region One, which stretched east from the South China Sea to the Laotian border and spanned 30 miles in width from North to South.

Just as 2nd squad thought they would be able to take it easy because they didn't have to be on point, if they had been taking it easy their whole company would have walked into a deadly ambush and many of them would have been killed. Instead, because of Wilson and Moose's extra effort, they saved their lives as well as the lives of many men in their company and their families are very thankful.

The extra effort to go a little farther out on recon not only saved the lives of American soldiers, but it disrupted part of the NVA regional command by capturing the captain and the lieutenant.

The cordial meeting between officers shows the senselessness of all the fighting; how governments waste our lives. The Captains didn't have any grudge against each other, it was just the governments who started the fighting and had the grudges.

Pitfalls, Risks, and Dungeons

Later in his tour of duty in Vietnam, on the afternoon of 27 March 1971, Sergeant Braithwaite's Company was helicoptered out of a Fire Support Base, known as FSB Mary Ann, as part of the regular rotation of troops. Captain Spilberg had been promoted and was part of the base command.

That night Mary Ann was overrun by Vietcong sappers who, under the cover of dark and fog, infiltrated the camp carrying explosives and other satchel charges. The results were disastrous: 30 GI's killed and 82 wounded out of 231 men. The only way the attack could be stopped was by calling in American artillery from a neighboring FSB on the perimeter of their own camp.

Captain Spilberg survived and later remarked that the reaction by visitors the next day was, "They were in a state of shock. The had just walked into Auschwitz."

http://www.arlingtoncemetery.net/psspilberg.htm

Sergeant Braithwaite, along with the other men in his platoon and company, risked his life in many very dangerous missions and survived. Many did not.

"These troops had faith in nothing much, least of all in men like Johnson and Nixon, [but still] served their country a lot better than it served them." Author, Geoffrey Perret. As described by author Al Hemingway, (2011) VFW, Sixty Minutes of Terror At Mary Ann.

Former Sargent Braithwaite is one to never complain about anything. It's people like him that should be running our governments but like with all of us, "The Man" teaches us to believe that we are not qualified or smart enough.

So, Marty stays quiet, to himself, and appreciates what he does have.

He wakes up every morning with his memories and knowing that he got another freebie.

Contact sports and football

I don't care what anybody says, these are dangerous activities—especially football. I just don't see any sense in why the players, especially young adults, would want to subject themselves to the risk of such severe injuries and why the schools, that are supposedly so concerned about student health and safety, let these hazardous sports activities continue.

While on a college campus tour recently, I met a healthy senior male who's left arm was immobilized in a sling. When asked about what happened, he said that he was playing high school football when he sprained his shoulder by hitting another player that was a lot larger than him. It was his first year playing football. I'm sure it was a painful and expensive lesson to learn. I think he was starting to reconcile that the experience probably wasn't worth it.

A few days later I was watching some of the football players at my local high school walk by me as they were returning to the locker room after practice on the field. I noticed that one player had his arm in a cast and another had his left arm tightly wrapped to his body, completely immobilized. It was a serious injury because his arm wasn't even in a sling. Why?

If you don't appreciate your body and all its functions now, go hang out at the waiting room of a hospital emergency room to get a good dose of everything that comes in. It isn't a pretty picture and you don't want to join the list of waiting injured.

There is enough trouble coming your way without even looking for it. I don't see any reason to go looking for more.

Credit cards

Don't sign up for the credit cards you receive in the mail.

When you do have a credit card, don't run up the balance.

Not being able to pay off the balance will quickly destroy you by destroying your credit score so you won't be able to borrow money when you need it. If you can't pay for something now you probably won't be able to pay for it in thirty days.

Don't get played by the credit card companies and have to pay up to twenty-four percent interest. Realize that the credit card companies are nothing more than legalized loan sharks and they will get

Pitfalls, Risks, and Dungeons

their pound of flesh.

While in Atlanta at a propane convention in April 2019, I happened to have a conversation with Madison, a 22 year-old from Roopville, Georgia who was helping coordinate charter buses for the event.

I was telling Madison about my writing of this handbook for teens and she said that she thought it was a good idea and that she was being careful with her future as she was transitioning from the crazy partying teen to the more responsible adult.

Madison explained, "But I'm really worried about how my best friend is destroying her future by not paying off the balance on a credit card she received in the mail. She activated it and ran it up its limit. I keep telling her to pay it off and now she says she needs the money she is making to live on.

"I keep telling her that she is going to ruin her credit score because the credit card company is going to report her delinquent payments to the credit bureaus which will make her credit history look bad and her look bad also, but she won't listen to me. And she isn't even paying the minimum amount.

"We have been best friends for 20 years and it is killing me that she is destroying her credit score and that she doesn't have the financial discipline to pay if off. I keep telling her that she needs to have discipline and cut back on her expenses and stop eating out and treating herself. I can't believe how gullible she was to accept that credit card in the first place, but that is how the bank preyed on her. She should have thrown it in the trash.

"It isn't right in how they will think nothing of setting us up so they can milk our money and destroy our credit at the same time. Either she can't hear me or she doesn't have the wherewithal to break free from the grip it has on her. It wasn't like she needed the money. It was just the temptation the card provided.

"All this trouble from a $300-400 credit limit. If you add my story in your book then I can tell her, *See, what I am saying is important.*

Delinquents

People that your parents would not condone your associating with are known as trouble—or delinquents.

Your mother and father have a lot more experience in judging people and their character than you so if they are not comfortable with who you are hanging out with, listen to them because you are probably going down the wrong road in the relationship and don't just try to hide it from them. Get out from their spell, even if you are temporarily entertained. You can do better.

Listen to your parents and move on so you don't have to pay a big price for your stubbornness later.

Dopamine - Part I

You have your own personal pharmacy in your body and one of the most dangerous drugs your personal pharmacist dispenses is dopamine. The best part is that you don't need a prescription from a doctor to get it. The worst part is that it is very easy to get addicted to it and it can cause your self destruction.

Most addictions are related to this chemical release in your body. Knowing how and being able to control it is critical to your well being and is a factor in determining your future success.

Drug Dealers

AKA "The scum of the earth." They destroy people and whole families. Do not associate with them. They are only out to use you so they can support their own addiction or know enough not to use what they peddle in. They are sinister and will die an early and tortuous death, are friends with the devil, and will rot in hell for eternity.

Drugs on campus

Drugs are not the answer to any problems. All they do is make things worse for you and better for the dealer. Look at the true stories—around you and online.

Pitfalls, Risks, and Dungeons

Illegal drugs

Always maintain control of your body and mind.

A freshman student fell or jumped from a window at George Mason University on a beautiful Saturday afternoon in the fall of 2017 and died. On campuses around the country, Deans of Students devote countless hours to fighting this curse.

His fraternity brother was convicted of selling him the drugs that led to his hallucinations and death and given a three year jail sentence. During the investigation it was learned that one of the selling points for joining the fraternity was because it was maintaining a database of tests for many classes which is against school policies. There are a lot of very bad influences on college campus so be careful that you don't get sucked into a bad scene.

Be high on life instead of drugs.

I was never interested in smoking marijuana because it seemed like the risks outweighed the benefits and my thinking was that if my mind didn't know what it was than it wouldn't be able to crave it. You can think the same way too. Please don't even try it.

**Stand up for yourself and avoid
anything that alters your clear thinking.**

I was always under the impression that if someone smoked pot or took drugs that they would have the will power to stop until about five years ago when I had a conversation with a former employee who worked for me part-time when he attended George Mason University in 1988. He explained that he had been addicted to pain killers for over ten years and it had destroyed all his relationships and his life. He explained what it is like to be addicted and how once you are exposed you have a gremlin that is always with you telling you it is OK to keep taking the drugs. He described how its impossible to shake the gremlin and how it takes over your life. He went through rehab in California and now he is a successful clean intake manager at the same facility.

He explained that part of the problem with drug use is that once you use them, the drugs stay in your system for a while and that is what the gremlin feeds off of.

Why do you think they call it dope?

You don't think it makes you smarter, do you?

Digital drugs

Digital distractions are destroying your brain.

See other sections on dopamine.

Ear buds

Do not use anything in your ears when you are outside and especially if you are running or walking along a road. You need to be able to hear warnings or approaching vehicles or bicycles. They are not good for your hearing either and you may pay the price later in life. If you use them a lot, you might want to start practicing the phrase, "What did you say?" or, "Excuse me, I'm picking up a lot of background noise." (Do I need clarification here?)

Recently, a hiker in Colorado survived a cougar attack because he forgot his ear buds that day and heard the stealthy cougar's paws rustling pine needles 10 feet behind him.

And, recently it was announced that pedestrian deaths are at a 30-year high. Use your ears and hear what is around you.

Falling down

You don't have to fall down 25 times to learn that you need to modify your behavior or process. You can learn it the first time if you think it through and learn from your mistakes. Don't be stubborn. Use your critical thinking skills to move ahead.

Pitfalls, Risks, and Dungeons

Gaming

Play video games after you have developed your mind to its fullest potential which hasn't happened yet. Once your mind is more fully developed, you might be surprised to find that the games are not as interesting or entertaining as they were before.

The monotony of games—or even the challenges scripted into the next level—are manipulators of boredom and time. Go to the gym. You'll feel, look, and act better. Maybe even meet your future spouse or somebody that knows them.

Gay and Lesbian Culture

As a young adult you are being exposed to an unprecedented explosive expansion of the homosexual community. This expansion is a new development in society and you need to be very wary of it to avoid getting sucked in at the time when you are most vulnerable.

A big shift has occurred in this alternative lifestyle for your generation causing me to ask, what caused the sudden change? Why are so many young adults from your generation questioning their sexual identity now, compared with the past from the beginning of time? Has this change occurred because so many more of your peers are having problems establishing relationships with members of the opposite sex? Is there a difficulty in communication between the sexes that is causing individuals to develop closer relationships with those of a similar sex as a safe haven in their emotional development?

To me, it appears that what has been known as traditional, in-person adolescent interactions between the sexes has been dramatically modified by the use of cell phones and the Internet such that in-person relationship building has become difficult and scary. Now, compared with the pre-cell phone era, it appears that it is very difficult to know who you can and cannot trust and what everyone might say about you, and whether something is true or not. Unfortunately, all of us, regardless of age, are most vulnerable to possible criticism and retaliation when trying to talk with members of the opposite sex. It's part of being human.

Teens, in particular, are most at risk from this phenomena because adolescence is the time where these heterosexual relationship skills are developed and practiced.

The advent of mass technology has magnified the threat of being bullied, criticized, and embarrassed so the best way to protect oneself is to not expose oneself and instead, seek refuge and safe haven with those of the same sex. This, in turn, leads to stifled development of interpersonal skills with the opposite sex which leads to the vulnerability of being lured into the gay and lesbian culture. A culture where, once you cross the line, you can't go back.

I believe that technology is the reason for this explosive growth of gay and lesbian relationships because technology has caused an indirect breakdown in adolescent heterosexual communication and interactions. Now, the boys are really afraid of the girls and the girls are really afraid of the boys. The homosexual lifestyle is further twisting minds to promote and take advantage of these fears.

Please be very careful with whom you associate.

Gremlins

Everyone has a Gremlin. It is the monster that sits on your shoulder who tells you it is OK to do things that you know you shouldn't do. Gremlins feed off of the dopamine your body creates when you are gaming so you want to keep gaming or from the high you get drinking alcohol or taking drugs. The more you feed the Gremlin with the food it likes, the bigger it gets and eventually it will beat up your Guardian Angel.

Protect your Guardian Angels by listening to them and by not giving the Gremlin food to eat. We all need our Guardian Angel(s).

Starve the Gremlin.

Hazards

Always be on the lookout and able to identify and avoid hazards as much as possible. Realize that even walking on the sidewalk

Pitfalls, Risks, and Dungeons

is a hazard because a car could jump over the curb and crush you or you may accidentally step into the street and get hit by a car. Some years ago, near our house, a car ran into the bus shelter and the people who were just sitting there waiting for the bus to arrive.

It is one thing to look, it is another thing to see. Don't just look, make sure you see the hazards and what might be coming your way.

Bike riding is a hazard and you need to be very careful. One father in the neighborhood was biking with friends and he was hit by a car an almost died. Another father was biking in an adjacent town and he didn't stop before he rode from the sidewalk into the street and he was killed by a truck making a turn at the intersection at the exact time he entered it. He was married with two daughters.

You always need to be thinking and be careful of what you are doing. Think about the risks associated with the activity ahead of time and be sensitive to any other variables that could occur.

Stop and just watch what you see at an intersection or on a road. Watch how people drive. Watch what people do and how they do and don't pay attention. See what you can learn from their behaviors and actions.

Sit and "people watch" and you can learn a lot about human behavior.

Infatuation

You have to be very careful with becoming infatuated with someone and remember there are lots of people out there. Observe closely how that person acts towards others. Take your time collecting observations.

Keep looking, you'll get over it.

Injuries

There are physical and emotional injuries and both of them hurt a lot and some can last for the rest of your life. You always have to be careful of what situations you are putting yourself in by thinking them through.

You can be injured playing sports or in relationships and all of them will take your time and energy and possibly your parents time and money to repair, so think through the risks.

Personal relationship injuries may be more challenging because you can't wear a cast on or stitch up your heart. Be kind to yourself and avoid abuse in all forms.

Interpretations

Realize that everything is subject to interpretation and that news reporting can slant or distort a story by leaving out certain facts. If an incident has 20 facts but only seven are reported, you don't get the whole picture.

Language - appropriate

It is not a good idea to start speaking and acting like the rap lyrics you are listening to. Doing so will cause you to provide the wrong impression of who you are or who you wrongly aspire to be. Keep your language clean.

Really, it is not a good idea to use the four letter words or substitutes for them such as "frickin" as part of your normal speech. They are going to slip out sometime when you want to make a good impression.

Keep you language appropriate. Don't embarrass yourself. You don't want to be perceived as uncouth.

Laziness

Lazy will trump your smarts every day—and usually on a day that counts.

Perezoso means lazy in Spanish
Pigro means lazy in Italian.
Paresseux means lazy in French

Lazy is a contagious disease throughout the world.
Wash your hands often so you don't catch it.

Pitfalls, Risks, and Dungeons

Don't think you are so smart that you can be lazy.
Lying
Don't lie to yourself, parents or anybody. If you can't say the truth then don't say anything at all. You don't want a reputation for lying because others will lose trust in you, and once you lose that you don't have much left.

Manners
Use them or lose them.

Mistakes
You are going to make mistakes and you are going to make a lot of them, but if you don't take risks and try, you are not going to get anywhere. The most important thing other than trying to avoid mistakes is to try and learn from your mistakes so you don't repeat them.

The best way to learn from your mistakes is to be able to create documentation as to what you were thinking at the time you made the decision listing all the pros and cons that you are considering. I have taught myself that when I am faced with a complex problem it is best to write out my thoughts on the problem and my options so I can try and organize and refine my ideas without struggling to keep everything in my head. This also helps me to remember my thoughts and prioritize them and once I make a decision the written narrative provides me with a solid basis for future review. Then I can examine my thought process and method I chose for solving the problem.

Writing things down also helps to quantify the risks relative to the gain. You can see the choices in black and white which often works like a balancing scale in decision making.

Motorcycles
These two—wheeled, engine—driven machines are clearly powerful and a great source for creating organ donors, according to doctors. Recently, a local hospital encouraged a heart—organ wait—listed 50-year-old by telling him the donor region was now expanded

to a state with no helmet laws. Obviously, the number of organ do-nors was expected to increase, sadly.

Pornography

There are a lot of detrimental consequences from watching porn and it will not teach you anything about healthy sex or healthy living. If anything, it will have a detrimental affect and cause disastrous consequences on your current and future relationships. It can even destroy your marriage and/or indirectly you.

Porn dehumanizes intimacy and the need to feel desired.

Dopamine is at work here, just like with gaming, and there is discussion that engaging with porn can cause your brain to become rewired in unhealthy ways, which is especially detrimental during this stage when it is still developing.

Recently I was discussing this handbook with a female friend of mine who thought this subject should be mentioned because she had first hand experience with how the use of pornography by her former spouse destroyed her marriage. I wasn't sure how to include it but her perspective helped me to put the hazards associated with pornography into context.

She saw and experienced the emotional affects of what happens when a spouse becomes addicted to it and she expressed her concern that so many young adults are not able or prepared to protect themselves from this new indiscriminate hazard. She is fearful for them because she knows it can lead to addiction and then cause brains to spiral down into an emotional wasteland.

She said, "Engaging with pornography will make you feel miserable and it will impede your ability to enjoy the many opportunities you have for emotional connections and relationships. It will change your perspective of what it really means to be human, what relationships are really about, and how to get in touch with others all of which are important aspects in having a better understanding of your friends as well as yourself.

"Pornography depicts the horrible abuse of others and you should understand it for what it really is, instead of what it appears to

Pitfalls, Risks, and Dungeons

be. Tell your readers that they need to protect themselves so it doesn't have the chance to rewire their brains and cause them to think and act in ways that are not who they really are or who they want to be."

I know from personal experience that being able to understand who you are as you are growing up is difficult enough to do without today's bad influences. Bad influences that will make it even harder to establish meaningful relationships than when I was growing up.

A significant personal story to try and illustrate this point occurred to me in the summer of 1972 when I was 13 years old. It was a stage in my life when, as all of us go through, I was still trying to sort out my attributes and characteristics about who I was.

What were my internal principles, values, character, personality, integrity and other traits as well as how did I conduct myself towards others? Who was I relative to the way my peers, parents, family, TV and society were influencing me to act and behave with all its external influences? How was I supposed to act and behave and what I was supposed to believe about myself and others?

I am embarrassed to say that I even almost most got suspended from junior high school for fighting because I was hanging out with the wrong crowd. These are very hard developmental times for each of us and they can last until our late teens to mid-twenties.

Getting back to the story, it was a summer right out of the movies for me because I was fortunate to met a girl named Laura, who was from Florida. Laura was visiting her Aunt in my neighborhood for a month during the summer and I really liked her. She had a very friendly personality and she was really cute. I met her because one of my best friends at the time, John, was her cousin.

We hung out together for a month and eventually for some reason I guess I began to feel possessive of her. I was very young and naive. She was my first close girl friend as a teen. I guess you can call it teen or puppy love and it must have hit me like a brick. I remember thinking, "Wow, if this is what being a teen is about then life can't get any better."

Then, the day before she was going to leave she went to see a movie and I wasn't included so I felt snubbed and I got mad at her just before she left to go back home. She said it wasn't anything intentional and that they just forgot to include me but I was mad at her just the same. Boy, was I stupid.

I never went to say goodbye to her to prove my point, whatever it was, but then I missed her a lot after she left and I did a lot of soul searching to try and understand why I acted the way that I did? Why did I give her such a hard time and make her feel bad?

It took me a week to realize that I was only acting the way I did because I thought that was the way I was supposed to act as dictated by society and the influences I was being exposed to at the time. As I reflected on the summer relationship and the breakup I realized that I had acted very juvenile and that my actions did not represent who I really was or who I wanted to be.

I felt bad that I had acted so immaturely and realized that my actions were not representative of my real character. I wrote Laura a letter of apology and we wrote letters to each other a few times and I think I even talked to her on the phone once a few months later

I said I was sorry in that I felt that I had ruined what had been a fun summer relationship and she forgave me. I was so embarrassed by how I acted that I think I even called her Aunt and apologized for my conduct also. Unfortunately, I never saw or talked to Laura again.

Like I eventually figured out the hard way, you have to be able to develop an awareness of how society impacts your life and your thoughts. It was hard for me in 1972 without all the noise from technology then. Today it is so much harder for you.

Take extra care in being able to understand how outside influences can and will cause you to make similar mistakes in how you define your personality and your relationships like I did in my mine.

Relationships are the neatest part of being alive and they are very hard to develop and they are very fragile. They were complicated before with just written letters and telephones, now they are so much more so. Feel fortunate and cherish them when you have great ones and always remember to be nice to each other no matter what.

Pitfalls, Risks, and Dungeons

**It is very hard to learn how to separate what you think
you are supposed to feel from what is really inside you,
but that is part of growing up.**

You will get it, hopefully sooner than later.

Take charge of yourself and recognize dopamine for the powerful drug it is so it doesn't destroy you and the beautiful world that surrounds you and all the fun and mutually enjoyable relationships that are waiting to engage with the responsible and mature you.

Rebelling

Rebel in ways other than dying your hair, piercing, tattoos, fighting, and vaping.

**Try rebelling by becoming extra smart
so you can earn more money than everyone else.**

That will show them in a more constructive way that they shouldn't mess with you because you have what it takes.

Scholarships - academic

A fancy name for discounts to the sticker price, scholarships are often free money. There are many varieties and many opportunities. Explore them. There's one for you. Ask your admissions officer for help.

Selfies

Creating continuous streams of selfies, which are just pictures of yourself in different environments, is a very unhealthy habit to get into. And you should be very concerned if you feel the need to alter the photos to improve your idealized self image and attributes.

Narcissism is a disorder, the term of which originated from Greek mythology, where the young Narcissus fell in love with his own image reflected in a pool of water.

In extreme circumstances, many people are being injured and even dying from falls as they try to take the perfect selfie. Selfies are not worth the physical or emotional risk they pose. Relax and just enjoy the experience and the view instead of trying to become part of it.

Don't value yourself, others, or your experiences based on the response from your social network. You don't have to prove anything to anybody except yourself. Your life and your feelings should not be about them and what they think. Your life should be about you and what you think. What you think is right for you. It's not easy to figure out, but work at it slowly.

Relax and don't worry about trying to get validation from others that you are special by seeking attention and admiration.

You can find your inner peace if you look inward instead of outward. Your inner peace is there, its just getting drowned by all the static that surrounds you.

Once you can tune out the static
you will be able to hear the peace.

Sex

This biological activity is fun but very risky and surely a choice with lots of potential for bad consequences until you have completed the prior step of commitments, not to mention the risks associated with sexually transmitted diseases which are really nasty and dangerous.

Guys, keep in mind that you will be presumed to be guilty until proven innocent. It is more dangerous than ever to be a male. Be responsible. Remember *The Golden Rule*.

Don't allow yourself to be pressured or tempted into having sex. If that is what someone is after, then take it as an indicator that you are probably not as compatible as you think because they are not as interested in your person. They are interested in your body or they could be using the allure of sex to help them manipulate and control

Pitfalls, Risks, and Dungeons

your mind. Avoid confusing lust for love.

Slacker

Be careful that Mr. Strickland from the movie *Back to the Future* doesn't label you as a "slacker."

Sports

Another big change since I was in school is the huge emphasis by parents and schools on the importance of sports which creates physical risks of injury and mental risks for drug addiction once injured. Sports also provide a distraction from what is supposed to be your primary objective which is your education.

Exercising your brain is more important than injuring your body. It is hard to have the energy to exercise your brain when you body is exhausted from sports. Sport activity is not a good excuse for poor grades. Scholar-athletes are less common in team sports. Think of why that might be the case?

Your parents may have been sucked into promoting your pursuit of sports excellence under the guise or auspices that the investment of time and money will be rewarded with a fulfilling college scholarship at some prestigious school when in the end you would probably be better served using your time and energy to condition and train your mind instead of your body. And there is always the possibility of getting an academic scholarship instead of an athletic scholarship.

Another option is to save all the money your family will spend on travel sports or cheer competitions by putting what you would have spent it into a 529 college savings plan. The savings plan will act as your own private scholarship, you won't get hurt, and you can have more control of which school you decide to attend.

I ran cross country for three years in high school and it was a lot of fun. My right knee would bother me sometimes when I ran and recently the damage finally caught up with me and my knee needed arthroscopic surgery to cut away tears on my meniscus which is the pad in the knee between the two leg bones. It was a relatively simple procedure for the times, but now I have to be very careful with how I use my knee so I don't destroy what is left and end up with bone-on-bone pain and then need a knee replacement.

You might be told that you will fully recover from an injury, but then sometime in the future it can cause pain again such as arthritis or other discomfort. You may have to live with the pain every day for the rest of your life or that part of your body might not be as functional as it was before the injury. Facial scars are another risk and they don't look good. My middle son was too aggressive in a basketball game against the wrong person and ended up with 16 stitches under his eye and the medical bill cost me thousands of dollars.

Remember, it is just a game.

I think that the culture of sports has grown because of the proliferation of sports programming and the exorbitant salaries that the players get paid but very few people attain that level of success. Look at the statistics.

If you want to play a professional sport try building a company and making a lot of money so you can buy your own team and then you can play yourself if it is still that important.

Don't beat up your body; it's the only one that you have and you might be faced with future consequences and discomfort from repetitive use or an injury.

In my high school, Dusty was well liked, friendly to everyone, and he stood 6'3". He was our school's track star in the hurdles. Dusty was so fast that he even received a full scholarship to Idaho State University.

In April of 2019, Dusty had his first knee replacement and the second knee will be replaced once he recovers from the first.

In April 2019, I saw Harold who I have known for many years because he used to sell me propane when he worked for a major oil company. At 80-years-old, when I said hello and asked him how he was because I had not talked with him in about 10 years he winced a little and said, "Not too good. My lower back is really bothering me and I might need surgery."

I asked him inquisitively, "Did you play sports in school?"

"Yes, I was a lineman," he said and after a pause, "there was

Pitfalls, Risks, and Dungeons

a game where while I had someone laying on the back of my legs I was hit from the front bending me back and over. I was out for a few games."

I think Harold now regrets playing football.

Another hazard to watch out for are the high school coaches that will try to recruit you and even your eighth grade siblings for their sport. One of the football coaches from the high school tried to entice my very muscular, 6-foot, 185-pound son to tryout for the Freshman football team. My wife was willing to give in a little and let him work out in the weight room because he was so interested in playing.

She agreed to sign the permission form so he could use the high school weight room periodically under the supposed supervision of a coach or other physical education teacher.

Then we started to notice how, what had always been a very friendly and pleasant disposition, started to change towards us. I suggested to Kathleen that we visit the weight room to see what was going on.

Kathleen and I were both surprised, shocked might be a better word, at the size of the weight room compared to the very small one we were familiar with from when we were in school. The music was blaring so loud you couldn't even have a conversation. The supposed "adult supervisor" was lifting weights himself and the lack of personal supervision explained why our son had created stretch lines across his lower back from over exerting himself.

John was very disappointed that I would not sign the form for him to play football but it wasn't long thereafter he stopped going to the weight room that his friendly, pleasant and happy disposition returned.

It all worked out for the best.

During this period I spent a lot of time reflecting on what seemed to have changed in sports since I was in school. I started to realize, whether it was or wasn't true when I was in school, that the priorities of the coaches had possibly shifted from what I thought was supposed to be participating in athletics for personal development to winning games at all costs. From various conversations I started to put together the sense that some coaches have an ulterior objective of having an exemplary win/loss record so they can have the credentials to advance to a more prestigious and/or competitive team at a more prestigious school.

I concluded that school sports was being promoted as a meaningful growth and developmental activity for the players but the reality had become helping the coach get promoted to a more prestigious team.

Playing wasn't about helping my child, it was about using him to help advance the coach.

One big problem with sports is that once you've conditioned your body you don't want to stop the activity because you lose your conditioning so you have to keep going and going. And if you are injured you will have to reduce your regimen and after a while you might just be getting bored with looking at the bottom of the pool or running in circles, literally and figuratively.

Keep asking yourself if the commitment is worth it or if you should or would like to be doing something else and whether continued participation is your or your parent's passion.

Exercise, conditioning, and physical fitness in general is important for all of us, but they need to be pursued in moderation.

You might think that your body is indestructible and resilient but it isn't and sooner or later you will pay the price for its overuse.

Smoking/Alcohol/Drugs

When my first child was a sophomore in high school, I had a conversation with Lisa, the school resource officer, to try and understand how and why today's high school experience was different than it was for me. She explained that cell phones were having a detrimental effect on attitude, language, and behaviors and that students were moving more quickly to alcohol, marijuana, and hard drugs because they had lost the smoking of cigarettes as their means of

Pitfalls, Risks, and Dungeons

rebelling and expressing their independence. I thought her analysis was very profound.

I remember trying to prove that I could run with the crowd by buying a few packs of cigarettes from 7-11 when I was in the 8th grade. It wasn't easy, but sixteen was the legal age then and if you were tall enough and acted like you were of age you could get away with it. Back then, cigarettes were even available in unattended vending machines.

I think I bought a total of two packs and after experimenting with them I made my own decision that it wasn't for me. I had long hair and a jean jacket and that was enough for me to be cool. I didn't need cigarettes also.

Once I realized it, I was much more comfortable being myself instead of trying to be somebody I wasn't, but it takes a while to figure it all out. Also, I could easily classify the kids that were smoking into the group that didn't seem like they were going very far in life either. It helped that I didn't like the cigarettes and the smoke made me smell funny. I could see that it was a yucky habit I was best to avoid.

A lot of students smoked cigarettes when I was in high school and many of those started in junior high. Very few students smoked marijuana or drank beer relative to today and now it seems that vaping is starting to take the place of cigarettes but it isn't the same kind rebellion and bonding that occurred with cigarettes forty years ago. And, where do kids get the money for these expensive habits?

Yes, kids were buying beer and getting drunk on liquor they took from their home then, just like they do today, but from the stories my children are telling me, I think the problem is much worse today.

More importantly, the use of marijuana and hard drugs seems to be much more prevalent now than when I was in high school. And I was in high school at the time of the Vietnam War with all the talk of hippies, dope, LSD and the new culture of drugs, but the drug and drinking problem then was no where near as ubiquitous as it has become today.

I get the sense that these risky behaviors are two to three times worse now than when I was in school and the need to have police officers at all high schools supports my premise that today's students are more disrespectful and harder to control than my classmates. Today, in extreme cases, the threat of guns even comes into the equation. In my time it was very rare that a police cruiser was seen parked at the front of the school.

Stress

Stress is a barrier to good health. A lot of stress comes from paying attention to and thinking about social media. What is more important, to have good grades, to look like you have a lot of friends, or to be carrying on many simultaneous and/or continuous digital conversations?

Your parents did not have social media stress in their lives so they can't necessarily help you through it, but it is not required and you can turn if off. None of it matters anyway, and you just need to have confidence in yourself.

In the end confidence is all that counts. Of course, how you develop and gain that confidence is the quandary you face.

In-person friends are an investment of effort and time, but they are real.

Tattoos

Don't do it. You don't need to prove anything to anybody and it will probably become an embarrassment later in life and work against your advancement.

Tattoos are a visible sign that you are rebellious in nature because that is why you went to get one in the first place, to rebel, and that might not be something you want to publicize because you might become more mellow as you get older. Also they all blur with age and sometimes they can lead to an infection. Your skin does not need ink in it.

Pitfalls, Risks, and Dungeons

Texting

You are committing virtual suicide if you are driving a car at the same time you add another distraction of trying to read and/or send a text. Your car could easily kill you or someone else in an instant. Be disciplined. Use the Force and resist the Dark Side.

Only text after you have pulled the car off the road in a safe place to park, stopped moving, put it in park, and removed the keys. If you don't remove the keys then technically you are still in control of the vehicle and could be cited by a police officer for texting while driving.

Don't use texting as a substitute for a conversation. You and your relationship will be better served by having a conversation with speech versus digitally. Texting me makes me think that you really don't want to talk to me, which can be detrimental to our relationship.

Don't appear or act like you are so busy that people are afraid to call and talk with you. Be patient and nice to everyone. Have conversations with them and keep relationships at the top of your list.

Traffic

Washington, D.C., is a region full of traffic. I tell my children that a lot of people must enjoy sitting in it because they do it for many hours each day. Other people ask how we can live here with all the traffic?

I explain that we adjust our day and only go certain places certain times of the day and if necessary I would take a small house closer to my job than a larger house that requires me to waste a lot of time and energy. Small houses in convenient areas work great.

Traffic lights

Be careful as you approach them.

Always approach controlled intersections as if the light is going to turn yellow just as you get there. Let your car decelerate as you approach the light. Watch for surprises if there is a crosswalk with a countdown timer displayed for pedestrians, it may give you an indication of when the light is about to turn yellow.

When stopped at a red light and you are going to be the first to enter the intersection when the light turns green, pause and look to the left first, and then to the right as you enter, to make sure somebody isn't running the red light. It is extremely dangerous as excessive speed is usually involved by those who ignore changing lights or are in a hurry. If you are at the front of two lanes of stopped traffic that is going to enter an intersection on the green light, take your time and let the other person enter it first a little ahead of you.

Traffic tickets

Don't disregard paying traffic or parking tickets. It is best to avoid getting them in the first place but if you get one be sure the jurisdiction receives the money before it is due to avoid a doubling of the cost or even an eventual suspended license which could lead to an unexpected arrest during a traffic stop.

Smart phones

This necessary evil is a dangerous device that is destroying your generation's potential for achievement. Your generation is going to be known as the lost generation—lost in your cell phones.

Do you sense that your attention—span shortens when you have your phone handy?

Swiping

Stop looking for your life in your phone. It doesn't live in there.
You have to break the spell yourself.
You are the only one that can do it.

Chapter five

Coming of Age

**Understanding the real world
and how it does or does not work and why.**

There are a lot of things in the world that we are not taught in school or ever discussed and many that most people probably haven't thought about or even know. These are the things that you learn from experience.

This section also includes just general advice and information that is important to know and think about but it doesn't have a good fit in any of the other sections.

Topics listed alphabetically

Advice

Do not automatically believe what older people tell you, me included. As young people we are conditioned to believe what older people say as correct even if it doesn't seem logical. We will usually defer to them because they have more experience, but this can be a mistake. Even with this handbook, the goal is to raise questions and to help you think.

Take what you are told into consideration but it is up to you to use your problem solving skills, ask questions, exercise your brain, and think.

A big part of growing up is having the education, experience, maturity and critical thinking skills so you can trust your judgment and not be automatically accepting what others tell you and being misled or played out of something. You need to be able to learn how to solve problems and then take responsibility for your decisions and not blame someone else if it doesn't work out like you hoped or expected.

You can improve the success rate of your decisions if you write them down with a justification, the important decisions as well as the not important decisions. This will allow you the opportunity to review the basis for your decisions later and see what you got right and what you might have missed.

Critical thinking skills are always challenging but applying a kind of review process will help you to make better decisions in the future. (I have mentioned this process before.) It takes time and effort but it will help in the long run: kind of an ongoing self-improvement program.

I had many incidents where I made mistakes and got played. My first big one occurred when I was 24 years old at my fledging used car rental enterprise.

I had a new employee named Gary who was a good employee and kind of kept to himself. Gary enjoyed working on his own and was very meticulous in how he cleaned the rental cars when they were returned and tried to pay attention to all the cosmetic and mechanical details that they might need. He was a detail guy but I didn't have enough experience to appreciate his talent. He even knew how to buff the paint, without burning it, as a way to rejuvenate the older cars so they were more presentable and looked better.

He was a pleasure to work with in that he didn't waste time, was industrious, and seemed to be comfortable with his work even though his silence seemed a little odd. It was hard to tell what he was

Coming of Age

thinking.

He was dependable as he went over the cars in one bay of a two-bay garage.

Lonnie Mountcastle was the car mechanic who repaired and maintained the cars in the adjoining bay with a car lift. Lonnie liked to talk. Lonnie had been my mechanic for about two years. He got the job done, but it took supervision to keep him on task.

Lonnie was a short redneck straight out of the 1950's with greasy jet black hair that was combed back. He stood about 5'4" and always wore black boots. He drove a blue 1968 2-door Chevy Chevelle with a four-speed on the floor.

Lonnie knew enough about car mechanics to get by. He was not gifted with a lot of intelligence or motivation. He smoked cigarettes and always had that stale odor of someone that doesn't take many showers around him. His eyes were always a little glassy and he didn't want anybody to know where he lived in Aldie, Virginia. He wasn't perfect but he came to work and could get the job done eventually. He was a rebel at heart but always talked of honor. He had more experience with cars and life than I did.

Lonnie's hero was Col. John S. Mosby, who was also known as the "Gray Ghost," the leader of a Confederate army cavalry battalion in the American Civil War. Col. Mosby and his men marauded the Union Army in Northern Virginia during the civil war with their lightening-quick raids and an ability to elude by blending in with the locals. Lonnie loved to recite stories of Col. Mosby's escapades, especially how he captured Union Brigadier General Edwin H. Stoughton while he was sleeping in a house, in the City of Fairfax. Along with the Union General, on March 9, 1863, Mosby's men captured two captains, 20 enlisted men and 58 horses in the City of Fairfax, just up the street from where we were, without firing a single shot.

I relied on and trusted Lonnie, as I did with other employees, always thinking that they would treat me as I treated them and that we were all working toward the same objectives of helping our customers with their temporary rental car needs. I was about 24 years old and Lonnie was about 35 years old.

The garage was located on Lee Highway in the City of Fairfax and the year was 1982. The garage also had gasoline pumps and sold gasoline.

One day Lonnie came to me with a very concerned demeanor. He had difficulty with what he wanted to say to me, which was unusual for him.

Lonnie said, "I don't know how to say this but I caught Gary stealing today and now I don't trust him. I'm not sure what you should do about it but I am concerned about my tools. It is difficult for me to work with him."

"You caught him stealing what?" I asked.

"He was siphoning some gasoline from one of the cars in the back. I was surprised to see it and I didn't say anything to him."

"What did he do with the gasoline?"

"I think he put the gasoline in his car."

"That is odd. Thanks, I guess I'll have to talk to him."

"Well, keep in mind that I can't work with somebody like that who steals."

"I understand," I responded.

I thought about what Lonnie had told me but I was caught. I wasn't there when Gary supposedly helped himself to the gasoline which wasn't right even if we were going to scrap the car and Gary had been doing a good job and I needed his help too. I also needed Lonnie's help fixing the cars so the next day I decided that I would tell Gary that he was fired.

I dreaded the conversation because Gary had filled a need of paying attention to the cars and he didn't ask for much or seem to bother anybody. I had not had too many conversations with him and didn't know him very well either. He had been working for me for about a month. In the short time I worked with Gary he had done very well and Lonnie had to be right. I trusted Lonnie more than I trusted Gary.

I called Gary over the next morning.

"I understand that you siphoned some gasoline from the car in the back yesterday and put it in your car so I am going to have to let

Coming of Age

you go. I'm really sorry but I can't have people here that steal."

He was a little surprised but accepted my analysis and said, "I'm sorry."

I asked, "So why did you take the gasoline?"

"Lonnie told me to," was Gary's response.

I was shocked and trapped. Gary was a good guy and we both got played.

It was a tough life lesson that taught me several things.

Aging

The good thing about aging is that you survived.

The problem with aging is that you see all the opportunities you missed and you can't go back and start over.

Ugh...The good news, next time you are more perceptive.

Appearances

A classmate of mine became a Manager of a Town which is a position held based on the trust of the community. He told me that he quickly learned that as the Town Manager you never buy beer in your town. I didn't understand what he was talking about and then I figured it out.

It doesn't look good if the Town Manager is drinking alcohol and in his town everybody knows who he is and will notice what else he purchases. People have vivid imaginations.

Appearance says a lot.

Bank/University relationships exposed

Everything is not as it appears especially when it comes to schools and financial institutions. At some colleges, banks are paying the schools to promote the bank's accounts where the students will pay more on average in fees.

It is unfortunate that our public and educational institutions will conspire with financial institutions to be able to try and exploit students that are vulnerable and looking for guidance.

270

Shame on you both.
https://www.marketwatch.com/story/after-controver-sy-trump-administration-releases-report-showing-deals-be-tween-bankscolleges-cost-students-27-million-2018-12-10.

Bureaucracy

A system of administration that naturally resists change and strives to protect itself—avoiding accountability at all costs, is called a bureaucracy.

Bureaucracies administer the system of rules that can be interpreted and applied in different ways and they are a necessary evil.

They administer a system of rules that have gotten so complicated that, "If you ask, the answer is no and if you do it you are a violator" unless you have special connections and protection. Remember, it's all about money and power by the people that make, interpret, and enforce the laws and rules. For many of those employed in bureaucracies it's about manipulation and job security.

Bureaucracies are a necessary evil and you just have to recognize where their power comes from and how they are really controlled. Then, hopefully, when you do have to work with them, everything will work out for the best but don't hold your breath. Be prepared in case they tell you no.

Businesses

Enterprises that have to keep changing to try and stay ahead of the competition while keeping up with changing consumer wants and needs. This is a contrast to a bureaucracy that resists change and wants to maintain the status-quo.

Running a business is like a never ending chess game.
My analogy between being in business for yourself and being a student in school is that in school you are told what you need to know, given a test on the material, and it is graded for you. In business you have to figure out what you need to know, test yourself, and grade your test every day.

In business you can't wait for assurance before you try some-

Coming of Age

thing because once everyone else figures it out you're too late.

Cash

If you don't keep a close eye on your cash, somebody else will and unscrupulous people will gladly separate you from it—if you give them the chance. You need to keep honest people honest.

Always watch your cash and protect your money.

Change

The only thing that doesn't change is that there will always be change.

Change creates opportunities and since so much is changing and quickly there are a lot of opportunities. You need to teach yourself how to identify and be part of the opportunities when they arise, especially the future big ones.

Cell phones

Advances in technology have made cell phones and the Internet available to all of us for a minimal financial cost; they are basically free. Phones are so cheap that as of 2018, even sixth graders were bringing them to school.

These devices might seem innocuous, but as you know they empower you with access to unlimited information and an ability for instant communication, not to mention the options for high quality audio, photo and video recording. Smart phones are a tool that gives you instant power. Power over others and a power that can come back to be used against yourself.

There is no minimum age requirement for carrying a phone, and when you received yours, it was with the hope and understanding that you would be able to use it responsibly and maturely irrespective of the inherent dangers, power, and capabilities of the device.

Please exercise good emotional maturity with yours.

Society and your parents say it is OK for you to have a phone, but they are not giving you all the instructions about how the world really works that should go along with it.

I hope that this handbook can fill in some of those missing holes so it can work for you instead of against you.

Complexity

Depending on which side of the fence you are on, complexity can work to your advantage. Complexity is working to the advantage of young adults today because it is creating more and more opportunities with which to create things and opportunities to maintain and manage all the new things that have been created. And the more complex everything becomes, the harder it is to understand how it works and to keep it integrated with everything else which is a contributing factor to the growth in complexity also.

We have entered a vicious era of digital industrialization and it is playing to your benefit because the older people can't keep up with all of it and they are up against diminishing returns for their efforts when they do.

Controversy

It is unfortunate that there is so much controversy in the world and it takes a special perspective to keep from getting caught up in the mess as everyone is fighting for your attention and a piece of someone else's or your pie. For survival sake, you need to be able to stay focused on your objectives that are important to you and conserve your mental energy so it can be applied in areas that will benefit you.

You, nor I, can save the world, but you can create big trouble for yourself by getting involved in matters that are better left to others, no matter how strong your feelings because we are surrounded by propaganda which is continually trying to manipulate us. Be careful because you are probably being manipulated and don't recognize it or know the full picture of how institutions are trying to influence you.

Corrupted - defined

A process that does not work as it is supposed to or one that

Coming of Age

loses its integrity.

Diversionary tactics

These are the tactics that are used to divert an enemy's attention so they can be caught off-guard when attacked or to hide or obscure something that is really important. The government, politicians, and lobbyists are very skilled in creating diversions and deploying diversionary tactics to obscure or hide what they don't want you to know.

Dopamine - Part II

Dopamine is the biggest barrier to your future successes.

Dopamine is a neurotransmitter that can overstimulate and create addiction in your brain. It creates the happy feeling you get from playing online games or looking at social media or sports highlights or Snapchat photos.

Dopamine has a lot of power and can alter habits just like what happens to smokers and drug users. The excitement of being online stimulates the production of dopamine which provides the good feeling which leads to the addiction.

Do a self-analysis of yourself by comparing how your brain functions and thinks and how you feel when you don't have your phone with when you are looking it. What's the difference? Is it a real or imaginary difference? Is your phone like the pack of cigarettes my grandfather kept reaching for? Why is the information that you see on your phone so important to you? Will you ever be able to get enough?

Try an experiment to assess yourself. Run it as if it were a lab for a science class at school.

Write down your hypothesis and then record your feelings about your phone and how important it is to you. Start the experiment by giving your phone to someone else to hold so you don't use it for twenty-four hours. You can start with six or twelve hours if you think twenty-four is too long.

Add to your original thoughts by recording what you do with your time and what you are thinking and how you feel every hour or so. Once you get your phone back, write down how it feels to have it back in your possession and a short summary of what information you missed. You can also write up an analysis as to whether it was a stupid experiment and you didn't like it or it gave you some insight into your behaviors and how your brain functions.

Did you feel a surge of dopamine when you got your phone back?

Did your Gremlin fight with your Guardian Angel before and during the experiment?

Did you hear them yelling at each other?

If so, who won?

Double standards of life

There are many double standards in life which means that there is one set of rules for one group of people and another set of rules for anther group of people because they are supposedly special for some reason so they get special consideration that doesn't seem fair to everyone else.

My best example of a double standard is how drug tests are not required of elected officials, just everybody else in important government positions such as those that have security clearances. So it doesn't make sense that if people with security clearances are required to take and pass a drug test, why aren't elected people held to the same standard.

Does this double standard mean that elected officials are less important than those that hold security clearances or does it mean that they are above everyone else?

Of course, why would the rule makers want to subject themselves to drug tests and what would happen if they failed anyway? They wrote themselves an exception.

And we all know that they would never use any drugs anyway, don't we?

Coming of Age

Double standards for elected lawmakers

Elected lawmakers and their senior staff are the epitome of an application of double standards. They get to live and conduct themselves by a different standard than society in general because they regard themselves as a special breed and as an elite group. Their attitude is based on the incestuous family they belong to— they are all inbred from the same parents of Deceit and Deception.

They are basically similar to an organized crime syndicate, but a special one that makes the laws and controls the prosecutors and the judges, all of whom have pledged allegiance to the "Family" in order to be qualified for advancement. The Family is called the "Iron Triangle" and I rapped about it in my third rap video.

The Iron Triangle isn't much different than any other organized crime syndicate except it is better organized, hidden, and most importantly, legal.

A double standard applies because the syndicate of relationships can do whatever it wants since they are protected in their ability to make, interpret, and enforce the laws. And where does that leave all of us?

Elected officials

These individuals operate as legalized gangs that sell a lot of products to businesses by proposing to manipulate laws for them. The ability of money to influence legislators and their legislation is the underlying problem with all governments.

President Ronald Regan, in a speech at Hillsdale College, on November 10, 1977 said, "You know, it has been said that politics is the second oldest profession and I've come to realize over the last few years, it bears a great similarity to the first."

The United States has a legal mechanism of local sheriffs to prevent this form of legalized prostitution from occurring, but the mechanism has been obscured by the Iron Triangle and its bureaucracy in the name of maintaining control.

Employment

Essentially, employment is the way you are going to provide employers with your problem solving skills so they can apply them in their enterprise. In return, your employer will pay you money that you can use to buy whatever you like.

If it was fun they wouldn't be paying you to do it.

Expendable

Mike Kennedy, a friend of mine that was in the military when he was young, decided to get out once he saw other people get hurt. He realized that, like the people that got hurt, he was expendable.

This is what you will become if you take the oath for military service. Before you decide to join you should watch the movie and/or read the book *Catch-22*.

A former WWII veteran said it was the most accurate book he ever read about the military.

Happiness

"Happiness is when you have someone to love and they love you back," as told to me by a Mexican married couple I visited in Torreon, Mexico. Of course, single people find happiness, too.

Money is not the only factor in the happiness equation.

International Trade

In the U.S., we traditionally only think domestically because our market is so big, but for most other countries in the world, businesses have to think and compete internationally because their domestic markets are so small.

I was guilty of this when I purchased my first CNC stone cutting machine from an American company. I thought, "How much difference could their be with a machine from another country," and the American company was much more convenient. It was a costly mistake and I paid the price for not making the extra effort and thinking globally.

Coming of Age

Italian stone cutting machines are superior to those manufactured in the U.S.

Look beyond your borders.
Broaden your horizons and think globally.
It is a big world out there.

Libraries

Libraries have a lot of answers about life.
Visit yours often.

Check out the biography section to learn about other people's lives. It's my favorite section even though I have been reading a lot of books lately about writing fiction.

Don't make the place a mystery. It is a really neat place that can be a lot of fun. There is a lot of knowledge parked on their shelves.

Commune with the books.

Love your library!
Now they are more important than ever.

Management

My earliest advice about management came from my shop teacher, Mr. Sam Derrick, in 9th grade when I took a class in carpentry and building construction. I still have the textbook. I was fourteen years old.

Mr. Derrick taught me three simple life lessons. Life lessons were the most valuable aspect to taking shop.

It was 1972 and Mr. Derrick was about sixty years old. He, like all shop teachers back then, was great for telling you like it was in the real world. He was that kind of shop teacher that had a crotchety demeanor, but if you took the time to know him and you weren't a trouble maker, he was really very nice, understanding, and considerate.

His rough aurora was enhanced because he was missing most of his pointer finger on his left hand. We never asked what happened and he never told us.

Like most vocational teachers, they have a freedom and flexibility to operate in their own world because their classrooms are usually located in an isolated separate wing of the school away from the traditional classrooms. The vocational wing always has a different feel to it because it is a place that most of the college tracked students never visit. It is more like a blue collar union hall where people actually work and make something with their hands and, unfortunately, more college tracked students are afraid to engage with them and the trades.

One morning when we arrived at class Mr. Derrick had a cardboard box on his desk. After he took attendance he closed the door and told us that he had something he wanted to share with us but that we had to promise not to tell anyone about it and it couldn't leave the classroom. Of course we all agreed curious to know what surprise he had for us and we were all captivated by the anticipation of his show-and-tell.

I can't remember what the tell was, but he pulled several handguns out of the box to show us and I vividly remember him holding a German Lugar pistol just like we would always see in the WWII movies and the TV. series Combat with Vic Morrow. He told us stories about each one and then let us come up and see all the handguns on his desk. I think they were part of his booty from his service in WWII. The guns solidified our image of him being as tough as a real combat veteran because from these captured guns we could see that he was.

This was a life lesson in that he thought enough of us that he wanted to share part of his life with us even at the risk of getting in trouble. He brought the war right into our classroom and put part of it on display right in front of us. This was 1972, only 28 years after WWII ended. After I left the classroom I never heard anyone say anything about his show-and-tell so everyone kept it secret.

The second life lesson was when he scolded me for not think-

Coming of Age

ing about what I was doing before I did something that could have been hazardous. One morning before class started and we were all milling around our benches, there was a bellows sitting on a table and I picked it up and used it to blow air towards a friend's face. He came over to me and very sternly pointed out that if metal fragments had been sucked up into the bellows before I picked it up that I would have sprayed my friend with them. The moral of the story was to think about the what-ifs before you do something. I'm not even sure why we needed a bellows in the class and why it was on our table unless it was a setup and part of the lesson on safety. Whatever its purpose, it worked for me.

The third life lesson was when he was talking about being a supervisor on a construction site, which is called a superintendent. He must have been talking about supervision and the need to be authoritative as well as firm and flexible and that in his story, the workers being supervised were probably being paid by the hour, such as bricklayers, which is a skilled trade so they would be earning a high rate of hourly pay. He was talking about the need for men to stop working periodically so they could use the outdoor toilet.

He started by explaining, "Bricklaying is kind of a team activity because each bricklayer works a section of the wall and everybody has to be able to lay bricks at the same speed in order for the wall to go up evenly. One slacker can create dissension in the crew. It is important that everyone pull their weight."

At 14-years-old I listened to his comment that left an impression on me regarding how you should treat and work with people: "And some days someone might not be feeling good so they might have to use it more often than usual and you need to be flexible to their needs."

His comment, for some reason, stuck with me as the best example of how supervisors always need to be flexible and able to take each persons unique situation into consideration with a very practical everyday example. And how everyone can't always be held to the same standard all the time. "Some days we just have to go to the bathroom more than other days and there isn't anything a supervisor can do about it." In other words, don't be a hard ass with your staff just because you have the authority to be one.

Niches

Sell what people want to buy, not what you want to sell.

Niches are what entrepreneurs try to discover so they can operate a business that will sell lots of products and services so they can earn a living and possibly make lots of money.

See if you can find a niche.

I found mine with propane fuel and cutting architectural stone.

Politics

By definition, politics means that which is related to a political party. Therefore, the term politician should only apply to members elected via the support of a political party.

Independent representatives, who get elected independently, should not be identified as politicians. Accordingly, they would not be part of politics because they are not associated with a political party.

I am making a point of distinguishing between politics and independence to illustrate the allegiance that a politician has to their political party versus someone without party allegiance or obligation.

Political controversy and fighting, per se, is just a big diversionary tactic (see definition) because, even though the Democrats and Republicans appear to be fighting each other, it is the fighting that keeps them funded.

If they got along and worked together nobody would send them money. The political parties need controversy to keep the money rolling in and average citizens get excluded from all the pandering.

If you could look behind the scenes at political parties, you would see that they operate in a very similar manner as organized gangs selling a form of legalized protection. It's all about the mon-

Coming of Age

ey so don't get sucked in to this quagmire of who's really right and who's really wrong because it is all deceit. They are all cut from the same mold and they are playing the same game with their own same set of rules. They are nothing more than actors on a stage.

You can become one of their gang members and be promoted to candidate and maybe even eventually an elected official—not by showing how much intellect you have—but by demonstrating how shifty you are. Political parties don't want do-gooders, they want people that are skilled at raising money by cheating and lying. You don't get chosen to be a candidate for your intelligence.

When, in 1980, presidential candidate Ronald Regan was asked, "How can an actor run for President?" his response was, "How can a President not be an actor."

Politics is all an act.

Watch political proceedings with this in mind, that it is more of a show than as something that should be taken seriously and you can see how you are being played. The controversy is a diversionary tactic by the political parties to provide cover for their primary business which is raising money by selling influence.

Power

**People end up in positions of power who are
not qualified for the power they are given.**

It took me a lot of money, work, and time to learn this reality, but it is one of the best to remember as you continue in life. It was told to me by an employee of the CIA. I didn't understand it at first so he illustrated it with a personal story.

He said, "My wife and I went on a cruise boat that traveled with stops in Mexico. While the cruise ship was anchored off shore in deeper water, us passengers interested in going on a daily excursion to see some ruins had to take a smaller boat, called a tender, to a small dock where we could then board a bus to visit the ruins.

"The dock was guarded by a young man who was armed in order to make sure that the dock was not used for illegal activities.

He was put in charge of the dock and had the authority for approving everyone that arrives and/or departs from the it.

The tender arrived at the dock, discharged us and we boarded the bus and visited the ruins. The young guard watched us the whole time. It's in the middle of nowhere. On the return the young man with the gun stopped us from boarding the tender. He didn't stop us because we were not allowed to use the dock, as it was obvious that we had all just arrived that morning and now we wanted to go back to the cruise ship. He stopped us because he could. He had the authority, and the gun, and he chose to exercise his authority.

Eventually we were allowed to board the tender and return to the cruise ship. We weren't doing anything wrong. He was just exercising his authority. Maybe he wanted to be paid a bribe.

The same thing happens all the time in life. Just because people are given power does not mean that they will exercise it properly or that they are qualified for the power they are given. The same applies to elected officials and the political parties they represent who together form their own check and balance.

The Federal and State Constitutions elaborate—and we are taught in school that the power is with the people—but in reality, the power lies with the money that is used to get people elected. Campaign contributions are, in actuality, treasonous because they diminish the power of the people.

Smart phones

Be careful of the power that your smart phone provides to you. They are a tool that provides instant communication for information and with other people but they have hazards.

The information they provide can manipulate your mind and make you think that you are not mortal and condition you to believe that everything can be instantaneous. Access to information gives you a sense of power.

The phones can cause you to alter or change your behaviors and they can cause you to become more narrow-minded as you communicate with more and more people with the same ideology as you.

Coming of Age

Search algorithms that present you information are designed and engineered to pull you into the extreme ideologies so you get hooked on the information that is being fed to you and you stay engaged longer and longer digging deeper and deeper.

Propaganda

You are inundated with propaganda and it is dangerous.

A book titled *Subliminal Seduction* was published in 1972 about what is incorporated into advertising to try and influence our minds. I thought it was an interesting subject so I wrote a book report on it for my sophomore English class. That was 46 years ago so the science has had lots of time to improve since then.

Many aspects in the world are trying to control you and your mind in ways that you need to be aware of so you can protect yourself from unwarranted influence as much as possible.

Everything from soda, sports, beer, credit cards, political parties and car manufacturers are trying to influence you for their gain. You need to be able to understand how you are targeted and why and try to separate fiction from fact and not let all of it drive you crazy which it will.

Rap and my campaigns for public office

Rap is an entertaining means of expressing yourself. It does not have to be vulgar or gross.

It is an interesting medium for conveying a message for those of us that can't sing because we don't have pitch.

I enjoyed learning how to write lyrics and how to rap them. It is really hard to do but I had a great teacher named Eric Weinberg.

Eric showed me how one of the keys to writing good lyrics is to use a rhyming dictionary which you can buy. You can also take a class in poetry for some extra help.

See my story of how when I was a candidate for office in 2008 I was excluded from high profile candidate forums so I decided to put my platform to fight corruption to rap and music and I produced my first campaign rap video in 2008. I continued to run for office each year and created campaign rap videos for each of my subsequent campaigns and they are all posted on my YouTube channel CDRapper1.

I was an independent candidate for Congress twice. The Library of Congress started archiving congressional candidate websites in 2012 so my campaign website, www.honestyandethics.com, was archived weekly by the Library of Congress from September 26, 2012 to December 12, 2012.

Rights

These are given to you at birth but that doesn't mean that you don't have to fight to keep them from being denied or taken away.

Your rights, and the expectations that go with them, are going to change as you turn 18 so you need be extra careful in how you conduct yourself after your eighteenth birthday.

Rules

As you learned in social studies class, society has rules and laws to bring order to our lives and it is important to try and adhere to them. If you don't agree with the laws, there is a process whereby when you are 18 you can run for office, draft legislation, and try to get the laws changed to the way you think they should read.

Regarding rules for students still in school, you can always talk with your principal and/or school board representative if you have a problem with a school policy or procedure. I am sure that they would be happy to hear from you.

Sheriffs Constitutional role in protecting democracy

Sheriffs have the authority and power to restore our trust in our local, state, and federal government's by stopping the flow of campaign money that corrupts the governing process. You can't fix something unless you know how it works and corrupted governance works because bribes have been legalized as campaign contributions.

Coming of Age

**The introduction of campaign contributions
into the election process is an oxymoron to the
democratic principles the Constitutions create.**

Sheriffs can and should fix America because they take an oath to protect the power of the people and they have the power of arrest both of which make sense in providing citizens a law enforcement mechanism that is accountable via election to them. But it seems that this concept may not be practiced because sheriffs are accepting contributions also.

High school students of America, please ask your government teacher about the constitutional powers of the Office of Sheriff, his oath of office and why he isn't protecting you from your governments that appear to have become dysfunctional?

Then ask your government teacher if there are any constitutional protections for elected representatives to accept contributions?

I am interested to know what their response is?

Then ask your government teacher if they have any idea why your school doesn't teach you about the powers of the sheriff or the other four local constitutional officers or about how your constitutional officers are supposed to function so as to prevent a scenario similar to that described in George Orwell's super-state Oceania in his novel *1984*?

And you can even go so far as to ask your School Board why your government textbook doesn't list the terms "corruption," "corrupted governance," or "Iron Triangle" in the index or discuss the terms in the body of the book?

I argue that a corrupt government is not going to educate its citizens about its dysfunction or to teach them about how it can be corrected.

I own a small business selling propane fuel in Virginia and I was a candidate for Sheriff in Fauquier County, Virginia, which is an hour's drive from Washington, D.C. Two years earlier I was a candidate for Sheriff in Fairfax County, Virginia. Both times I ran as an independent to fight political corruption. Corrupted governance is just the same here in Virginia and D.C. as it is in throughout America, well organized and well hidden.

In my campaigns I argued that disclosure of contributions does not make them constitutional. Nobody has ever questioned or disagreed with my thesis.

As explained to me by several sheriff deputies, sheriffs are our chief law enforcement officer in each county, and as Constitutional Officers, they have a higher authority than the local police, the state police and even federal agents such as the FBI. State and Federal law enforcement has to get permission from the sheriff before they can take action in a jurisdiction. This legal interpretation was explained to me by sheriff deputies who act at the pleasure and in place of the actual sheriff. The power of the sheriff is inherent in the aspect that they have personal responsibility and liability for the actions of their deputies.

Sheriffs are classified as Constitutional Officers. "Constitutional" referring to the jurisdictional State Constitution, not the Federal Constitution, but I believe their jurisdiction can translate to the Federal Constitution also via the State Constitution. All sheriffs take an oath to uphold and protect your State and Federal Constitutions, you and your power (the power of the people) and your rights (to control your government vis-a-via elected representatives). So I ask, with all the money flowing into political campaigns, where are our sheriffs when we need them and their authority the most?

As can be expected I did not win either election. The campaigns did provide me the opportunity to learn a lot, make new friends, and publicize the message that independent sheriffs are the only protection we have from corrupted governance.

Your local sheriff is supposed to be accountable to the citizens that elect him, or her, as protector of their constitutional rights because they are the only law enforcement officer that we elect and, via election, they are supposed to be responsive to your needs. By comparison, county police are controlled by a Chief of Police that is controlled by your County Board which is a political entity and the city police are controlled by a Chief of Police that is appointed by the

Coming of Age

City Council which is also a political entity.

**The sheriff is your only law enforcement officer
that is directly elected by the citizens.**

To help put the distinction and significance of having your chief law enforcement officer directly elected by the people in a better perspective, consider that when the Constitution was written that the guys who wrote it knew all about corruption and how they needed a decentralized way to help insure that the government they were creating wouldn't become corrupted. They also had the legal roles of sheriffs in England to serve as a guide.

It makes sense that the local sheriff had to protect the State as well as the Federal Constitution because who else was going to do it? Travel by horse took a long time and the sheriff was the best person to give the authority so he could make sure the government and its legislators did not subrogate the power the people gave them to monied interests. So the Office of Sheriff is molded as the decentralized protector of freedom and democracy. It all makes sense for the time of the 1700's and even more so for today.

By comparison, modern times for today's sheriffs are a lot different in that our representatives and our governments accept lots of money while the sheriffs in metropolitan areas are relegated to running the jails and protecting the courts. This leaves the government free to do as it pleases without regard for the power the people placed with their elected representatives each election cycle.

**I argue that citizens have been conditioned to think that the
Federal government is supreme and the schools don't teach
anything about State Constitutions and the roles of the local
Constitutional Officers as provided in the documents
to perpetuate the myth.**

For a country that says it is so concerned about promoting democracy it seems that it has skipped a few steps when it comes to educating its own. The citizens have been bamboozled out of their real constitutional power as provided in the Federal and State Constitutions even though it is still there. Citizens will be second class as long as influence money is available to the leadership. And if passive or incompetent sheriffs are recruited by the party elite, they are not going to challenge or bite the hand that feeds them. The real constitutional power of the sheriffs is still valid, its just been obscured.

I have always assumed that all countries had sheriffs like we do, only to find that they don't. It turns out that many constitutions, such as for central American countries, do not have a provision for sheriffs. This means that the citizens do not have any elected person that is accountable to them, vested with the legal authority to protect them from other legal authorities or threats. Maybe that is why corruption is so rampant in all the other countries and why so many of their citizens are driven to try and immigrate to America. And America keeps sending their governments money? I'm really confused?

I hope you can use this information to better protect your rights and have a better understanding of how and why your governments have become dysfunctional.

Your sheriff is your only hope for protecting your rights to have a truly representative government but it seems that few of the sheriffs can or are willing to fulfill all the duties of the Office as originally intended.

I did create and produce two campaign rap videos to promote my candidacies and illustrate these concepts. I posted the videos on my YouTube channel CDRapper1 as part of my campaigns for sheriff in Virginia. The rap videos are titled "Democracy Rides Again" and "Gunfight at the Fauquier County Corral." You can also visit my campaign website www.HonestyAndEthics.com for more information.

My website for my second, anti-corruption, independent campaign for Congress of Virginia's 11th District was even indexed by the Library of Congress.

Chapter six
Miscellaneous concepts

Governments

Introduction

Once good governance is compromised the government isn't able to give the citizens the tools they need to be able to police it, except for the authority vested in local sheriffs. The policing process becomes too complex and dependent on the government to administer and the self-policing process itself creates a conflict of interest for the government to pursue as it is a process against itself. In the extreme, loss of confidence in one's government is what causes citizens to riot. They feel caught in a catch-22.

Disclosure of campaign contributions might make them legal but just because they are legal does not mean they are constitutional. And what about contributions to political parties?

Are the political parties not the organized gangs that launder the protection money that is provided to influence the legislation?

Where are the lines drawn and who is in charge of drawing the lines between what is right and what is wrong?

These aspects are very simple but they are not discussed or promoted because so many of the channels for discussion are kept closed by the individuals and organizations that are part of the web of influence.

The problem is not the established legal frame work or structure of the government, whereby the citizens can control their government through elected representatives, the government itself is as perfect as it can be. It is the process of governing that is corrupted.

Money has compromised how the government is supposed to function. It is as if the citizens are caught in a catch-22 whereby once influence money corrupts the governing process, the checks and balances are politicized and then the citizens do not have any way to re-mediate the situation. They become captives of the political money machine because the checks and balances have been compromised by the influence of money so as to protect and maintain the status-quo.

People in the know don't have a platform to discuss these concepts because to do so would jeopardize their continued employment and/or their retirement payments whether they work in the government or in academia. So there are no supposed "authorities" that can or will speak honestly on the subject even though we all know the problem is there.

During one of my petition signing campaigns I was at a local farmers market asking for signatures on my petition for candidacy. To get on the ballot you don't just fill out a form and say I'm a candidate. How to get on a ballot is one of the things The Man will never allow to be taught in school because his machine won't condone it.

I approached a woman headed to the market and asked her if she could sign my petition so I could fight corruption. She was a little surprised about my approach to elected office and we talked for a few minutes. Then she said, "You are right, they use complexity to get away with what they want. I know, I work on Capitol Hill.

Conspiracy

Aren't political parties nothing more than a legalized conspiracy to undermine the legitimate governing process? Are not the legislators in conjunction with their political party conspiring to defraud the citizens of their constitutional right to control their government without the influence of money? Why are political parties even al-

Miscellaneous Concepts

lowed? Could the issues that political parties espouse just be another diversionary tactic to obscure their real modus operandi which is financial solicitation?

Conspiracy is doing something secret that is harmful. Is the solicitation and acceptance of campaign funds harmful to the citizens rights to have an equal influence in how votes are cast by their elected official? Who does the elected official really represent, the political party that supported their election or the constituents of their district? What happened to one-person one-vote Rule? It's MIA from the textbooks also.

Efficiency

I don't understand how the government got along before without the Internet and computers. I would have thought that the government would have become more efficient with computer technology but instead it seems like it has gotten more complicated and complex.

How did it ever survive before without computers?

Illegal border crossings - Easy solution to the problem of

There is a very easy solution to solving the problem of illegal border crossings and it lies in educating the captured illegal immigrants about how democracy is supposed to work before they are deported so when they are returned home they can have the political understanding to begin correcting the corruption in their country which is driving them to the U.S.

With this program in place, the political elite in Mexico and the other Central American countries would be on notice that all returned citizens will be schooled in how to fight political corruption in their home country such that once they get deported back to their country they will be qualified in how to run for office on a clean platform and threaten to overthrow the hold on power. This threat to their power would cause the political elite to be more restrictive about who can cross their borders on the way to the U.S.

The catch-22 for the U.S. in implementing such a program of detainee democratic education is that to do so would expose the corrupted democracy in the U.S., also.

Racketeering

Where is the line drawn for what is racketeering versus what is not racketeering as it relates to political parties and their candidates and elected officials?

Racketeering/Racketeer Influenced and Corrupt Organizations Act (RICO)

Racketeering occurs when organized groups run illegal businesses, known as "rackets," or when an organized crime ring uses legitimate organizations to embezzle funds. Such activities can have devastating consequences for both public and private institutions. The problem is that the government won't prosecute itself. So what are citizens left to do?

How are the citizens supposed to be able to control their government when it is controlled by influence money and the rules are adjusted to accommodate the continued flow of money?

Influence money is not supposed to be a protected right of the Constitution, is it? Was influence money a concern when the Constitution was drafted and ratified or has it become a fait accompli?

Are the political parties and Congress racketeers?

Treason

Defined: The offense of attempting by overt acts to overthrow the government of the state to which the offender owes allegiance or to kill or personally injure the sovereign or the sovereign's family. The betrayal of a trust.

According to the Constitution, whom is vested with the power over the government created by the document?

Is accepting supposed funding for a political campaign treasonous? Read the definition again.

Trust

Miscellaneous Concepts

Trust is the one thing we would like from our governments but it seems to be the last thing they can actually provide because of the way the power is vested in elected officials that can circumvent what we expect of them.

Irrespective of what we are told and taught, as citizens how do we believe an idealized government is supposed to function? In an ideal democracy or republic, whichever term one wants to apply, how do we think government is supposed to work and what do we expect of our representatives versus how all of it functions today? Is this the way it is supposed to work?

Miscellaneous

Alternative methods to achieve goals

As an example, if you want to be an actor or actress, first figure out how to make lots of money and then you can own your own studio and star in your own movies. Then you will be more in control of your destiny instead of other people. Granted you probably won't make lots of money so you can eventually start a studio, but…

What struggles did your ancestors go through and survive so you could be reading this today?

Complaints or opportunities for discovery?

Usually complaining is a waste of time and energy. Instead of complaining use your frustration to fuel your creativity to solve the problem that you have identified with a solution which might lead to you're discovering some new product or service that is needed or filing a patent for a new product that can be manufactured. Think about how you can turn lemons into lemonade.

Comment by a former weed dealer at a high school reunion who use to sell nickel and dime bags, "As many of those baggies as I rolled I could have come up with the idea to put a zip on it. I don't know how I missed out on that."

Human component

The biggest challenge in life is trying to manage the human component of living. You have to be able to manage yourself as well as get along with everyone else and this is the hardest thing of all in life.

The human component is different from the machine component because a machine is predictable and engineered to do specific tasks and if it breaks it can be fixed. And it doesn't have emotions.

Humans by comparison are the opposite of machines, unpredictable and can't be fixed which makes understanding yourself as well as being able to get along with and working with others so difficult. A lot of your happiness is going to be derived from human interaction so the better you are with it, the happier life your life will probably be.

Your Generation - The Big Experiment

You and your generation don't realize it, but you are part of the biggest ever, ongoing social experiment, regarding the most dramatic societal changes ever and its effects. You should try to recognize and manage these changes because they are and will affect your future.

Change can be beneficial if you can figure out how to position yourself so it can work to your advantage.

Just as society is analyzing the effects of the Great Recession of 2008 on the millennial generation today, you are the next in line to be analyzed and it behooves you to pay attention. Pay attention so you can mitigate your exposure to the current hazards of life today and the ones coming your way while looking for the hidden opportunities that change creates.

Technology

Apple Computer - the start of

Miscellaneous Concepts

I met a man at one of my longtime customer's houses who was visiting from California over the Christmas holidays in 2017. He was a little older than I and we talked about all the crazy things we have seen and how much the world has changed since we were in high school and the regrets that we had about opportunities that we missed.

He won the missed opportunity prize when he told me that he was living in California at the time Steve Jobs was experimenting with computers and he read the invitation for the meet-up that Steve's computer club had placed in Byte magazine about 1975 for people interested in computers to come by and join their garage club meetings. He told me that he didn't bother going because he didn't think anything would come from his participation in the club's events.

Computers in the 1970's.

When I attended Georgia Tech I learned the programming language called Basic and used key punch cards to write my lines of code which I had to leave to be fed into an IBM mainframe computer. I was right at the beginning of the computer age and didn't know it because I didn't understand how to look for and identify opportunities.

Information overload

Schools should be teaching you how to deal with information overload but they are just adding to it.

You are being subjected to so much information without prior experience or training in being able to figure out what is and isn't critical that you are getting lost as to what is and is not important to you now and in the future. It is hard to stay focused when so much is coming at you and you think that you are going to miss out on something if you don't keep up and keep taking it all in.

You won't miss the important stuff if you can prioritize so you can see through the fog.

Life's never ending challenge

Trying to understand what others know and how they think.

Opportunities

What you should always be looking for whether they are related to making new friends, reading a book, taking a class, starting a conversation, staying in an old job or taking a new job, getting married, getting a divorce, having children, writing a book, starting a business or taking a nap.

Birds are metaphors for ideas or concepts whose time comes and goes. These are what you are always looking for and you want to know if you have one in your hand when it is there so you can take advantage of it when you have it because they are fleeting. The phrase that is in Chinese is something like,

> **"It is one thing to have a bird in your hand,**
> **it is another thing to know that you have it."**
> Ancient Chinese proverb

I heard this phrase from a famous inventor who was told it by one of his electrical engineering teachers when the inventor was looking for investors for his idea for a new speaker system. The inventor told the story that he was surprised when the teacher agree to invest $10,000 in his idea which was probably a year's salary in the early 1960's. When the inventor questioned how his teacher could take such a risk the teacher responded with the Chinese proverb.

The proverb means that not only do you need the right idea, but you need the right idea at the right time and you need to know what you have or it will get away.

Opportunity costs

You can't discuss opportunities without also discussing opportunity costs which are lost opportunities when you choose another opportunity. If you engage in one activity you lose the possibility that the avoided activity might have provided an alternative opportunity so you took advantage of the first opportunity at the cost of the second opportunity. You will never know what could have been from the second opportunity but those are the decisions that we make every day and we live with the consequences or unknown cost or benefit of those decisions.

Opportunity - Positioning for

Try to position yourself in the right place with the anticipation that the other events will occur so you will be in the right place at the right time. But don't set too high a goal that you lose credibility because your expectations are too high and always be expecting more. And don't start jumping around to different jobs trying to find the sweet spot. Have reasonable expectations and see what comes along. Consistency is just as important as finding opportunities.

Vineyard Vines is an interesting story of how the two brothers didn't like their jobs in New York so they quit and decided to start selling ties. Mr. Knight, the owner of Nike had an idea for importing running shoes from Japan and he came up with the name of his fictitious company, Blue Ribbon Sports on the fly when he was in a meeting at a shoe factory in Japan in 1962.

I started a propane company not because I wanted to start one, but because people were asking directions for where they could get their propane cylinders filled for gas grills as gas grills were becoming popular in the early 1980's. I had a gas station at the time and gas stations were a convenient place to go when you needed directions. One weekend, probably Memorial Day weekend, when a lot of people use propane at their cookouts, several people asked me where to go and I put together that there was a lot of demand for propane so I investigated selling it and it worked.

The gas station and car rental concept that I had started with wasn't going anywhere but the propane worked. I had started selling propane for new gas grill cylinders at the time everyone was looking to buy propane for their new grill. When the competitor sold his property and retired all his former customers came to me for their propane but then many years later, cylinder exchange cabinets were installed as another alternative for propane refills and my sales fell into a precipitous decline.

Schools

School Boards

School Board members do not realize what it is like to be in school all day every day as a student today. They know what it was like when they were in school but times are different.

To make them more in touch with the reality of today's school life and classroom environment, all elected officials should be required to attend classes for two weeks and to eat the same food with the students and do the same homework. No bringing their lunch.

How long would they be able to survive getting up early, catching the bus and sitting in the uncomfortable chairs with the fluorescent lights and taking notes (and they can't use cursive for notes if they take any) from the white board that is hard to see or the hand written notes that are hard to see because the lights are out so the white board is more visible? And they would have to complete their homework online without looking at social media also. Could they do it successfully and survive?

The harsh environment would probably cause them to be redirected to alternative education facilities very quickly and they wouldn't even have the extra social and peer pressure present today.

Schools, and your unknown super powers

Don't think that schools are teaching you everything you need to know. There are a lot of important lessons about life in general that are being excluded because "The Man" doesn't want to scare you and collectively, you and your classmates would be a serious threat to his base of power if you had too much knowledge about how the real world works and what real super powers you and your friends possess as described in my *Calling All Jedi... Rap Song #2* at 2:36 on YouTube.

Schools promote the fact that they want you to be smart, but they only want you to be smart about specific subjects for applica-

Miscellaneous Concepts

tions that they can determine and control.

What would happen if you and your classmates had the experience and knowledge of forty-year olds with the powerful interconnectivity that you hold in your hands?

What could or would you be doing differently now, and how differently would you be approaching your education, life, and the world in general if you knew about your real super powers?

Schools and the use of technology in the classroom

More and more technology related nuances for education are driving parents and students crazy. What about going back to paper textbooks and tests and sending everything home with the student as a means of facilitating parent involvement with one's child?

An extreme approach is to discard all the technology in school and go back to blackboards and in person teaching as a way to reengage with the students.

Where is the improvement from such a push and investment in technology? It seems like the students are going backwards more than they are going forwards.

School's continued push to incorporate technology in teaching systems is a movement towards educational disaster. It is similar to how doctors feel technology is pushing them towards insanity.

Students need to be saved from all this technological teaching that is supposed to make them better students and adults.

It is appearing that the more technology is utilized, the worse the test scores become as measured in the continued decline in the most recent ACT test scores.

Refer to the 2018 Annual Report and as reported in Education Week, https://www.edweek.org/ew/articles/2018/10/17/math-scores-slide-to-a-20-year-low.html.

And how about the tests that measure emotional maturity? Is it improving or getting worse? What do you think?

Schools are Working at Cross Purposes to the Parents and Students

The schools have gotten to the point where, in spite of everything they say, in actuality their words do not meet with their actions.

As an example, it is easy for schools to say that more instructional time is necessary in class, but then many teachers waste the time they have with filler movies etc, especially after standardized testing is completed and the school year is concluding.

More importantly, parents know what their kids need but the schools say this is how we are going to educate your child and you have to accept it because we know what is best for them. We are the experts.

The educational industry has adopted technology to try and teach and work more efficiently, under the auspices that students can adapt and learn the same with it as they did without it. The overall problem is that these changes are actually making it harder to learn and students are learning less. But nobody will say anything because they can't or they don't have a voice in the discussion.

Teachers are showing more online videos because it's easy, wasting more good instructional time for many reasons, and responding to emails etc, because they have technology in the classroom. The classroom situation is further complicated because students have their phones at school so they are less engaged in the classroom. The problem is feeding back on itself.

I was introduced to a game called Kahoots in my Senior level Sports Communication class at George Mason University. It was used as part of student led presentations but I was shocked to learn that it is an acceptable classroom practice. I couldn't believe it was part of a college level, let alone a senior level class because it is so juvenile. When I mentioned it to my children they were familiar with its use in high school. It serves as just another example of poor applications of technology in classrooms and how schools are wasting learning time and opportunities for engagement.

The teacher in the same Sports Communication class wasn't interested in going over the mid-term with the students because he said, when I asked after class, that I was probably the only student that was interested in knowing what I got wrong. And in my work-

Miscellaneous Concepts

shop type creative writing class that cost $1,500 for the semester, my teacher never provided any written feedback to any of the students on any of the submitted pieces for the whole length of the class, providing instead, her verbal analysis as part of the supposed workshop experience.

College today, for all that it is promoted as being so great, is by far, not what I expected it to be. Where I was expecting, from everything we are told or lead to believe, that going back into the classroom as a student would be an invigorating experience; instead, it appears to me that the classroom experience and its environment has regressed. It is much worse than when I was in college 40 years ago. And I won't even get started on teacher evaluations and the school's lack of interest in trying to gain anything meaningful from the results.

It appears to me, from what I remember and from what I would have expected, that technology is destroying classrooms, education, and the learning experience. It is occurring in small little bites that gnaw away at what is supposed to be the most enlightening and important experience for each of us.

The biggest bite of all is coming from the diminishing lack of human teacher/student engagement with the course work. This is coupled with student's interest in scamming the system and doing the minimum, which is human nature. The requirement for so much to be online defeats the core human component of education that we know works because that is how all of us were educated. All of these new, non-human and non-tangible tools of learning are working at cross purposes to what is supposed to be occurring in the schools.

The situation is even more complicated because there is no check and balance in the educational system. Parents are not allowed in the schools or the classrooms and are only left holding a bag of wasted opportunities when they finally wake up, at some future time, and realize that their child isn't able to perform as they would have hoped and expected.

All I can say is "Buyer Beware."

Chapter seven
My Story and Regrets

My story

You never know what is coming and how it may affect you. There are so many things that will happen to you in life to influence your decisions or open doors that you can't even imagine.

One of the many big life changing events for me was toward the end of my Sophomore year at Georgia Tech. I was living in an apartment off campus with three other guys when one day my roommate, John, from Chapel Hill, North Carolina told me that he wasn't coming back to school in the fall. He was never very studious in the first place and he would sleep late in the morning and not go to class, but I told him that he was making a big mistake and that he should not quit school. He said he was not happy and so he was adamant that he wasn't coming back.

I was miserable at school also but the thought of quitting or going somewhere else had never even entered my mind. I was determined that I wasn't going to be a quitter and that I had to tough it out. It took me about two weeks to realize that if my roommate could quit school that I didn't have to return either. I was worried about what my parents would say and that I would be letting them down but when I mentioned it to them on the phone they said it was OK and I could go somewhere else.

I finished my sophomore year in Atlanta with a 3.2 overall gpa and came home and began taking classes in Business at George Mason University and thinking about starting a family business. I was twenty years old.

Then one day on the way to the class I saw a former gas station for rent and I was able to rent it and start selling gasoline to pay the

My Story and Regrets

rent. Then, since I knew a lot about cars, how they worked and how to fix them I started buying used cars for $1,000 that I rented for $10 per day and I started with five cars. The first car I rented was stolen so I lost twenty percent of my fleet in one day. It was hard going and I didn't have much money so my fleet grew very slowly.

One afternoon, a representative of Hertz Truck Rental stopped by and asked if I would be interested in becoming a commission agent for their trucks so I started renting trucks. I used the money I earned from renting trucks to buy more cars.

Then one Saturday I realized that several people had stopped for directions to a local propane cylinder refill location up the highway two miles to the west. I thought, "If there are that many people looking for propane gas maybe I should sell it."

I didn't know anything about propane so I investigated the business and six months later started selling propane in 1981. Several years later a tour of my propane suppliers propane terminal in a rural area led to my family being able to purchase an adjacent farm with industrial zoned land. The zoning allowed us to establish our own propane terminal that would support a greatly expanded propane business that could now include home delivery.

The car rental business model was not successful so I eventually stopped renting cars and later I stopped renting the trucks. Propane was the growing business and that is where I put my attention and efforts and it continued to grow.

I could have grown the propane business a lot bigger but between the family problems my father created, a need to diversify into more of a summer business, and the inherent problems in the seasonality of the demand for propane as a winter fuel, I decided to try growing fresh market vegetables. Being a farmer didn't work very well at all so next I tried setting up an online news company for the propane industry but that didn't work either. Eventually I started selling stone products which led me to buying CNC machines to cut large blocks of stone into architectural products like hearths, wall caps and fireplace surrounds. This has not worked very well either relative to the large learning curve and high investment in machines and facilities.

Since I had experience with CNC machines, I gained some experience with industrial robotics. Then, I happened to be sitting through some advanced swimming lessons at an indoor recreation center pool with Ralph Albrecht, a parent of Mary Jane's former classmate whose brother was in the class with my children. Mr. Albrecht is a patent attorney and while we were passing time he explained the criteria for patents, how sometimes they can become very valuable, and the process for filing one.

I decided I needed to come up with a patent so I started paying more attention to my environment to see what my imagination could come up with. Then, one afternoon while I was watching my son John practice shooting basketballs in the driveway, I came up with the idea for a moving sports goal by attaching a backboard to an industrial robotic arm. I called Ralph right away. One year later Ralph filed the patent application for me and two years later it was granted with some modifications. Since then I have received three more patents for take-offs of the original patent. On average, it costs about $10,000 to file a patent application.

Sheila Gunter, a friend of mine at Camp Friendship, the family camp we attend in Palmyra, Virginia, every August, told me about some successful novel writers so I thought about writing a novel even though we have all been conditioned to believe that writers don't make any money. Sheila mentioned the writers because I always bring an old electric typewriter to camp to document the story of our camp experience each summer and she would hear the sound of the typewriter from my cabin.

I researched successful novel writers when I got home and decided it was worth a shot. So I studied novel writing for a year by reading how-to books from the library and then I started writing a story about a sheriff, who is played by me of course, that is instrumental in fighting corruption in Washington, D.C. It is still in progress.

My interest in writing the novel combined with having met my wife which led to the kids which has led to my experience seeing

My Story and Regrets

them and all their friends growing up in today's digital and information overloaded environment has led me to start writing this handbook. Now I am finishing it. I am working on a Parents Guide also.

My conversation with Sheila was the impetus for writing.

As a side note, I am looking for students and adults that are interested in submitting their short stories or longer works for publication in a soon to be published series about the daily lives of high school and college students. I am also interested in stories from recent graduates about life after graduation, fiction and non-fiction. Other stories for the young adult reader will be considered also.

These are all things that I could never have imagined in my wildest dreams when I was your age. I don't think I have run out of time so hopefully there are still some interesting new adventures and things for me and my family on the horizon.

My Regrets

Regrets from my high school and college years.

Not making more friends in high school and participating in more activities like the school newspaper now that I see what a great experience it has been for my children.

Not working with computers and software a lot more because there were so many opportunities in this field and because they are the tools and machines of the future.

I also wish I had known to take classes in creative writing and to start writing stories sooner.

Regrets from my life and take-aways for yours

I like thousands of other people have many regrets that I can't do anything about except write about them.

I missed being able to take advantage of the computer and digital revolution. I wish I had been as interested in computers as I was in cars and engines but I did not have a window into the full potential of the industry nor did I have anyone to mentor me in computers. I

Chris DeCarlo

thought playing computer games were a waste of time but I missed the idea of trying to create them. I also didn't have any guidance in trying to look ahead to see how to position myself and I didn't have any mentors to guide me along such a path. When I was at Georgia Tech, I did meet with some electrical engineers during a break who were designing antenna systems for the Navy in small drab offices at Crystal City in Alexandria, Virginia, and that didn't look like much fun so that helped for me to throw in the towel on my career in electrical engineering. Maybe if I had met someone that was having fun and excited to work in computers or software at the time that I would have moved in that direction, but it didn't happen.

Innovation was much harder to learn about in the past compared with today. Innovation was never really taught in general or as it might be discussed in other places that are dependent on manufacturing and producing a product for sale. But it was never discussed in the media to the degree it is today. The industry, in Washington, D.C., is information and laws, not electronics or manufacturing which is tangible and which was growing rapidly in California with all the defense and aerospace contractors trying to innovate to stay ahead of the Russians. Schools have always taught us to follow the process; it is only recently that they have begun talking about creativity and innovation.

Part of your life is determined by where you happen to be born and another part is to whom you are born. These are some of your uncontrollables and it is a take it or leave it deal where you have to appreciate what you have and work with what you are given. You don't have a choice.

Steve Jobs was born in Michigan and then he was adopted by a family in California in an area that just happened to be the forerunner to Silicon Valley. I was in college just before Michael Dell began building computers in his dorm room, but I didn't have access to the insight, equipment, or the money to try and put something like he did together, but he caught the wave at just the right time.

Writing this book has just given me the realization that, just as the majority of innovation has been occurring in California's Silicon

307

My Story and Regrets

Valley to support the defense establishment, over the last 50 years, that a lot of that development is now shifting to my back yard in Northern Virginia because cyber weaponry and security is the new frontier and that is why this area has seen so much recent growth in cyber.

The technological development frontier for the military is shifting from the West coast to the East coast and now I am right in the middle of it just as Steve Jobs was right in the middle of the surge in hardware and software development forty years ago. Northern Virginia is the new Silicon Valley East and it is being driven here by the proximity of the CIA, the Pentagon and the location of MaeEast which is the big east coast Internet trunk line that originates in Ashburn, Virginia near Dulles Airport.

Controllable's are things that you have in your power to control like how to apply your time, books to read, places to visit, things to learn about and people to associate.

Thinking ahead you have to use what you have to try and put yourself in the right place at the right time so you can be in possession of the knowledge and experience at the time that there is a realization and sudden need for what you have and than you can supply it because there won't be much competition. There won't be much competition because the new products will be in, what is called, a growth phase.

Cyber security is probably one of the fastest growing areas with the most demand and, it has the least amount of supply. It is a well kept secret, even here in what I call the cyber security corridor that pretty much runs between the Pentagon, the CIA in McLean, Virginia and Dulles Airport. It has the least amount of supply because it is changing and growing very rapidly and because it is very complex subject matter.

Another industry that is growing a tremendous amount in this area of the country is the data center facilities that hold all the servers. This region is currently home to 30% of the data centers in North America.

If you have a security clearance and experience in either of these areas, and you don't necessarily need a college degree though that will give you a better start, you will always be able to find employment and job security. Other areas that you can also consider are networking and of course computer programming and software development.

Don't avoid these careers just because you think you won't like working with computers all day or because you think they are too complicated. These perceived negatives can work in your favor as they scare others from considering the profession. If it is not easy then everyone else is going to avoid it and you will have less competition. In reality, it isn't that hard once you get the hang of it. If you follow such a career, path you will probably find that in the long run the positives will greatly outweigh the negatives.

As an example of job security, if you have experience in how a particular software was developed then you will have job security as changes need to be made to it and as a computer programmer you can probably work from anywhere so you won't have to waste a lot of time sitting in traffic.

Computers and software programs always need to me maintained as things change so look at software and computers like I looked at engines and machines in the 1970's because that was what was driving the world then. Computers and software are driving the world now.

Computers and the data they process are the machines of the 21st century and you can easily still be part of the computer revolution and its continued evolution if you just point yourself in that direction.

However, none of this is going to happen automatically. You will have to put out the effort and take advantage of the fact that the best time to get yourself established is in your teens and early twenties.

This is the time for you to be building your solid foundation so you are as well prepared as possible to move into your next phase of, not only your career, but your new family life as you will probably be getting married and having children in the near future.

Conclusion

Please, please, please take your time and be careful in what you do. I hope you can put this information to use and it has improved your understanding of how the world really works, your place in it, and the many things that you need to take into consideration so you can have the best life possible in your own pursuit of happiness.

I hope that you find ways to apply and make good use of many of these aspects and concepts. In addition, I hope that you have gained a better understanding of how and why you need to take as good a care as possible of yourself and those around you. And I hope that you will make efficient use of your time so you are prepared to seize the opportunities that await you along the road of your long and prosperous life.

Life is complicated with lots of variables and that is what makes it fun and interesting. You are positioned to navigate your way through your life in even a better way then I have navigated through mine.

Prepare yourself as well as you can now for whatever adventures happen to be coming your way and enjoy the ride.

I wrote my story and now you are starting to write yours.

Have fun…

As part of life, you are always going to be balancing the risk reward equation and since risk is inherent in everything, you won't know unless you try.

Don't be afraid to keep trying because if you don't try you will never get anywhere. Don't be too hard on yourself either when you meet failure. With persistence and perseverance you'll do just fine.

None of us is or ever will be perfect. It's impossible and there is no such thing as perfection. We are all human, living our own individual human experience with our specific family, genes, emotions, heritage and environment.

The one thing we can control is what we do with what we each have. Whatever it is and however it is composed, we alone are responsible for how we behave and apply ourselves. Don't worry so much about the uncontrollables. Stay focused on the controllables and make them the best they can possibly be and you will always come out a winner.

As I put the finishing touches on this manuscript before I send it to the printer for its first printing, I hope that you can use my work in creating it, as another example of what you too can accomplish if you put your mind and energy to your goals.

As I read through all the chapters I am amazed that, with some help and support from a lot of people, I was able to come up with all these ideas and write all these words. I didn't do it alone. My editor was a big help and I couldn't have done it without her. Thank you.

Look around and see what you can find to achieve and accomplish if you put your mind to it and drop me a line sometime to tell me about it all. I would love to hear from you.

Thanks for reading.

Enjoy your life. It is yours to create.

"Uncensored" explained

This handbook is labeled as "Uncensored" to clarify that it is a blunt assessment of the state of youth, the educational system, and corrupted governance while also trying to provide appropriate guidance and concepts for the reader and society in general to try and remedy the issues at hand.

Its content encompasses and is similar to themes from four books. Three of the books mirrored by this story line portray a dystopian society. The fourth was banned because it was believed to be a bad influence on youth in that it reflected real life in ways that made some people uncomfortable.

This handbook is a little of all of the books and much more.

This handbook reads as a treatise on the state of youth, education, and our governments today, in a manner that tries to warn the reader about how the world really functions, how they are being molded, and why and how youth need to pay attention to what is going on around them so they can make the most of their lives and don't get taken advantage of.

The topics discussed in the handbook present a continuing real life story line that, as written about in the past, is actually becoming more prevalent today.

In George Orwell's *1984*, set in the fictional super-state of Oceania, citizens are not allowed to read or write so you can't remember all the details, and you get all your news (propaganda) from a screen on the wall that has the ability to see and watch you wherever you go. The lack of paper, pencils, and books causes citizens to become so confused as to what is real or fake or what they were told, that they become immune to emotions, compliant and gullible with whatever Big Brother tells them.

Fahrenheit 451 has a similar dystopian theme in that it is against the law to read books and if they are discovered they are burned, sometimes with your home. Like in *1984*, the past and its stories cannot be recorded and are lost and the citizens become mesmerized by the television screens in their homes.

Fahrenheit 451 further serves as a simile for where youth are headed today with their decline in reading, and from it, a developing sinister role of the media and its intricate relationship with the leaderships. Also, the increasing difficulty of youth to be able to separate fact from fiction and the diminishing teaching and learning of history.

Catch-22 portrays the insanity of "personal relationships in bureaucratic authority," now partly represented by The Iron Triangle, and how governments function with unwieldy bureaucracies and can enact laws and rules that don't make sense except to those special groups for whom they are enacted which are usually not the citizens in general.

Catcher in the Rye was censored and banned because of concerns that the main character, Holden, acts as an insolent role model for youth towards authorities with bad language and a bad attitude. Holden describes society for what it is, and many people have difficulty with its portrayal.

This handbook encapsulates a little of all these works through explanations of the problems that today's youth face. It calls out today's problems for what they are.

The handbook also tries to propose and offer analysis, solutions, and remedies, as deemed appropriate, for many of the risks and problems identified to help and/or better inform and position youth for their life journey.

The Many Forms of Subtle Censorship

Subtle censorship exists in many hidden ways. As an example, it can be an implied condition of continued employment.

Just because you haven't heard of a problem or a possible solution doesn't mean that they are not present or possible. Do not necessarily take silence as an indicator of harmony even within the realm of the so called "Freedom of the Press".

Yes, the Press is free, but freedom to publish does not mean the Press is free of financial or federal licensing dependencies or oth-

Uncensored explained

er "access to information" relationships. Additionally, employees of primary and higher education, and governments, in particular, are legally precluded from publishing without censorship.

There is always an element of what one knows and what one thinks needs to be disclosed versus the risks in making the disclosure. And as our society with its obscured and complex rule making becomes more litigious, deep pocketed, and politically biased judicially, the element of a truly Free Press will become more and more polarized and narrow in scope.

And all the drama without any clear or understandable outcome continues...

Sales Methodology

Wholesale: to buy in bulk quantities for purposes of selling in smaller quantities to the end user.

Retail: sales to the end user.

Margin: the difference between the cost and the selling price.

To truly become empowered, you need to be able to master many of the skills explained in this book as well as having a source of funding to further your growth and development and pursuit of your objectives.

Therefore, the channels of distribution for this handbook are going to be very restricted and tightly controlled as a means of insuring that you and your classmates can use sales of this book as your means to generate the funds that you can use collectively to further the pursuit of your collective educational group or club objectives. At the same time you will be learning important practical lessons about the power and use of money, other principles of economics, and about business in general. All of which could become one of your most valuable and practical lessons as a young adult.

There is a very large market for this book but distribution to retail stores will be limited. Student clubs will be the primary channel of distribution for this publication. One non-school club related point-of-sale will be my online retail store, where it will be priced at retail plus shipping and handling. You will be able to retail it without the added shipping and handling costs of online sales. Libraries will be able to buy direct in bulk quantities at a discount.

Qualified educational student clubs, both high school and college, will be able to buy the book at a wholesale cost of 50% of the retail price, plus shipping, which will provide plenty of margin for the effort to stock and sell it. The book should serve as an excellent product for efficient fund raising for your club projects and goals.

Simon Thompson
Death Certificate
July 6, 1976
Passenger in Car That Struck Tree
June 19, 1976
Graduated High School
June 11, 1976

COMMONWEALTH OF VIRGINIA — CERTIFICATE OF DEATH
DEPARTMENT OF HEALTH — BUREAU OF VITAL RECORDS AND HEALTH STATISTICS — RICHMOND

MEDICAL EXAMINER'S CERTIFICATE

STATE FILE NUMBER: 76-020048

FULL NAME OF DECEASED: SIMON H. THOMPSON — SEX: male

DATE OF DEATH: June 30, 1976 — AGE OF DECEASED: 19 years

NAME OF HOSPITAL OR INSTITUTION OF DEATH: Fairfax Hospital

COUNTY OF DEATH: Fairfax

CITY OR TOWN OF DEATH: Falls Church — inside city or town limits: yes

STREET ADDRESS OR RT. NO. OF PLACE OF DEATH: 3300 Gallows Road

COLOR OR RACE: WHITE

STATE (OR FOREIGN COUNTRY) OF DECEASED'S RESIDENCE: Virginia

COUNTY OF DECEASED'S RESIDENCE: Fairfax

CITY OR TOWN OF RESIDENCE: Vienna

STREET ADDRESS OR RT. NO. OF RESIDENCE: 1508 Cerritos Court — ZIP CODE: 22180

NAME OF FATHER OF DECEASED: Joseph B. Thompson

MAIDEN NAME OF MOTHER OF DECEASED: Pamela M. Plumbly

DECEASED CITIZEN OF WHAT COUNTRY: USA

MARRIED / NEVER MARRIED: NEVER MARRIED

IF VETERAN, name war, or if peacetime only, so state: None

BIRTHPLACE OF DECEASED: England

DATE OF BIRTH: May 17, 1957

USUAL OR LAST OCCUPATION: Student — KIND OF BUSINESS OR INDUSTRY: High School

INFORMANT OR SOURCE OF INFORMATION: Joseph B. Thompson

CAUSE OF DEATH:
PART I.
IMMEDIATE CAUSE (A): Injuries, multiple, extreme
DUE TO (B): Motor vehicle accident
DUE TO (C):

AUTOPSY AUTHORIZED: no — BY: ME

EXTERNAL CAUSE OF DEATH WAS: PRIMARY

DESCRIBE HOW INJURY OCCURRED: Passenger in car that struck tree

TIME OF INJURY: 4:39 P.M. 6-19-1976

INJURY OCCURRED: not while at work

PLACE OF INJURY: Highway — Fairfax County, Va.

I CERTIFY that I took charge of the remains described above... resulted at or about 6:45 PM

NATURAL CAUSES / ACCIDENT: ACCIDENT

ACTUAL SIGNATURE: Claude E. Cooper, M.D. — MEDICAL EXAMINER FOR Fairfax County — 7/6/76

BURIAL REMOVAL CREMATION: CREMATION

PLACE OF BURIAL, REMOVAL, ETC.: Metropolitan Crematory, Alexandria, Va.

NAME OF FUNERAL HOME AND ADDRESS: Money & King Funeral Home, Vienna, Va.

FUNERAL DIRECTOR signature: R. W. Robinson

REGISTRAR signature: Janet L. Carlborn

DATE RECORD FILED: 7-6-76

See pages 68 and 101 for more information about Simon Thompson.

Presented,
January 15, 2013
National Memorial Park
Falls Church, Virginia

My Eulogy for Karl Eisenschmidt

Good morning, my name is Chris DeCarlo and I grew up next door to Karl and his family. I am honored to say that he was my best friend.

As a child my sister and I played with his children and our two families grew up together. As I started driving and getting interested in cars and mechanics, Karl and I became much closer friends.

He was my best friend for many reasons. He was just fun to be around whether it was watching TV, going to the hardware store or going for a ride somewhere. As a young adult we spent many hours watching different TV shows together, building and fixing things, and commenting on and about life in general.

I have always reflected on how fortunate I was in the coincidence that my parents purchased their house next door to Karl and his family. I grew up believing that the most important part about purchasing a home should not be the location, size, schools or layout. It should be finding neighbors like the Eisenschmidts. But now I know that the people and the world have changed and that growing up next to someone like the Eisenschmidts is something that could never be done again.

For those of you that don't speak German, Eisenschmidt translates to iron worker.

Karl was instrumental in my having the knowledge, skills and confidence to start a small family business at an abandoned gasoline station in the City of Fairfax in 1979. I began the business by selling gasoline and renting used cars and after giving directions so many times to another business eventually began selling propane which I still sell today.

I could not have done it without the training and opportunities he provided me. He was always very supportive of my endeavors and willing to help whenever asked. I am sure that as Karl was a mentor and teacher to me that he was a mentor and teacher to many of you.

Karl worked at American Service Center in Arlington for most of his adult life. He arranged a job for me at American Service Center in the summer of 1975 as a porter parking cars. It was the first summer I had my driver's license. It was an honor to be associated with him there where he was held in very high regard.

The second summer I returned and was promoted to the very important job of dispatching the work to the mechanics. I was only able to perform the job as a 17-year-old because of all the training and experience Karl provided me. I am sure that at 17 I was the youngest dispatcher ever but for me it was an unexpected education in managing grown men. Riding to work on the back of a motorcycle, eating lunch in the lunch room with grown men, being part of the adult working world, and working with Karl at American Service Center are memories of two summers I will always cherish. I was very proud to wear my blue automotive mechanics shirt with a Mercedes emblem just like Karl.

After he retired Karl and Margrit took his long dreamed trip across the country and back pulling a camper trailer. He survived the trip even though a passing tractor-trailer almost caused him to flip the trailer over. When he returned, he worked with me at Fairfax Propane. He refilled propane cylinders, drove heavy trucks, and tackled various other projects on a farm such as building a road with heavy equipment. We had a lot of fun together.

As I am sure all of you know, Karl was unique person for many reasons. He was from the old school and the old country. He took calculated risks and was always up for adventure. He was a person of honor and he was smart. I am sure that if he was a child growing up today he would have been labeled as GT, gifted and talented and been in accelerated learning programs. There is no question that he would have been a very successful mechanical engineer. Machines are in his genetics.

318

But, Karl didn't grow up today, he grew up in the shadows of WWII which he survived. Prior to the war, his parents had a very successful business selling and repairing automobiles. The war destroyed everything they had. He told me stories of living without food or fuel and how they would get by modifying whatever was left to get by. How they never even threw a bolt away because it could always be rethreaded down to a smaller size. He came from a time and place that most of us younger people can't even imagine.

I am sure that Karl got by on his smarts, his problem solving skills. He would look at a problem and study it before jumping in to solve it. He explained to me, "You can't fix something unless you first understand how it works." I use his training every day. I always ask myself, now how would Karl solve this problem? What would he do? The neat part is that it usually works, I just have to think like he taught me.

Karl was a survivor. He survived the war and escaped Germany before you couldn't get out. His brother remained and became trapped in East Germany.

Karl told me stories about how he had to be resourceful to survive after the war. He explained how he took the seats of his car out or it would be hijacked. Once the hijackers saw it would only seat one person they didn't want it and would let him continue.

Karl and Margrit had just been married and were frustrated with the limited housing opportunities for them in Germany and were looking for other options when a friend told him about an ad in a German newspaper for mechanics at a garage in Ohio. He arranged for their passage to America as passengers on a freighter. It was 1958. The reason there were limited housing options in Germany was because the American bombers had destroyed so many buildings.

Karl never complained and when I asked him if he could go back and change something in his life what it would be he said that more than anything he wished he had never started smoking.

He may have not been able to survive the smoking but he did survive a lot after WWII. He survived several heart attacks and received several stets and a defibrillator. He survived a serious motorcycle accident on Wilson Boulevard where he broke his collar bone and leg and was given up for dead. In January, 13 years ago, he passed out twice with me in the snow in Gainesville, Virginia; he survived a ruptured aorta where the chances of survival are only 1 in 10. He survived because I made the decision to risk driving him to the best hospital directly instead of waiting for an ambulance that would have taken him to a different hospital and then he would have had to survive long enough in a helicopter ride to the one I took him.

Karl loved his motorcycle and would take it on Sunday afternoon rides and he belonged to the BMW motorcycle club. Margrit would always worry about him on the motorcycle and she had good reason to worry to worry even though he tried to be very conscientious and safe. He loved lighting his cigarette each time before he began a ride.

I will always remember one of the few times I went with him for a recreational Sunday ride on the back of the BMW. It was a time when route 66 began outside of route 495 and there was no traffic as you left 495 and got on 66. It was three lanes of wide open interstate.

As we got on 66, he started to open it up and I held on to the back. I could see over his shoulder as the speed kept increasing. There wasn't anything I could do or say so I just held on trying to take in the experience as the speedometer kept climbing past 70, 80 and 90 all the way to what I remember was 100 miles an hour. Once we hit a 100 he slowed down and we headed home.

I never told my mother.

Karl was a person that would never complain and he was always on time. He was the neighbor and friend everybody wants, they just don't know it.

I am sure that his spirit will continue to live on with each of us and hopefully we can pass it on to our children.

He was a remarkable man, husband, father and friend and all of us will miss him dearly but we can rest assured that he will always be circling us on his BMW in the clouds above.

Sequential List of Inside Book Quotes

Your Real Challenge

It is important for you to understand that the choices
you make now will affect your options for choices in the future.

Chapter one

Who are You?

Don't fill your brain with trash.
Keep it clean. Keep it sharp.

Think about tomorrow's happiness today
instead of about today's tomorrow.

Solving problems is the name of the game
in the competitive world of adulthood.

Plan your objectives for the day,
Don't idly waste your life away.

Be careful with how you allocate your free time.

An unkempt appearance reflects an unkempt mind.

Money becomes the currency of life.

If all you are after is money you will never have enough.

The sum of your relationships make up your unique network.

Focus on the positive instead of the negative.

Sequential List of Inside Book Quotes

Books should be your best friends
and you can never have enough friends.

You won't know unless you try.

Time is fleeting and there's never enough of it.

Time gives good advice.

You don't want your life to be a sprint to the end.

More skills, more money.

Use words to unleash the true power of your brain.

Programming is the best foreign language you can learn.

Don't be afraid to learn programming.
Try it, you might like it. It's really not that hard.
It may even become one of your best friends.

A journal is a great way to document
what you did and your concerns.

So many ways to learn, lots of money you can earn.

If you want to remember something, you have to write it down.

Clear and concise writing is essential for communication.

The goal of driving is to deliver the load safely.

Chapter two

Phases of Life

Think about tomorrow's happiness today.

Timing is everything.

Listen to the establishment but you
need to be able to think on your own.

What trails are you blazing for yourself?

There is only one person that can make
you successful and that is you.

Shakespeare builds comprehension skills that YA novels don't.

Campaign finance and speaking fees of hundreds
of thousands of dollars are two of the biggest con jobs
being run on the American public.

Always remember: The political network uses
legislative complexity to achieve its ulterior goals.

How careful are you going to be in choosing your spouse?

What will your career ladder look like?
Can you find it?

Careers don't happen on their own.
You will need help and lots of it.

You need help with all of this because you don't have the experience and depth to be able to put it all together. Ask!

Sequential List of Inside Book Quotes

Remember, complacency is your enemy.

How much do you want to be paid
and how hard do you want to work?

Military service does not come
with a "Get out of Jail Free" card.

Now I want you to remember that no bastard ever won a war by
dying for his country. You won it by making the other
poor dumb bastard die for his country.
General George S. Patton
3rd Army's 6th Armored Division, France, May 31, 1944

When I was in school we didn't have a ton of information showing
us that everybody else was happy when we were slogging it out and
the world was not moving as fast.

Be careful that you don't get sucked into thinking that going to a
prestigious school is going to make your life easier. You may find
that it can easily work the other way around.

It is all available to you, you just need to make the effort.

Education is the key to scoring in the big game.

It is your time, money, life and future.

Your education should continue throughout your life.

Reading is the only way you can unlock the
real power of your brain.
Make time for it.

Books provide a lot more in depth knowledge
then you will ever find online.

Reading is great food for your brain.
Feed it.

"Just enough, just in time," is not a good mantra.

Social media is your real enemy because
it has a detrimental affect on your brain's natural ability
to process information and reason.

Social media overloads your brain and causes it to lock up.

Many changes are created in a bureaucratic and political
environment where these changes take on a life of their own since
there is no direct accountability and then they are
impossible to get rid of once enacted.

College is a test in discipline and in keeping yourself motivated.

Today you need to go to college "smart".
Do you think you have what it takes?

When I was in school we didn't compare our self to everybody else
because we couldn't and we took everything one day at a time.
We established a small circle of friends, got our grades,
went home over break and that was all that mattered.

No students in a program, no jobs for the teachers.

Keep long term practicality in mind as you
construct your short term building blocks.

Once the money is accrued, the passions can be pursued!

Sequential List of Inside Book Quotes

Go for the gold now and you can always adjust
or scale back or play more later.

Chapter three
Soul Deep - Relationships

"Family" is the nucleus of society.

Grandparents won't be around forever
and they have many life lessons to offer for free.

Neither guys nor girls should expect their prospective
mate to be a crutch or solution to one's own insecurities.

Remember, instructions are not included with newborns.

Relationships are the special keys to linking all the pieces.

Men think that the women won't change and the women think they
can change the men and they're both wrong.

Happy wife, happy life.

Nobody wants to marry a loser.
The load will be unbalanced.

You want to marry someone that you can steal horses with.
German proverb.

Who are you going to trust with your
emotions, money, life and children?

Can your selected spouse take care of
herself or himself or is that person needy?
You don't want to marry needy.

Children are a big responsibility and they cause big changes in your
life so it is best to have as much in place as possible before you go
down this road of making them.

Chapter four

Pitfalls, Risks and Dungeons

Cheating now cheats you out of a lot more later.

Always maintain control of your body and mind.

Be high on life instead of drugs.

Stand up for yourself and avoid
anything that alters your clear thinking.

Digital distractions are destroying your brain.

Please be very careful with whom you associate.

Starve the Gremlin.

Don't think you are so smart that you can be lazy.

Try rebelling by becoming extra smart
so you can earn more money than everyone else.

Once you can tune out the static
you will be able to hear the peace.

Sequential List of Inside Book Quotes

You might think that you are indestructible and resilient but you are not and sooner or later you will pay the price for overuse.

It is very hard to learn how to separate what you think you are supposed to feel from what is really inside you, but that is part of growing up.

Chapter five
Coming of Age

Appearance says a lot.

Dopamine is the biggest barrier to your future successes.

If it was fun they wouldn't be paying you to do it.

Look beyond your borders.
Broaden your horizons and think globally.
It is a big world out there.

Libraries have a lot of answers about life.
Visit yours often.

Love your library!
Now they are more important than ever.

Sell what people want to buy, not what you want to sell.

People end up in positions of power who are not qualified for the power they are given.

The introduction of campaign contributions into the election process is an oxymoron to the democratic principles the Constitutions create.

The sheriff is your only law enforcement officer
that is directly elected by the citizens.

I argue that citizens have been conditioned to think that the Federal
government is supreme and the schools don't teach anything about
State Constitutions and the roles of the local Constitutional Officers
as provided in the documents to perpetuate the myth.

Your sheriff is your only hope for protecting your
rights to have a truly representative government but it
seems that few of the sheriffs can or are willing to fulfill
all the duties of the Office as originally intended.

Chapter six
Miscellaneous Concepts

Are the political parties and Congress racketeers?

Change can be beneficial if you can figure out
how to position yourself so it can work to your advantage.

"It is one thing to have a bird in your hand,
it is another thing to know that you have it."
Ancient Chinese proverb

Index